Getting It Wrong

Regional Cooperation and the Commonwealth of Independent States

Martha Brill Olcott,
Anders Åslund, and
Sherman W. Garnett

Carnegie Endowment for International Peace
Washington, D.C.

DK
293
.056
1999

© 1999 by the
Carnegie Endowment for International Peace
1779 Massachusetts Avenue, N.W.
Washington, D.C. 20036
202-483-7600
www.ceip.org

Getting It Wrong: Regional Cooperation and the Commonwealth of Independent States
ISBN 0-87003-171-6 (paper) $19.95

To order, contact Carnegie's distributor:
The Brookings Institution Press
Department 029, Washington, D.C. 20042-0029, USA
Tel: 1-800-275-1447 or 202-797-6258
Fax: 202-797-6004, E-mail: bibooks@brook.edu

Library of Congress Catalog Card Number: **99-65601**

Cover: Zamore Design
Map: Dave Merrill

Contents

Foreword

The swift yet peaceful collapse of the Soviet Union in 1991 produced fifteen newly independent states and a sudden change in citizenship for 250 million people. More by default than by design, the demise of the USSR left an enormous vacuum in a vast region, from Kaliningrad in the west to Khabarovsk in the east.

To fill this vacuum, two contradictory impulses emerged. The first was the eagerness of a number of the new states to establish themselves as independent entities, liberated from Soviet control. In some cases, this meant reestablishing their identity as free nations; in others, it meant independent existence for the first time. The second impulse was the desire of several of these new states to create some type of superstructure to take the place of the moribund Soviet Union. This impulse was driven by doubts some leaders held about surviving independently and by hopes of others to maintain order amidst the chaos.

It is the first impulse, eight years after the breakup of the USSR, which has prevailed. The second, which led to the creation of the Commonwealth of Independent States (CIS) in December 1991, even before the Soviet Union was formally dissolved, has amounted to little. The CIS, expected to be an organization dominated by Russia and designed to maintain formal cohesion among the post-Soviet states, has been a failure by almost any measure.

In the West, there has been significant confusion about the CIS and its importance as a regional organization. This book offers the first clear analysis of why and how the CIS has been a failure and what the implications of that failure have been for regional cooperation on security, trade, economic development, migration, and other key issues.

Getting It Wrong: Regional Cooperation and the Commonwealth of Independent States is a joint project bringing together three of the West's leading experts on the former Soviet Union. Martha Brill

Olcott and Anders Åslund are current senior associates at the Carnegie Endowment for International Peace and co-editors of a recent Carnegie publication, *Russia After Communism*. Sherman W. Garnett, a Carnegie senior associate until July 1999, is now dean of James Madison College at Michigan State University. We are grateful to the Smith Richardson Foundation for its support, which made this important study possible.

Jessica T. Mathews
President
Carnegie Endowment for
International Peace

Acknowledgments

This book would not have been possible without the assistance of a number of people and organizations. The Smith Richardson Foundation initiated the idea for this study of the Commonwealth of Independent States and provided the Carnegie Endowment for International Peace with generous support to conduct the project; the culmination is this book. Smith Richardson's support allowed the authors to carry out primary research, conduct numerous interviews in the region, and sponsor working groups, conferences and roundtables in Almaty, Bishkek, Minsk, Kyiv, and Moscow.

The volume also benefited from other projects with which the authors have been involved. Anders Åslund received support from the Open Society Institute for economic advisory work in Ukraine and from the UN Development Program for economic advisory work in Kyrgyzstan. Sherman Garnett co-chaired a project on security issues in Belarus with Professor Robert Legvold of Columbia University. And Martha Brill Olcott travelled extensively in Central Asia as a director of the Central Asian American Enterprise Fund.

We are especially grateful for the invaluable input from our Carnegie Moscow Center colleagues, present and former, including Irina Kobrinskaya, Dmitri Trenin, Aleksey Malashenko, Tatiana Maleva, and Mikhail Dmitriev. We also want to thank Vladimir Yevstegneyev of the Institute of World Economy and International Relations in Moscow for his research contribution, and Andrei Zagorsky of Moscow State Institute of International Relations for sharing his published and unpublished materials with us.

Our research assistants—Marcus Fellman, Rachel Lebenson, Maria Popova, Oksana Sinyavskaya, Judith Smelser, and Marat Umerov—all made major contributions. Marcus Fellman also deserves particular recognition for seeing this volume through all the technical hurdles of publication. Special thanks also go to Elizabeth Reisch and Sherry Pettie for their help in the final stages of the publication process. To Natalia Udalova, who acted throughout as the coordinator of our efforts gathering valuable material and bringing the whole project together, we extend our special gratitude.

We cannot possibly list everyone who had an influence on this volume, but we would like to single out the following individuals who generously shared some of their own research with us: Sabit Bagirov, Nadija Badykova, Sabit Jusupov, Ilya Tevzadze, Ben Slay, Timothy Heleniak, Constantine Michalopoulos, and David Tarr. We greatly value the work of Anthony Olcott, who took our three diverse styles of writing and melded them into one.

As always we had superb support from the staff of the Endowment, in particular from the Russian and Eurasian Program and from Carnegie's library. We are also grateful for the support and encouragement of Paul Balaran, Arnold Horelick, David Kramer, Alan Rousso in Moscow, and of course, our president, Jessica Mathews.

Getting It Wrong

Regional Cooperation and the Commonwealth of Independent States

THE COMMONWEALTH OF INDEPENDENT STATES

ARMENIA
Chief of state: Robert Kocharian
Territory: 29,800 sq km
Population: 3,798,500
Currency: Dram (introduced November 1993)

AZERBAIJAN
Chief of state: Heydar Aliyev
Territory: 86,600 sq km
Population: 7,700,000
Currency: Manat (introduced January 1994)

BELARUS
Chief of state: Aleksandr Lukashenko
Territory: 207,600 sq km
Population: 10,226,800
Currency: Belarusian Ruble (introduced July 1993)

GEORGIA
Chief of state: Eduard Shevardnadze
Territory: 69,700 sq km
Population: 5,445,000
Currency: Lari (introduced September 1995)

KAZAKHSTAN
Chief of state: Nursultan Nazarbayev
Territory: 2,724,900 sq km
Population: 15,491,300
Currency: Tenge (introduced November 1993)

KYRGYZSTAN
Chief of state: Askar Akaev
Territory: 199,900 sq km
Population: 4,729,600
Currency: Som (introduced May 1993)

MOLDOVA
Chief of state: Petru Lucinschi
Territory: 33,800 sq km
Population: 3,648,300
Currency: Lei (introduced November 1993)

RUSSIA
Chief of state: Boris Yeltsin
Territory: 17,075,400 sq km
Population: 146,700,000
Currency: Ruble

TAJIKISTAN
Chief of state: Emomali Rahmonov
Territory: 143,100 sq km
Population: 6,164,000
Currency: Tajik Ruble (introduced May 1995)

TURKMENISTAN
Chief of state: Saparmurat Niyazov
Territory: 491,200 sq km
Population: 4,990,000
Currency: Manat (introduced November 1993)

UKRAINE
Chief of state: Leonid Kuchma
Territory: 603,700 sq km
Population: 50,090,900
Currency: Hryvnia (introduced September 1996)

UZBEKISTAN
Chief of state: Islam Karimov
Territory: 447,400 sq km
Population: 24,232,000
Currency: Uzbek Som (introduced June 1994)

Source: Inter-State Statistical Committee of the CIS, as published on its website (http://www.unece.org/stats/cisstat/macro0.htm).

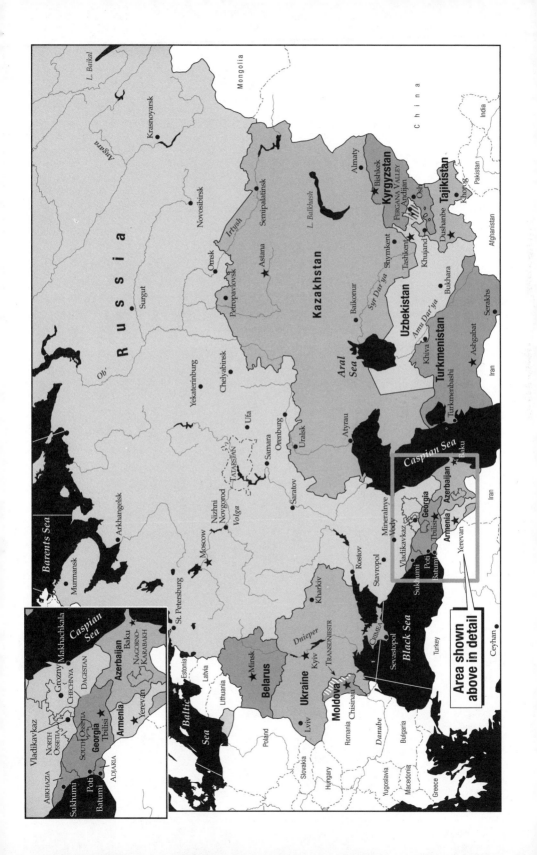

1
The Failure of the CIS

The speed with which the Soviet Union collapsed created mind-boggling challenges. The Soviet Union effectively imploded between August and December 1991, and a single country was replaced by 15 newly independent states, all soon to become members of the United Nations.[1] The problems raised by such a breakup would still have been monumental if there had been many months of advance warning, as the British had given before their withdrawal from India and Palestine in 1948,[2] and would have been eased somewhat even if there had been just three months' prior notification, as there was of the separation of Czechoslovakia into the Czech and Slovak republics.

It took just weeks, however, if not days, to turn millions of Soviet citizens into citizens of various new countries, some of which had not been independent states in living memory, and others that had never been states before. Many people were content with their new citizenship, but others were not, which meant that most of these new states were born with new diaspora populations, some of which had powerful foreign patrons. None of the new states had fully delineated boundaries, and most of them had no means to defend those boundaries even if they had been defined. Paradoxically, the shared territory of these new states also contained more than four million soldiers who were sworn to preserve and protect a nation that no longer existed. No one, not even the soldiers themselves, really knew where the loyalties of these strategic and defensive armed forces, which possessed both tactical and strategic nuclear weapons, really lay.

The new states faced enormous economic challenges. Some economic authority had already been transferred from Moscow to the republics before the breakup, but at the time of independence the new national leaders did not yet know either the full inventory of their national economic assets, or how to assert control of them, since many of these assets were administered by people whose loyalties to the new political entities were dubious. Even if all potential sources of revenue could be identified, it still remained unclear how most of these states could meet their payrolls and social service obligations, since they had no banking systems, and currency emissions had always been controlled in Moscow. The new states shared a single transportation and communication system, which had been designed to integrate the USSR, not to serve or supply its now-independent subunits.

In part because of the immediate need to manage the complexities of this vast political divorce process, the leaders of these new states quickly, and with almost no controversy, agreed to the formation of the Commonwealth of Independent States (CIS). At least as pressing, though, was the universal desire—in Moscow, in the capitals of the member states of the North Atlantic Treaty Organization (NATO), and in the newly independent states alike—to determine what Russia's relationship to these new states would be, since it was still taken as a given that, whatever the process, Russia would play a dominant role.

Policy makers in Moscow generally assumed that Russia's preeminence in the post-Soviet space was a foregone conclusion, even if they had no clear idea of how it could be achieved or what form it would take. Leaders in the new national capitals expected that their countries would be treated like Russia's "little brothers," an outcome that some Western policy makers also hoped for, fearing that economic and social chaos would ensue without strong Russian involvement. Many others in the West were willing at least to delay judgment of Russian domination until they saw what form it might take.

The passage of time, however, has put the CIS in many new lights. Moscow's bilateral and multilateral ties with the successor states, which it chose to call the "near abroad," have proven to be paternalistic at best and clearly adversarial at worst. As the first shock of independence began to fade in the other national capitals, their leaders became more aware of the opportunities that their new status offered, and some became much less enthusiastic about and less resigned to remaining in Russia's orbit. Many in the West also came to question earlier assumptions that Russia would prove to be a benign regional influence after Moscow strong-armed states like Azerbaijan, Georgia, and Moldova that had either refused to join or to participate actively in the CIS.

The CIS has also not evolved in ways that serve Russia's purposes. All of the Soviet successor states except the three Baltic nations eventually joined the organization, but most members have opted out of one or more of the key political, economic, and security agreements that were intended to be the main instruments of integration. The heads of the CIS states have all met regularly, but the agreements drawn up at their meetings have had no real force; indeed, the only reason that such sessions continue to be held seems to be that most of the leaders find some other utility in regular summit meetings.

The failure of the CIS to manage them has not made the interconnections of the post-Soviet space disappear, as all of the member states seem to understand. Some of the states have begun to find other ways to group together, sometimes with Russia and sometimes without. To date, though, such efforts have had only limited success, since weak states joining up with other weak states usually cannot create strong, effective unions and organizations.[3] None of the newly independent states has been willing to reduce its autonomy of decision making, preferring to maximize its own national interests rather than to delegate authority to multistate arrangements.

Most of the problems for which the CIS was created remain unresolved. Each of the CIS member states is trying to define itself primarily in relationship to a broad international community, although all of the post-Soviet states remain closely intertwined. Economic competition among CIS member states remains keen, but all are still interconnected enough to suffer the economic crises of their neighbors and, even more so, of Russia. The greatest security threats to these states come from within, or from former Soviet neighbors, yet member states are not competent either to cope with security needs on their own or to form an effective multilateral security force.

This book offers a perspective for understanding both the failure of the CIS and the continuing challenges of integration. It traces the evolution of CIS institutions, showing why they have failed to achieve most of their initial purposes. It describes the challenge of integration, as understood by Russia and by the other newly independent states. It looks at the national strategies adopted by several CIS member states, at efforts of some of the new states to group together in ways other than through the CIS, and at the integrating role played by other regional or multilateral organizations. Finally, this book shows how the failure of the CIS has contributed to the reconfiguration of the former Soviet space, and offers advice to U.S. policy makers who wish to promote good relations with Russia, but who simultaneously want to see each of the other Soviet successor states secure independence and sovereignty in a way that maximizes their own economic and political potential.

THE BIRTH OF THE CIS

Beyond giving long advance warning of their intentions, the British did little to prepare their colonies for postwar independence, failing among other things to resolve competing land claims. This guaranteed a bloody transfer of power. Intercommunal violence broke out immediately in India and Pakistan, as Hindus and Muslims tried to move to their respective new states. Israel's Arab neighbors refused to recognize the partition of Palestine and went to war with the new Jewish state, inadvertently wiping Palestine from the map in the process.

By contrast, the dissolution of the Soviet Union occurred with greater preparatory consultation, which helped make it a relatively peaceful process. Fighting did escalate after independence in Georgia, Armenia, Azerbaijan, Moldova, and Tajikistan, but the underlying disputes had either begun smoldering before independence, or had already become violent. Only the war in Chechnya[4] was the direct result of the USSR's demise; it would have been unlikely to develop had the leaders of the Chechen republic not demanded of Russia the same rights of national self-determination that the titular peoples of the former Soviet republics had been granted.

This is not to suggest, however, that the breakup of the USSR was a considered act. Similar to the demise of the British Empire in 1947, the USSR was not so much dismembered as allowed wearily to collapse, with little thought for what would come next. In a March 1991 referendum, tens of millions of people had shown overwhelming support for the continued existence of the Soviet Union, but the precise form of that future union was unspecified in the question put to voters.[5] Some regions of the USSR refused to conduct the referendum at all, while others modified the question slightly so that support for the union also meant support for local sovereignty, while still other regions voted for continued union with such unanimity as to raise suspicions of election fraud. The only parts of the USSR that had large, potentially uncontrollable mass movements in favor of independence were the Baltics, which were formally permitted to leave the Soviet Union in the aftermath of the failed coup of August 1991.

Soviet cohesion, however, had been compromised well before that time. The Congress of Peoples Deputies of the Russian Federation elected Boris Yeltsin as its chairman in May 1990. In part because of the personal rivalry between Yeltsin and Soviet President Mikhail Gorbachev, the Russian republic declared its sovereignty on June 12, 1990. In June 1991, Yeltsin was popularly elected president of the Russian Federation, after which Yeltsin claimed his administration had more political legitimacy than that of Gorbachev.

Gorbachev's authority evaporated entirely after the failed Communist Party putsch of August 1991, and the banning of the Communist Party seemed to obviate any remaining legitimacy the Soviet Union may have had. Between August and November a number of the republics issued declarations of independence through votes in their national legislatures.[6] Most of these declarations were more expressions of a goal than statements of intent, part of an escalating struggle for control of strategic economic assets between Moscow and the periphery, rather than a serious push for independence.

The behavior of the republic presidents in this period suggests that they viewed the formal collapse of the Soviet Union as a real possibility, but not as inevitable. Each of the Soviet republic leaders, however, seemed more concerned with retaining power than with holding the union together. Their fears had justification; political dissident Zviad Gamsakhurdia became Georgia's president even before the 1991 coup, while another political dissident, Levon Ter-Petrossian, came to power in Armenia just after it;[7] in the aftermath of the coup an unruly crowd had also toppled Kakhar Makhamov in Tajikistan, and Ayaz Mutalipov, a Communist supporter, was barely hanging on to power in Azerbaijan.[8]

Outlawing the Communist Party was a popular measure in many republics, as it transferred important assets to the personal control of their leaders, while also making the republics appear to be even more quasi-statelike than they had before.[9] In October 1991 eight Soviet republics agreed to the creation of an Economic Union that would have made the Soviet Union a free trade zone with the ruble as a common currency, to be managed by a banking union headed by Gosbank. The debt of the Soviet Union would be divided among member republics on a formula that was agreed upon at a December 4, 1991, summit of republic leaders.[10] Tellingly, four republics (Azerbaijan, Georgia, Ukraine, and Moldova) refused to attend that October 1991 meeting, because the proposed union usurped more power than these quasi-states were willing to cede.

The results of the referendum in Ukraine held December 1, 1991, made it clear that the Ukrainians were serious about wanting to withdraw from the union, and effectively made the dissolution of the Soviet Union inevitable.[11] Still, it is far from clear whether the leaders of Russia, Ukraine, and Belarus had dissolution as their intention when they met on December 8, 1991.[12] That Kazakhstan's President Nursultan Nazarbayev was invited to join the meeting suggests that they did not, for Nazarbayev had been actively trying to redefine the union in a way that would satisfy most republic leaders. Nazarbayev declined to attend the December 8 meeting because he disapproved of circumventing Soviet President Mikhail Gorbachev, which also suggests that he did not know that dissolution was on the meeting's agenda.

It is equally unclear whether Boris Yeltsin, Leonid Kravchuk,[13] and Stanislav Shushkevich[14] actually expected the decisions they made that Saturday in a dacha outside Minsk to become binding. The men claimed the authority to dissolve the 1922 Treaty of Union, which had formally organized the Union of Soviet Socialist Republics, on the grounds that the entities that they each headed (which also happened to be the three surviving signatories of the 1922 Treaty[15]) were sovereign republics. The same claim had been made in other contexts, but what distinguished the Minsk Agreement (also known as the Belovezh Accords) from earlier declarations was that, for the first time, the Soviet elite was ready to support a radical redefinition of the Soviet political and economic space.

President Gorbachev tried frantically for several days to find support for holding the USSR together, but without success. The country's military and security forces were formally still under his command, but there was great doubt that his orders would have been obeyed. Tellingly, no crowds took to the streets demanding the preservation of the USSR, and the leaders of the Soviet republics finally seemed ready to dissolve the union.

This does not mean, however, that they were prepared to abandon all their former ties. President Nazarbayev in particular was concerned that Kazakhstan and the other four Central Asian republics had been excluded from the Commonwealth of Independent States, the post-Soviet structure that had been agreed to at the Minsk meeting. Convening a summit of the five Central Asian republics in Ashgabat on December 13, 1991, the leaders of these states asked to join the new commonwealth. Another summit was held in Almaty[16] on December 21, 1991, which was attended by the leaders of eleven Soviet republics; the three Baltic states and Georgia declined to attend.

There the leaders all signed a protocol that was declared to be a part of the Minsk Agreement of December 8, and eight "high contracting parties" joined the three initial members as founders of the new Commonwealth.

The stated goals of the new organization were straightforward. The purpose of the Commonwealth of Independent States was to allow member or participating states to coordinate their foreign and security policies, to develop a common economic space with a common customs policy, to maintain orderly control over the military assets of the former USSR, to develop shared transportation and communications networks, to preserve the environment and maintain environmental security, to regulate migration policy, and to take coordinated measures against organized crime.[17]

The men who dissolved the USSR accepted each other as representatives of a single elite that had interests in common, even as other of their interests increasingly diverged. They believed they had time to work out institutional solutions for their lingering interconnections, and saw it as their first priority to establish themselves as leaders of independent states that were subjects of international law. There was little interest at the time to look backward and to decide whether what they had dissolved was a state or an empire, because it seemed far more pressing to define what would come next.

THE ROCKY START OF THE CIS[18]

The first CIS structure was very simple, deriving directly from Gorbachev's final State Council, which had been formed in 1991 to bring together the republic presidents.[19] It consisted of two councils, one of Heads of State and the other of Heads of Government, and a working group to prepare materials that these two councils would discuss.

The leaders of Armenia, Azerbaijan, Belarus, Kazakhstan, Kyrgyzstan, Moldova, Russia, Tajikistan, Turkmenistan, Ukraine, and Uzbekistan recognized the need for continued coordination of the new states. They believed that a summit setting provided the best opportunity for it. In the next two years, between December 1991 and 1993, there were thirteen meetings of the Council of Heads of State and twelve sessions of the Council of Heads of Government.[20]

These meetings may have served an important communications function, but they were unable to promote the CIS as a decision-making organization. Discussions in the corridors were often more important than those at the formal sessions, while the press conferences after most summits projected discord over the nature of the organization, its presumed or projected institutions, and their presumptive functions.

At the first meeting of Heads of Government, held in Moscow in February 1992, the Russian delegation accused the Ukrainians of hindering the council's efforts to reach agreement on pressing questions. The specific topic was whether Russia was the legal successor to the Soviet Union and the guarantor of the foreign creditor agreements of the Commonwealth member states. Of those who attended, all but the Ukrainians were willing to cede Russia such status.[21] A different formulation was offered at the next meeting, in March. The Council of Heads of Government agreed to accept joint responsibility for repaying the USSR's debt;[22] Russia would repay about 61 percent, Ukraine, 16 percent, and the remaining members were to split the rest according to their economic strength. After this agreement, however, Russia negotiated bilateral agreements over the next two years with every state other than Ukraine that transferred its debts and assets to Russia on a "null-null" basis.[23] Ukraine formally refused to grant Russia the authority to administer its portion of the former Soviet debt, but Russia still took de facto control of all USSR assets.

At the March 1992 summit, Armenia, Kazakhstan, Kyrgyzstan, Moldova, Uzbekistan, Ukraine, Belarus, Turkmenistan, and Tajikistan signed agreements on taxation policy, pension provisions, price setting, customs policies, the internal debt of the USSR, and a protocol on banking. Azerbaijan only sent an observer to the meeting.

There was so little confidence in the potential efficacy of any of these agreements that just a week later, at a summit in Kyiv, President Leonid Kravchuk was already describing the CIS as completely ineffective.[24]

Nevertheless, the Kyiv summit produced a number of agreements, including a Declaration on the Non-Use of Force or the Threat of Force in Relations between CIS Members and an Agreement on Groups of Military Observers and Collective Peacekeeping Forces. Ukraine signed these agreements, but vehemently opposed a plan for the creation of an Inter-Parliamentary Assembly, which was subsequently supported by seven member states at an inter-parliamentary conference held in Almaty, also in March 1992.

That such major differences surfaced so quickly should have made clear that the CIS was doomed as any sort of formal political organization, but the organization nevertheless started work on a formal charter. Completed in January 1993, the draft document closely resembled the agreement that had been signed at the first Minsk meeting, with two important additions. The 1993 draft charter expanded the organization's duties to include protection of human rights and fundamental freedoms, and, most importantly, it added the coordination of defense policy and border protection. Despite the five months of contentious negotiation that had gone into drafting the CIS Charter, its presentation to the Heads of State Summit in Minsk on January 22, 1993, led to further disagreement. Only Kazakhstan and Russia fully supported the draft, while Belarus had reservations about the collective security provisions, and Uzbekistan objected to the inclusion of human rights issues, which it considered to be the internal affair of member states. Ukraine, Moldova, and Turkmenistan refused to sign the charter, while Azerbaijan and Georgia did not even come to the meeting.

Member states were given a year to ratify the charter, after which it would come into effect in January 1994. Only nine nations did so, including Georgia, which did not ratify the charter until March 1994. Moldova, Turkmenistan, and Ukraine have never ratified it. Of these nine signatories, only Armenia and Uzbekistan fully met the criteria for founding membership that the charter set forth, by endorsing the Minsk Agreements and Almaty protocols prior to ratifying the charter.[25] Azerbaijan, Georgia, Kyrgyzstan, Tajikistan, and Turkmenistan never ratified the Minsk agreements, while Moldova did so only in April 1994, when it ratified the Almaty protocols as well. Moldova, however, specified that it would participate on economic questions only, and so accepted associate member status. Belarus, Kazakhstan, and Russia never ratified the Almaty protocols, which then necessitated the creation of a new category of participating states to parallel that of member states.

Well before even this partial ratification, the CIS had begun to elaborate a number of formal institutions. The Inter-Parliamentary Assembly was created on March 27, 1992; its powers were subsequently enhanced at the Minsk meeting of May 26, 1995, when the formal convention outlining its responsibilities was adopted. Not all member states agreed to participate in the assembly; the most crippling refusal was that of Ukraine, an absence that limited the potential effectiveness of this body from its inception. Ukraine did eventually join on March 3, 1999.[26]

Two new coordinating councils were established, the Council of Defense Ministers (Heads of State summit, February 14, 1992) and the Council of Foreign Ministers (September 24, 1993). The CIS established a formal Executive Secretariat in September 1993, with headquarters in Minsk. A Committee for Consultation and Coordination (of the economy) was also established in 1993, but was effectively replaced by the Inter-State Economic Committee of the Economic Union in October 1994.

In all about sixty institutions were set up, most with highly specific coordinating functions (see tables 1.1 and 1.2). A few of these, such as the Inter-State Aviation Committee and the Council on Railroad Transportation, had tasks of vital importance, but most of the employees of the CIS, who at one point numbered about 2,500, were essentially wasting their time. The CIS institutions prepared approximately a thousand different agreements for signature by CIS members, of which only a handful were ever implemented.

The institutional design of the CIS was in conflict with the goals of many of its members from the beginning. Many of the goals set out in the Minsk Agreement and CIS Charter were explicitly integrative, but the institutional structures meant to implement them were either exclusively consultative or were not empowered to impose legally binding decisions. Indeed, Article 1, paragraph 3 of the charter states that, "The Commonwealth ... possesses no supranational authority," a limitation that had been inserted to satisfy Ukraine and some other CIS states. The charter also contains no instruments of enforcement. An Economic Court was proposed in July 1992 to insure the fulfillment of economic commitments made within the CIS framework and to settle economic disputes among member states, but its powers were exclusively consultative and member states generally preferred not to avail themselves of its services.[27]

The Inter-Parliamentary Assembly holds consultations and elaborates proposals on legal issues; since inception it has recommended sixty-three legislative acts, including model civil, criminal, criminal-procedure, and criminal-enforcement codes, but the national parliaments of member states are not required even to look at such proposals.

Nothing in the CIS Charter encourages consensus; in addition to signing a given agreement, members also have the options of abstention, of signing with reservations, or of refusing to sign. Instead of encouraging members to seek compromises or to modify their positions, this procedure allows all of the contradictory stances on a given question to be brought to the conference table.

NO TRUST OF RUSSIA

In part this proliferation of positions was the fault of overly ambitious CIS institutions, which threatened to usurp sovereignty that member states had not yet really exercised, but it also reflected the differing visions of the member states about the role of the CIS and the degree of integration that each wished to achieve. Theoretically there was a wide variety of forms that integration might have taken; even deep integration may have been achievable in the first years of independence, before member states began reform programs and otherwise ruptured Soviet-era linkages.

The only vehicle for integration put forward, however, was the CIS, which Russia strongly advocated, thereby making the other states cautious and suspicious. Russian leaders pushed immediately for the organization to increase its formal powers. The failure of CIS leaders to reach consensus on important issues only intensified Russian pressure, as in the April 1993 special meeting at which Boris Yeltsin, assisted by Nursultan Nazarbayev, attempted to force the leaders of Ukraine, Moldova, Georgia, and Armenia either to accept greater CIS control or to leave the organization.[28]

Table 1.1
CIS Institutions: Main Bodies*

Institution	Date of Formation	Occasion of Formation
Council of Heads of State (CHS)	21 December 1991	Summit on including Central Asian and Caucasus republics in CIS, Almaty
Council of Heads of Government (CHG)	21 December 1991	Summit on including Central Asian and Caucasus republics in CIS, Almaty
Council of Defense Ministers	14 February 1992	CHS meeting, Minsk
Customs Council	13 March 1992 (inactive due to lack of progress on CIS customs union)	CHG meeting, Moscow
Inter-Parliamentary Assembly of the Participating States of the CIS	27 March 1992	Meeting of representatives of CIS parliaments, Almaty
Economic Court	6 July 1992	CHS meeting, Moscow
Council of Ministers of Foreign Affairs	24 September 1993	CHS meeting, Moscow
Executive Secretariat of the CIS	24 September 1993	CHS meeting, Moscow
Council of Commanders of Border Troops	24 September 1993	CHS meeting, Moscow
Commission on Human Rights	24 September 1993 (inactive due to lack of support from participating states)	CHS meeting, Moscow
Staff for Coordination of Military Cooperation of the CIS Participating States	24 December 1993	CHS meeting, Ashgabat, Turkmenistan
Inter-State Economic Committee of the Economic Union (ISEC)	21 October 1994	CHS meeting, Moscow
Meetings of Attorneys General	December 1995	
Council of Ministers of Interior	19 January 1996	CHS meeting, Moscow
Council of the Heads of State Information Agencies (Informcouncil)	3 November 1996	CHG meeting, Moscow

Source: Andrei Zagorski, *SNG: Tsifry, fakty, personalii* (Minsk: PRS, 1998).

Table 1.2
CIS Institutions: Specialized Bodies*

Inter-State Currency Committee

CIS Inter-State Committee on Statistics

Consultative Legal Council of the CIS

CIS Center for Research and Consultation on Private Law

Inter-State Council on Anti-Monopoly Policy

Council of the Heads of Foreign Trade Agencies

Council for Protection of Industrial Property

Council on Railroad Transportation

Inter-State Aviation Committee

Inter-State Council on Outer Space

Inter-State Commission on Military-Economic Cooperation of the Participating States of the CIS

Inter-State Council on Machine Building

Inter-State Euro-Asian Association of Coal and Metals

Inter-State Council on Oil and Gas

Inter-State Council for Cooperation in the Area of Chemistry and Petrochemistry

Intergovernmental Council for Cooperation in the Construction Field

Eurasian Patents Organization

Council on Electric Energy

Inter-State Council on Exhibiting Activities

Inter-State Association "Electro-Trade-Union"

Inter-State Committee on Science and Technology

Inter-State Council for Coordination of Information on Science and Technology

Inter-State Council on Geodesy, Cartography, Cadastre, and Distance Sounding of the Earth

Inter-State Council on Standardization, Meteorology, and Certification

Inter-State Council on Agro-Industrial Complex

Intergovernmental Coordination Council on Seed-Growing

Council on Cooperation in Veterinary Medicine

Inter-State Consultative Council "Radionavigation"

Consultative Council on Labor, Migration, and Social Protection of the Population of the Participating States of the CIS

Council on Cooperation in Health Care

Council on Cultural Cooperation of the CIS Participating States

Sports Committee

Council on Tourism

Inter-State Ecological Council

Inter-State Coordination Television and Radio Company "Mir"

Inter-State Coordination Council of the Inter-State Television and Radio Company

Office for Coordination against Organized Crime and Other Dangerous Kinds of Crime on the Territory of the CIS

Coordination Council of the Heads of the *Feldjaeger* Agencies of the CIS States

Coordination Council for the Security of Means of Communications and of Their Use in the Communication Systems of Governments and Classified Communication in Agencies of the CIS Participating States

Inter-State Council on Emergency Situations

Joint Commission on Evacuation

Coordination Committee on Air Defense

Fund for Assistance to the Republic of Tajikistan

Inter-State Fund for Assistance to Refugees and Forced Migrants

Inter-State Commission on Food Importation

Source: Andrei Zagorski, *SNG: Tsifry, fakty, personalii* (Minsk: PRS, 1998).

* The distinction between main and specialized bodies is that, theoretically, the former are derived from the CIS Charter while the latter are auxiliary bodies established by separate agreements among member states. The distinction has become blurred, however, as many main bodies have been created through procedures similar to those established for the formation of specialized bodies.

The costs of doing the latter had already been made clear in Georgia, Azerbaijan, and Moldova. The Azerbaijanis pulled out of the CIS in October 1992 after the nationalist Abulfaz Elchibey was elected president in free and fair elections in June, replacing Ayaz Mutalipov (who had been forced from office in March). Within the next year well-armed Armenian troops took control of Karabakh and much of the territory surrounding it, essentially annexing 20 percent of Azerbaijan.[29] The Armenian government position is that the fighting was done exclusively by soldiers from Karabakh. Similarly, Georgians claim that Russia supported and armed Ossetian and Abkhaz separatists.[30] The Transdniestr region, where Russia's Fourteenth Army was stationed, continued to seek secession from Moldova, which had refused to sign the CIS Charter or founding documents.

The Russian government sought to distance itself formally from its surrogates active in Abkhazia, Armenia, and Transdniestr, but most observers remained unconvinced that it had done so. Withdrawal from the CIS seemed to insure that internal security problems would worsen. All of the new states were multinational (see table 1.3) and thus were vulnerable to ethnic tensions. Ukraine in particular was susceptible because of its eastern regions, which are heavily ethnic Russian.

States thus acquiesced to the CIS, as Azerbaijan and Georgia did in September 1993 and December 1993, respectively, but they had no interest in empowering its institutions, since these appeared to be vehicles for Russian domination. Suspicion of Russian motives for the degree and type of integration Russia desired was universal among the other members of the CIS. The behavior of the Russian elite, as well as that of the Russian government, seemed to justify these suspicions. From late 1992 on, when the Russian government was energetically pursuing CIS integration, many Russian commentators were tying CIS integration to Russia's vital interests and its claims to be a world power. A number of prominent Russian figures, including Ruslan Khasbulatov, speaker of the Russian Supreme Soviet, Vladimir Shumeyko, first chairman of the Russian Federation Council, and Vladimir Zhirinovsky, the leader of the newly triumphant Liberal-Democratic Party,[31] were vociferously critical of what they described as Russia's abandonment of ethnic Russians and Russian speakers in the other new states, or were loudly decrying

Table 1.3
Ethnic Breakdown of Former Soviet States (1989 data)

Armenia	
Armenian	93%
Azeri	3%
Russian	2%
Other	2%

Azerbaijan	
Azeri	82.7%
Dagestani	3.2%
Russian	5.6%
Armenian	5.6%
Other	2.9%

Belarus	
Belarusian	77.9%
Russian	13.2%
Polish	4.1%
Ukrainian	2.9%
Other	1.9%

Estonia	
Estonian	61.5%
Russian	30.3%
Ukrainian	3.2%
Other	5%

Georgia	
Georgian	70.1%
Armenian	8.1%
Russian	6.3%
Azeri	5.7%
Ossetian	3%
Abkhaz	1.8%
Other	5%

Kazakhstan	
Kazakh	41.9%
Russian	37%
Ukrainian	5.2%
German	4.7%
Uzbek	2.1%
Tatar	2.0%
Other	7.1%

Kyrgyzstan	
Kyrgyz	52.4%
Russian	21.5%
Uzbek	12.9%
Ukrainian	2.5%
German	2.4%
Other	8.3%

Latvia	
Latvian	51.8%
Russian	33.8%
Belarusian	4.5%
Ukrainian	3.4%
Polish	2.3%
Other	4.2%

Lithuania	
Lithuanian	80.1%
Russian	8.6%
Polish	7.7%
Other	3.6%

Moldova	
Moldovan/Romanian	64.5%
Ukrainian	13.8%
Russian	13%
Gagauz	3.5%
Bulgarian	2%
Other	3.2%

Russia	
Russian	81.5%
Tatar	3.8%
Ukrainian	3%
Chuvash	1.2%
Dagestani	1.2%
Other	9.3%

Tajikistan	
Tajik	64.9%
Uzbek	25%
Russian	3.5%
Other	6.6%

Turkmenistan	
Turkmen	73.3%
Uzbek	9%
Russian	9.8%
Kazakh	2%
Other	5.9%

Ukraine	
Ukrainian	73%
Russian	22%
Other	5%

Uzbekistan	
Uzbek	71.4%
Russian	8.3%
Tajik	4.7%
Kazakh	4.1%
Karakalpak	2.1%
Tatar	2.4%
Other	7%

Source: *New States, New Politics: Building the Post Soviet Nations,* ed. Ian Bremmer and Ray Taras (Cambridge, U.K.: Cambridge University Press, 1997), pp. 48, 706–7.

the security risks to Russia posed by the unsecured international borders of its near-abroad. Speaking at a June 9, 1994, session of the Inter-Parliamentary Assembly, Shumeyko argued that the CIS would evolve into a single confederate or even a federal state, while Zhirinovsky went even further to say that Russia should reacquire the most desirable parts of the former Soviet territories by force.[32] Even Russia's State Duma, the first post-independence parliament, which was elected following the dissolution by force of Russia's Soviet-era legislature,[33] passed formal resolutions demanding the reconstitution of the USSR, a stance the legislators reiterated as recently as March 1996. In the early 1990s, even many moderate Russians held the view that, while the sovereignty of the newly independent states should be preserved, the CIS should become an eastern version of the European Union, with a single currency, a strong supranational parliament, and a single security system.

No serious political actor in Russia, however, ever advocated that the CIS become a union of juridical equals, as the European Union is. The EU has two or three strong nations at its core, but it was Russia's intention that the CIS would have only one. Indeed, most influential Russians believed that the CIS states were incapable of sustaining independence, so membership in the CIS would be beneficial to all parties by minimizing the hardship of transition in the new states, while helping to insulate Russia from its neighbors' problems.

Such a geostrategic vision was never stated openly by President Yeltsin, former Foreign Minister Andrei Kozyrev, or former Prime Ministers Viktor Chernomyrdin and Yevgeny Primakov, but leaders elsewhere in the CIS understood the implications of Russia's integrationist desires even though they were not openly articulated. All of the CIS leaders were products of the Soviet system and were accustomed to a world in which public pronouncements had little to do with *Realpolitik*. Whatever the challenges of independence, these leaders were reluctant to concede power to a large powerful neighbor that had contempt for their independence.

THE GOALS OF THE CIS

Fears of Russian domination and the desire of each country's leader to be free to shape the domestic politics of his state made it equally difficult for the CIS states to move toward realization of the organization's stated goals. Attempts at cooperation in economics and security are discussed at length in the following two chapters; those chapters show that efforts in both of these spheres bogged down from the beginning in a combination of suspicion of Russia and the insistence of each leader to maximize his nation's interest, even if that came at the expense of a neighbor.

The ways in which this combination made it difficult for the CIS states to work for common goals may also be seen in other spheres. The CIS Charter, for example, calls for member nations to coordinate their foreign policies, but the issue of NATO enlargement, which infuriated Russia, initially caused barely a ripple in any other CIS states except Belarus, which supported Russia. Ukraine even welcomed NATO enlargement, and some Ukrainian politicians voiced hopes that their country might also join the alliance some day.

Another case in point is the civil war in Afghanistan. The Afghan-Tajik border has been the site of frequent attacks both by Tajik opposition forces and by Afghan Mujahideen rebels; one such incident in August 1994 left seven Russian border guards dead and fourteen injured.[34] Russian leaders unsuccessfully tried several times to mobilize the five Central Asian presidents to adopt a common stance both on defending the old Soviet-Afghan border and on bolstering the Northern Alliance of Afghanistan's combatants as the alliance was being overwhelmed by the Taliban.[35] The five states understood the threat in different ways, however. Turkmenistan did not even attend the summit held in Almaty to discuss the problem in October 1996 and then, one year later, gave de facto recognition to the Taliban government, when two senior Taliban officials were received in Turkmenistan's capital. By contrast, Uzbekistan openly supported the ethnic Uzbek opposition in Afghanistan, which was locked in bloody struggle with the Taliban.

It has not proven any easier to coordinate policies on what might seem to be less contentious issues, such as environmental policy. Usually this is because what seems to be an environmental question to one state is an economic question to another. In the case of water, for example, the comparatively richer states of Turkmenistan and Uzbekistan are especially big users,[36] while the comparatively poorer states of Tajikistan and Kyrgyzstan are Central Asia's major suppliers. However, water is supplied free to the users, while the individual states must pay to maintain all dams, reservoirs, and other water-storage facilities found on their territories.

Similarly, the Caspian littoral states of Russia, Azerbaijan, Turkmenistan, and Kazakhstan have been unable to reach formal agreement on the legal status of the Caspian Sea or on how it may be divided. Ownership of the fossil fuel reserves in and around the Caspian is a major concern for most of the littoral states, but Russia initially tried to frame the discussion in terms of ecological management. The CIS has proven a wholly inadequate forum in which to debate such issues, let alone to resolve them.

The CIS Charter is also marred by the amorphousness of some of its goals, especially in the cultural sphere. The charter mandates common support for the spiritual unity of citizens, based upon respect for identity, cultural exchange, and close cooperation in the preservation of cultural values. This goal, however, contradicts the desire of most CIS states to strengthen the role of the core ethno-national community in what is usually seen as a national homeland. The CIS states have failed to reach agreement on protecting the rights of national minorities, in large part because Russia has defined protection as synonymous with the Russian minorities retaining their privileged position, including the retention of Russian as the dominant language and as a medium of education in the Soviet successor states. The other member states have resisted this position, because the right to set policies of language and culture is crucial to these new states, touching as it does the heart of national identity and state sovereignty. Only Belarus and Kyrgyzstan have been willing to give Russian formal status as one of their national tongues.

The issues concealed behind such questions are of enormous importance because of the unsettled waves of migration that have rolled across all of the post-Soviet expanse. Some of this population movement has been caused by war. Armenia and Azerbaijan both have large refugee populations, constituting 6 percent and 3 percent of their total populations, respectively; per capita, these are the largest refugee populations in the former Soviet Union.[37] Kyrgyz have fled Tajikistan's civil war, as have some Uzbeks, even though the Tashkent government has tried to limit their flight wherever possible for fear that it might provoke reprisals against local Tajiks. Georgia and Russia both have serious refugee problems as results of their respective internal conflicts.

Peacetime migrations, though, involve even larger numbers of people. Individual motivations for relocation are complex, but ethnicity generally plays a major role. Some migrants feel that their nationality limits their economic prospects. As national languages gain hold in the new states, many feel that they have become second-class citizens, while others are reluctant to become citizens of what they now view as foreign states, even if in some cases they, or even their parents, were born in the former Soviet republic that they are now leaving.[38]

Ethnic Russians seeking to return to Russia make up by far the largest group of migrants, but there has been a migration in and out of every post-Soviet state. From 1991 to 1997 there was a net migration to Russia of more than 2.6 million people.[39] According to data compiled by demographer Zhanna Zayonchkovskaya, of all the other CIS states only Belarus shows a small but steady net in-migration of some 86,000 people. Ukraine had a net in-migration for 1991–1993, but since 1994 has had more people leaving the country each year than coming in.[40]

Frequently, non-Russians are returning to a "historic homeland," but often the motive for relocation is economic. The domestic economies of Armenia, Georgia, and Azerbaijan depend heavily upon remittances from workers living in Russia; it is estimated, for example, that about a third of the Azerbaijani labor force is employed outside of the country.[41] Large numbers of Belarusians and Ukrainians are also employed in the Russian economy, but their presence does not provoke the same kind of race hatred there as do the so-called people of Caucasian nationality. In Moscow in particular, there have been periodic roundups of "illegal aliens" from CIS states, which have led to deportations of even long-term residents who had failed to secure the proper registration during the Soviet era.[42]

Russia put strong pressure on all the CIS leaders to adopt policies of dual citizenship, but without wide success. Turkmenistan and Russia signed a dual citizenship agreement in December 1993, at which time Boris Yeltsin demonstratively accepted Turkmen citizenship. Anecdotal evidence suggests, however, that while this treaty made it easier for ethnic Russians living in Turkmenistan to get Russian citizenship, it never became easy for Turkmens to do so. Moreover, when relations between Turkmenistan and Russia later began to sour over the question of pipeline access for Turkmen gas, Ashgabat allowed this treaty to fall into disuse. Turkmenistan then became the first CIS state to restrict entry to citizens of other Commonwealth members when it introduced a visa regime on June 9, 1999.

The Tajiks also came to permit local Russians to hold dual citizenship, although Russians living in Tajikistan have complained that it is hard to obtain Russian passports. Kazakhstan, Russia, and Kyrgyzstan all reached bilateral agreements on interchangeability of citizenship among their states, but the Kazakh-Russian agreement was debated for two years by the Russian State Duma before it was ratified.

Citizenship questions were part of the "deep integration" agreement signed by Belarus, Kazakhstan, Kyrgyzstan, and Russia on March 30, 1996.[43] The signatories all pledged to preserve "a common cultural and educational space" and to facilitate the granting of citizenship. While there is regular talk of this agreement becoming a model for other CIS states, only Tajikistan has shown any interest in participating; it was accepted with apparent reluctance, having had to wait until February 1999 to be granted full membership. This treaty, however, has yet to achieve its stated goals. Citizenship is not proving easy to exchange, except for ethnic Russians returning home.

The CIS Charter commits member states to various principles of international law, including respect for territorial integrity and border inviolability; noninterference in other members' domestic affairs, either by force or through the threat of force; priority of international law over national legislation; peaceful resolution of conflicts; right to self-determination; conscientious discharge of commitments; and various other human rights decrees.

The CIS has had as much difficulty in meeting these goals as it has had in setting standards for ethnic tolerance. Russian officials have downplayed or denied official involvement, but Georgian, Azerbaijani, and Moldovan officials have all complained of Russian interference in their internal affairs. President Eduard Shevardnadze of Georgia has claimed several times that "outside groups"—generally understood to mean Russians—are responsible for several assassination attempts against him, while Azerbaijan's President Heydar Aliyev accused Russians of being behind the failed insurrection led by Surat Hussein.[44]

For most of the CIS states, it is not necessary that Russia's hand actually be visible in such interventions; it is sufficient only that Russia does not seem displeased by them. After all, at one time Russian Foreign Minister Andrei Kozyrev stated openly that Russia reserved the right to intervene militarily to protect ethnic Russians living in the former republics.[45] To be sure, he subsequently tried to reassure concerned senior officials from the rest of the CIS that Russia planned no unilateral actions. Kozyrev's foreign policy nevertheless saw the protection of the rights of Russian minorities as falling explicitly within Russia's domain, rejecting claims that these were domestic or internal problems. Although Russian law defines such "foreign" Russians as co-nationals, not citizens, the Russian Duma has nevertheless attempted to legislate privileges and rights for them. Russia preferred to apply pressure on states that it considered to be violating the rights of local ethnic Russians through international bodies, such as the Organization for Security and Cooperation in Europe and the Council of Europe, but Moscow refused to rule out more direct responses, if it deemed them necessary.

CIS members have demonstrated little inclination to respect mutual interests, frequently employing economic levers against one another for larger political gains. Russia, for example, has played "pipeline politics" with all the CIS fossil fuel oil producers, but it is not the only country to link energy supply with political aims. Uzbekistan has done the same with Kyrgyzstan, Kazakhstan, and especially with Tajikistan. Even though the two countries are part of a formal economic union, Uzbekistan has not hesitated to cut off gas supplies to Kyrgyzstan regularly.

The CIS has done little to promote consistent legal and human rights standards throughout the former USSR. CIS member states exhibit a wide spectrum of political regimes and demonstrate significant differences in human rights standards. In Belarus, Uzbekistan, and Turkmenistan, authoritarian leaders have already consolidated power, so the citizens of these states have few rights or liberties. The performance of the rest of the CIS members is more mixed. Russia, Ukraine, Georgia, and Kyrgyzstan offer better protection of human rights and civil liberties than do Kazakhstan, Moldova, Azerbaijan, and Armenia, while Tajikistan's record approaches that of the three authoritarian states.[46]

Ironically, the restriction of human rights is one of the few areas of reasonably good cooperation within the CIS. The state security services do cooperate with one another on both a formal and an informal basis. Uzbek and Turkmen opposition figures have been detained in Moscow at the request of their national authorities. Uzbek officials were given the right to detain an Uzbek opposition figure who was visiting Kyrgyzstan,[47] which they did with consider-able force, and Kazakh security officials are rumored to have been responsible for the beating of a prominent Kazakh opposition figure who was attending a conference in Bishkek.[48]

Cooperation on crime fighting has been less systematic. Law enforcement officials have signed a series of agreements on coopera-tion in criminal investigations and in controlling narcotics trafficking. One example is a 1998 initiative that calls for the creation of an Inter-State Center for Combating Drug Trafficking subordinate to the CIS Executive Secretariat. The center has yet to be organized, however, because CIS member states disagree on several issues, including the important question of how the center will be funded. Unless an international sponsor is found, this initiative is likely to join the legions of other stillborn CIS proposals.

Despite the failure of these agreements to produce an integrated crime fighting program for the CIS, cooperation among the various Ministries of Interior must be seen as one of the CIS success stories, for it is well institutionalized, has generated a common database, and takes place on a regular basis. It should be pointed out, however, that one of the reasons why this form of cooperation has been rela-tively successful is the persisting influence of close personal ties among Soviet-era law-enforcement professionals, which extend across the new national boundaries. The structure of the CIS is such that the rising generation of law-enforcement professionals, who are now receiving different types of training in their various states, have no venue in which to develop similar relationships for the future.

NEW UNDERSTANDINGS OF SOVEREIGNTY

During the first years of the CIS's existence, the degree to which the various CIS leaders wished to see integration work was largely a function of how they thought it would impact national sovereignty of their particular states.

In many ways Turkmenistan has been the most adamant opponent of integration. Ashgabat adopted a doctrine of positive neutrality immediately after independence, which was recognized by a UN resolution in 1995. The state prefers bilateral relations to multilateral structures and has avoided participation even in regional Central Asian bodies.

The stand of Ukraine is of greater impact though, for it has from the beginning limited the scope and effectiveness of the CIS, making it impossible for the CIS to take action on any of the myriad issues on which Ukraine and Russia disagree. Ukraine understands the CIS to be a mechanism for the civilized divorce of the Soviet Union's constituent republics. The Ukrainians resist political integration of the post-Soviet states both because of the threat this poses for the country's current positions and because they seek greater integration with Europe. The Ukrainians prefer to strengthen the organization that they created with Georgia, Azerbaijan, and Moldova, which was originally given the acronym GUAM, and renamed GUUAM after Uzbekistan joined in April 1999.[49] Kyiv is also eager to promote new trade routes that would pass south of Russia and use Ukraine's territory to link China with Europe.

Since the formation of the CIS, Uzbekistan's position has moved toward that of Ukraine; Presidents Karimov and Kuchma have also developed a close personal relationship; they have even vacationed together.[50] Uzbekistan is more open to the development of multilateral relations than is Ukraine but it also seeks a strong regional role for itself. For this reason it formed a Central Asian Economic Community with Kazakhstan, Kyrgyzstan, and Tajikistan.[51] It has openly opposed attempts to have the CIS act as a suprastate.

The Aliyev government in Azerbaijan is becoming an increasingly reluctant CIS partner as Western interest in the country's petroleum resources has grown. Azerbaijan is especially interested in developing transit routes for oil and gas that bypass Russia. As long as its dispute with Armenia remains unsettled, however, Azerbaijan will have to take Russia's geopolitical demands and concerns into account.

Georgia and Moldova are also reluctant participants in the CIS, having been dragged into the organization by economic helplessness, the possibility of civil collapse, and Russian pressure. As already noted, Moldova formally limits its participation in the CIS to economic questions, while Georgia has concentrated on reducing, and if possible eliminating, Russia's military presence in its country.

The leaders of Kazakhstan and Kyrgyzstan, who did not want to leave the USSR, saw the CIS as an instrument by which to preserve as many of the Soviet Union's features as possible and thus were among the most enthusiastic integrationists. After Russia, probably the strongest advocate of integration was Kazakhstan, because President Nursultan Nazarbayev was convinced that the economic integrity of the USSR's geopolitical expanse had to be preserved. But Nazarbayev would not accept integration that sacrificed the juridical independence of each of the member states. He proposed instead that the CIS be replaced by a new organization, the Euro-Asian Union (EAU), in which member states would adopt common policies at an intergovernmental assembly and share a common currency and mutually beneficial foreign economic policies. EAU decisions would require a four-fifths majority vote, with each member state having an equal vote.

Nazarbayev offered this proposal at the CIS summit in April 1994, but it evoked little response. That did not stop him from pushing forward with the idea, which he formally introduced as a public document at the United Nations.[52] Some 200 articles were published in CIS newspapers in support of the proposal, which was also debated at conferences in Russia and Almaty. The EAU, however, never generated a groundswell of public support. For a time both Kyrgyzstan's Askar Akaev and Georgia's Eduard Shevardnadze expressed interest in Nazarbayev's proposal, but both eventually backed away when it became clear that Russia's leadership would not endorse it.

The CIS's other presidents, who were not as willing as Nazarbayev to trade sovereignty for security, were even less enthusiastic. Russia's formal response to Nazarbayev's plan was presented at the October 1994 CIS summit. The response plan asked member states to agree to a six-point program for strengthening the CIS, demanding closer integration of economic, political, and security relations within the CIS's existing institutional arrangements. This counter proposal left little doubt that Nazarbayev's proposal for the creation of a Euro-Asian union was dead, although the Kazakh leader continues to hold out hope that eventually it will be revived.

Over time, Kazakhstan's and Kyrgyzstan's approaches to integration have become more pragmatic. Kyrgyzstan sees the CIS as a source of economic assistance, while Kazakhstan perceives it as a means of mollifying its large Russian minority. The last remaining CIS enthusiasts are Tajikistan, Armenia, and Belarus, all of which are keenly interested in pursuing actively integrative national development strategies. The Tajik government has used the CIS to help hold the state together against the pressure of its several warring factions. Armenia has consistently supported Russia's political integration initiatives because it needs economic and military help from Russia to maintain an advantage in its conflict with Azerbaijan over Karabakh. Belarus understands the CIS mainly as a means for reintegration with Russia. Other than the need that each has to continue to rely upon Russia, however, there is little that unites these three states.

THE LATE CIS: HOLDING ON TO SOVEREIGNTY

This combination of passive resistance by most member states and enthusiasm without resources by others has prevented the CIS from developing into an effective organization. In fact, Russia's continued determination to make the CIS work is the only thing that has kept the organization from dying entirely.

Moscow has been actively trying to resuscitate CIS institutions since spring 1994, but has found little enthusiasm among CIS members for reworking the charter. At the February 10, 1995, summit in Almaty, Russian President Boris Yeltsin pressed hard for new forms of integration and consolidation of CIS member state policies to compensate for the failure of CIS institutions, implying menacingly that there would be other consequences if such measures were not adopted. Since the Russian army was then mired down in Chechnya, Yeltsin's threats were not taken seriously.

Yeltsin made another effort to reform the CIS at a closed-door session held during the March 28, 1997 summit, trying to invigorate CIS institutions by scaling them back. The same meeting saw serious discussion of the need to systemize specialized institutions and to merge specialized committees.[53] Yeltsin was reelected chairman of the Heads of State Council for the fourth time at this summit, after promising that Russia would increase its efforts to treat all CIS members as equals. In the course of the meeting, however, Presidents Kuchma (Ukraine), Shevardnadze (Georgia), Aliyev (Azerbaijan), Nazarbayev (Kazakhstan), and Lucinschi (Moldova) all argued that bilateral relations had proven to be more effective than multilateral ones and contended that the CIS had failed to justify itself as an instrument of cooperation.[54]

The changes that Yeltsin engineered improved neither the effectiveness, nor the popularity of CIS institutions. At the next CIS Heads of State meeting, held in Chisinau in October 1997, none of the documents presented for approval was signed, and Russia was attacked by the other member states. The presidents of Georgia, Azerbaijan, Uzbekistan, and Ukraine all argued that the CIS policy of multitrack integration was hindering, not helping, the development of harmonious relations among the member states. President Karimov of Uzbekistan said that the CIS states had to solve their internal problems and strengthen their individual economies before it would be possible to move toward integration; most attendees held Russia at least partly responsible for those persistent problems. President Aliyev declared that Azerbaijan would support no further integration until the Karabakh conflict was resolved. President Shevardnadze went one step further, saying that Georgia would consider leaving the CIS if Russia did not stop impeding the peace process in Abkhazia.[55]

Yeltsin's failing health dealt a further blow to the CIS. A Heads of State meeting first scheduled for January 1998 was postponed several times before it was finally held on April 29 in Moscow. In an effort to give greater credibility to the ailing Russian leader, it was agreed at that time that Yeltsin would remain chairman of the council until 2000. To a certain extent this demonstration of essentially personal support also was extended to the CIS as an organization. The Heads of Government Council had also delayed its meeting for several months, not for health reasons, but because of an inability to agree on the text of several key agreements that were being prepared for presentation. At the meeting of this council on March 6, members agreed to delegate authority both to the Council of CIS Foreign Ministers and to the Inter-State Economic Committee. This prompted Anatoly Adamishin, then Russia's minister for cooperation with CIS members, to remark, "All this indicates is that the CIS is proceeding to the next stage, a stage of normal work, and that relationships among the CIS member countries are acquiring an increasingly business-like character."[56]

The April 1998 summit appointed Russian businessman Boris Berezovsky the executive secretary of the CIS. Believing that he possessed the charm and skills necessary to save the organization and to make it more business-like, Berezovsky launched an ambitious program of travel and consultation with CIS leaders, trying to find ways to make CIS functions more clearly defined and mutually acceptable.[57]

Plans were made to hold an interstate forum on reforming the CIS, and a number of working groups were appointed to review the functions of the various councils and to suggest new mechanisms for implementing the decisions of various CIS bodies. Berezovsky focused on two issues: the creation of a functioning free trade zone and a reorganization of the CIS apparatus. He proposed the creation of a Coordinating Consultative Committee that would unite the existing Executive Secretariat, the CIS Inter-State Economic Committee, and thus the whole CIS apparatus. Berezovsky also advocated a dramatic cutback of the CIS bureaucracy and a streamlining of the organization; all administrative structures except those that provide support for the Heads of State Council would be consolidated and the number of CIS employees would drop from 2,340 to 600 or 700.

Work along these lines moved forward while Berezovsky remained in this post, but the changes he proposed encountered broad resistance. In particular, the presidents of Turkmenistan and Uzbekistan opposed restructuring because they had no wish to strengthen the CIS administration. Many feared that Berezovsky wanted to use the executive secretaryship to build himself a position of power; President Lukashenko of Belarus in particular seems to have objected to Berezovsky personally rather than to the position as such. Not surprisingly, the CIS staff was strongly against the proposed personnel reductions and also objected to Berezovsky's market approach to economics.[58] Others objected to Berezovsky's proposal that the representatives be seated hierarchically at summit meetings according to their countries' contributions to the organization.[59]

Disagreements over Berezovsky's proposals, especially those for organizational changes, caused a CIS summit to be rescheduled several times in early 1999, until President Yeltsin made the disputes moot by firing Berezovsky in March 1999. While several CIS leaders maintained that the Russian president did not have the authority to do this,[60] they seemed in fact to approve of the dismissal. Berezovsky's firing was confirmed at the April 2, 1999, summit in Moscow, where he was replaced by Yuri Yarov, a low-key former Russian deputy prime minister. Substantiating the charge that the CIS presidents objected to Berezovsky himself rather than to his proposals, the council adopted what essentially were Berezovsky's plans for reorganization of the CIS apparatus, although they only endorsed reducing its staff by half. They also accepted the amendments that Berezovsky had proposed to make the CIS protocol on the Free Trade Zone more effective.

A NEW KIND OF UNION

A political union by definition requires contracting national governments to delegate power to some kind of supranational institution. The European Union's experience with integration demonstrates the reluctance with which even secure and well-established national governments will delegate power to a supranational body. Experience also suggests that successful political unions rarely include members who may pose direct threats to the independence of other member states. In successful unions members are reassured by the degree of leverage that they acquire from the supranational institutions, rather than fearful that such institutions are a disguised form of one member's hegemony. The development of the CIS has been severely hindered by the imbalance of power among its members. In the EU, France and Germany serve as two power centers, with Italy and England also playing major roles. This configuration has allowed even small member states to matter in the EU by forming coalitions around at least one of these four larger states.

The situation in the CIS is not a comparable one. There is no state or group of states in the post-Soviet space that can counterbalance Russia in a supranational decision-making body. The Soviet experience constantly reminds the new elites of the CIS that Russia could effectively usurp their independence in any supranational body in which it is the only major power center. Russia's understanding of that same Soviet experience, however, equally reminds it of the costs that Russia might incur by ceding its own sovereignty to a supranational body. Fear that the other members of such a body could take more from Russia than they would contribute has made Russia try to prevent the CIS from developing into an organization in which sovereignty is yielded equally.

In addition to a remarkable degree of mutual suspicion, the CIS states share a profound reluctance to part with any of the sovereignty they so recently have gained. The newly independent states are slowly developing new kinds of cooperative institutions and associations, but they remain nearly as reluctant to yield sovereignty to smaller bodies as they have been to yield it to the CIS. Russia has been moving slowly to develop its union with Belarus, despite Belarus's official enthusiasm for the merger; even in Belarus, though, the ruling elite seems to be developing a greater appreciation of its own sovereignty. The "deep integration" of Kazakhstan, Kyrgyzstan, Belarus, Tajikistan, and Russia has yet to develop into an effective union, while the economic union agreed to by Kazakhstan, Kyrgyzstan, Uzbekistan, and Tajikistan has not lowered the customs barriers that have risen between these states. Economic competition among the members and the region's acute shortage of capital greatly limit the ability of this union to function. The same is true of the GUUAM union, which Georgia, Ukraine, Uzbekistan, Azerbaijan, and Moldova would like to be used to limit Russia's ability to be a gatekeeper for transportation and trade.

These smaller unions were formed with greater enthusiasm and clearer need than was the CIS, yet they seem to suffer from the same inability to create workable institutional bases of integration. This supports theoretical arguments that new states have more difficulty coming together in successful multilateral groupings than do older states. If the CIS states were to face a shared external challenge, this might provide sufficient incentive for integration, but for now most threats to the internal stability of the post-Soviet states lie either within the borders of each state or within the CIS. Even such external threats that do exist, such as the Afghan civil war, do not affect the entire CIS.

At the same time, though, the inability of these states to integrate politically does not mean that any of them can afford to abandon entirely the goal of integration within the CIS. They may embrace this goal to varying and ever diminishing degrees, but the post-Soviet states still occupy a shared economic and security space. The political institutions of the CIS, especially those that provide for regular meetings of the heads of state, prime ministers, and foreign ministers, make it easier to regulate life within this common space. These regular multilateral sessions also help each of these states to hold their own in bilateral encounters with Russia.

Changing economic circumstances may well alter the balance in future bilateral relationships, and the passage of time will continue to erode the common elite culture that the present leaders still share from Soviet times. The appearance of new elites in the member states will increasingly mean that leaders will not even share a common language, and if they do, it is just as likely to be English as Russian. In present circumstances, the CIS serves an obvious purpose in providing regular meetings of the member states' presidents and other elites, even if these meetings accomplish little of formal consequence. As the many legacies of the Soviet Union continue to disappear, however, the purposes of the CIS will continue to dwindle and eventually to disappear.

NOTES

[1] Dates of each state's admission to the United Nations are as follows: Armenia, March 2, 1992; Azerbaijan, March 9, 1992; Belarus, October 24, 1945; Estonia, September 17, 1991; Georgia, July 31, 1992; Kazakhstan, March 2, 1992; Kyrgyzstan, March 2, 1992; Latvia, September 17, 1991; Lithuania, September 17, 1991; Moldova, March 2, 1992; Tajikistan, March 2, 1992; Turkmenistan, March 2, 1992; Ukraine, October 24, 1945; Uzbekistan, March 2, 1992; Russia, October 24, 1945. The USSR was an original member of the United Nations from October 24, 1945. In a letter dated December 24, 1991, Boris Yeltsin informed the secretary general that the membership of the Soviet Union in the Security Council and all other UN organs was being continued by the Russian Federation with the support of the eleven member countries of the Commonwealth of Independent States.

[2] Britain submitted the Palestinian issue to the United Nations in February 1947. In November of that year, the United Nations passed a resolution on the partition of the territory into Israel and Palestine, and Britain relinquished control in May 1948. On February 20, 1947, Britain announced that it would withdraw from India in June 1948. On June 3, 1947, the withdrawal date was moved back to August 14, 1947.

[3] For two excellent discussions of alliance formation and state interactions within alliances, see Stephen M. Walt, *The Origin of Alliances* (Ithaca, N.Y.: Cornell University Press, 1987) and Glenn H. Snyder, *Alliance Politics* (Ithaca, N.Y.: Cornell University Press, 1997).

[4] Chechnya and Ingushetia split into two republics in 1992.

[5] The referendum took place on March 17, 1991. The breakdown of the vote by republic, in terms of support for preserving the USSR,

was as follows: Russia 71 percent, Belarus 83 percent, Ukraine 70 percent, Azerbaijan 93 percent, Kazakhstan 94 percent, Uzbekistan 94 percent, Tajikistan 96 percent, Turkmenistan 98 percent, Kyrgyzstan 95 percent. The Baltic republics, along with Moldova and Georgia, did not participate in the vote; however, Moldova's Transdniestr and Gagauz regions and Georgia's Abkhazia region allowed the referendum to continue. Support for the union in all three of these areas was almost universal. Ian Bremmer and Ray Taras, eds., *New States, New Politics: Building the Post-Soviet Nations* (Cambridge, U.K.: Cambridge University Press, 1997).

[6] In August the parliaments of Ukraine, Moldova, Azerbaijan, and Kyrgyzstan declared independence, and those of Belarus and Tajikistan issued declarations of sovereignty. (The December 1 vote in Ukraine, as referred to in the text, was a popular referendum.) Uzbekistan's legislature declared independence in September and Turkmenistan's did the same in October.

[7] These leaders were elected president of their respective states in 1991, though both began the process of coming to power in 1990, when Ter-Petrossian was elected parliamentary chairman and Gamsakhurdia's Round Table-Free Georgia bloc won parliamentary elections.

[8] Makhamov resigned on August 31, 1991.

[9] For a discussion of quasi-states, see Robert H. Jackson, *Quasi-states: Sovereignty, International Relations, and the Third World* (Cambridge, U.K.: Cambridge University Press, 1990).

[10] Each republic's share of the former Soviet debt was to be based on its share of the Soviet Union's population, exports, imports, and national income. The agreement signed at the December 4 meeting also linked a republic's fulfillment of its debt repayment commitment to its ability to claim its share of the former Soviet Union's assets. Andrei Zagorski, *SNG: Tsifry, fakty, personalii* (Minsk, Belarus: PRS, 1998), p. 24.

[11] Ninety percent of the population voted for Ukrainian independence in the referendum. Bremmer and Taras, eds., *New States, New Politics*, p. 269.

[12] According to then-Soviet foreign minister Andrei Kozyrev, the Ukrainians and Belarusians came to the Minsk meeting—which was actually at a dacha in the Belovezh Forest—opposing the continuation of a Soviet Union-type structure that would demand

their subjugation to Moscow. The Russians leaned more toward preserving the union, at least among the three Slavic republics. Andrei Kozyrev, *Preobrazhenie, mezhdunarodnye otnosheniia* (Moscow: Mezhdunarodnye Otnosheniia, 1995), pp. 169–70.

[13] Kravchuk became chairman of Ukraine's Supreme Soviet on July 23, 1990, and was elected president on December 1, 1991.

[14] Shushkevich was elected chairman of the Belarus Supreme Soviet on September 18, 1991.

[15] The fourth signatory, the Transcaucasian Republic, was subsequently broken up to form the separate republics of Georgia, Armenia, and Azerbaijan.

[16] To reflect Kazakh pronunciation, Alma-Ata was formally renamed Almaty by a decree of the Supreme Kenges (Parliament) of Kazakhstan on May 13, 1993. Shirin Akiner, *The Formation of Kazakh Identity from Tribe to Nation-State* (London: The Royal Institute of International Affairs, 1995), p. 61. For the sake of consistency throughout this book, we are using the latter Kazakh language designation, rather than the Russian that it replaced.

[17] Minsk (Belovezh Forest) Agreement on Creation of the Commonwealth, Article 7, printed in *TASS International Service*, December 9, 1991, as translated by *FBIS Daily Report*, SOV-91-237, December 10, 1991.

[18] During the June 4, 1999, meeting, the Council of Heads of Government implemented some of the CIS reorganization plans and created two new administrative bodies: the Commonwealth Executive Committee, which replaced the Executive Secretariat, and the Economic Council, which has consolidated the Inter-State Economic Committee and most of the CIS economic bodies. However, at the time of this report, the agenda or the exact structure of these bodies was still unclear.

[19] This State Council, formed on September 2, 1991, consisted of Gorbachev and the heads of the republics that planned to remain in a confederation. Its actions included recognizing the independence of the Baltic states on September 6, 1991, and disbanding the Soviet KGB on October 23, 1991. Bremmer and Taras, eds., *New States, New Politics*, p. 81.

[20] For details on these meetings, see the Appendix.

[21] This meeting was attended by the prime ministers of all CIS members except Ukraine, which sent a deputy economics minister.

[22] Approximately $80 billion in 1992. See *1993 CIA World Factbook*, which can be found at http://cesimo.ing.ula.ve/GAIA/CIA/factbook/first_page/Russia.html.

[23] The newly independent states that transferred debts and assets to Russia on a "null-null" basis gave up any claims of a share of the USSR's assets in return for being forgiven any responsibility for the USSR's debts.

[24] *Postfactum*, March 20, 1992, in *FBIS Daily Report*, SOV-92-056, March 23, 1992.

[25] Zagorski, *SNG: Tsifry, fakty, personalii*, p. 9.

[26] Uzbekistan and Turkmenistan remain outside the group, although they do sometimes send observers to assembly meetings.

[27] The court has eight members: Armenia, Belarus, Kazakhstan, Kyrgyzstan, Moldova, Russia, Tajikistan, and Uzbekistan. By June 1998 just twelve of the sixteen judges had been appointed and the court had heard only twenty-eight cases, three of which had to deal with breach of contracts and the rest with interpretation of the existing economic agreements. *Belorusskaia delovaia gazeta*, May 27, 1998.

[28] All CIS heads of state attended this meeting, except the Turkmen president, who was ill, and the Kyrgyz president, who had a prior engagement. The stance on CIS issues of Turkmen President Niyazov was also a subject of criticism, although he did not attend the meeting. *Keesing's Record of World Events*, April 1993.

[29] See *The World Factbook 1998*. (Washington, D.C.: Central Intelligence Agency, 1998), p. 32.

[30] There is general acceptance that there was Russian support of the Abkhaz separatists during their successful military campaign in summer 1993 in which rebels routed Georgian military forces that had been stationed in Abkhazia and its regional capital of Sukhumi. Dodge Billingsley, "Georgian-Abkhazian Security Issues," *Jane's Intelligence Review*, February 1996, pp. 65–8. For a lengthier discussion, see chapter four of this book.

[31] During the December 1993 parliamentary election, the Liberal-Democratic Party of Russia won 22.9 percent of the vote and 54 out of 450 seats.

[32] Zhirinovsky is famous for his statement that Russian soldiers should someday wash their feet in the waters of the Indian Ocean. Vladimir Zhirinovsky, *Poslednii brosok na iug* (Moscow: TOO "Pisatel," IK "Bukvitsa," 1993).

[33] In October 1993, President Yeltsin sent tanks to fire on the Russian White House where members of the disbanded parliament were holed up.

[34] *Interfax*, August 19, 1994, in *FBIS Daily Report*, SOV-94-162, November 12, 1995.

[35] The Northern Alliance, the anti-Taliban opposition group within Afghanistan, included ethnic Uzbeks and Tajiks, as well as members of Afghanistan's Shi'ite Muslim minority. It was formed after the Taliban pushed government forces out of the Afghan capital of Kabul on September 27, 1996.

[36] As of 1996, Turkmenistan withdrew about 22.8 billion cubic meters of fresh water a year, and Uzbekistan withdrew about 82.2 billion cubic meters. World Bank, *World Development Report 1998/99* (Washington, D.C.: World Bank, 1999), p. 207.

[37] Martha Brill Olcott, "Pipelines and Pipe Dreams: Energy Development and Caspian Society," *Journal of International Affairs*, vol. 53, no. 1 (Fall 1999), forthcoming.

[38] Galina Vitkovskaya, *Emigratsiia netitulnovo naseleniia iz Kazakhstana, Kyrgyzstana i Uzbekistana*, unpublished manuscript.

[39] Zhanna Zayonchkovskaya, unpublished study.

[40] From 1991 to 1993 Ukraine's net in-migration was 485,000 people. From 1994 to 1997 its net out-migration was 451,000. Zayonchkovskaya, ibid.

[41] Sabit Bagirov, "Sotsialno-ekonomicheskie aspekty perekhoda k rynku v Azerbaijane," unpublished paper (Baku, Azerbaijan: January 1999).

[42] According to the U.S. State Department's "1998 Human Rights Report for Russia," Moscow Mayor Yuri Luzhkov has repeatedly encouraged the deportation of Caucasians from the city. In 1996, the report alleges, Luzhkov signed a document mandating that anyone not registered to live in Moscow be forced to leave. Moscow denies the existence of such a document, and it also denies the State Department's assertion that 20,000 to 25,000 people are forced to leave the city each year. The State Department report also states that Moscow's special police unit OMON conducts regular document checks of dark-skinned people, often entering their houses without warrants and fining them excessively for not being registered to live in Moscow.

[43] This agreement was formally called the Treaty on the Intensification of Integration in the Economic and Humanitarian Areas.

[44] Since Aliyev came to power there have been two serious attempts to remove him forcibly from office. Then prime minister and former army colonel Surat Hussein was allegedly behind an October 1994 rebellion against Aliyev in Ganja, Azerbaijan's second largest city. *Paris AFP*, October 5, 1994, as *FBIS Daily Report*, SOV-94-194, November 12, 1995. In March 1995 then deputy interior minister Rovshan Javadov, with the alleged complicity of Surat Hussein, led a police revolt in Baku and in two towns near the border with Armenia. Former president Ayaz Mutalipov (who lives in exile in Russia) was also said to be tied to the March 1995 attempt. *Paris AFP*, March 15, 1995, in *FBIS Daily Report*, SOV-95-051, November 18, 1995; *Turan*, March 20, 1995, in *FBIS Daily Report*, SOV-95-054, November 18, 1995.

[45] Kozyrev stated on September 30, 1993, that Russia had a special right to intervene in the former Soviet republics to protect human rights, "particularly those of ethnic minorities." He was obviously referring to the many ethnic Russians living in the "near abroad." *Keesing's Record of World Events*, vol. 39, no. 10 (October 1993), p. 39693.

[46] CIS states do not always meet the Council of Europe's human rights standards. Ukraine, for example, is resisting the council's pressure to abolish the death penalty.

[47] Officers from the Uzbek Ministry of Internal Affairs arrested Uzbek opposition leader Abdurahim Polat in Bishkek, Kyrgyzstan on December 8, 1992.

[48] Opposition leader Petr Svoik was attacked in his Biskhek hotel room on December 1, 1997.

[49] This organization grew out of these four countries' cooperation on CFE Treaty revisions in late 1996 and early 1997.

[50] The two leaders met in Tashkent in 1995, in Crimea in July–August 1996, during the CIS Council of Leaders summit in Moscow in March 1997, again in Crimea in August 1997, and in Kyiv in February 1998.

[51] Until July 1998, it was called Central Asian Union.

[52] *ITAR-TASS*, July 1, 1994, in *FBIS Daily Report*, SOV-94-128, July 1, 1994.

[53] Zagorski, *SNG: Tsifry, fakty, personalii*, p. 16.

[54] *Komsomolskaia pravda*, March 27, 1997, in *FBIS Daily Report*, SOV-97-068, April 10, 1997.

[55] Information about this summit was taken from *Chisinau basapress*, October 23, 1997, translated in *FBIS Daily Report*, SOV-97-296, October 27, 1997; *Rossiiskaia gazeta*, October 24, 1997, in *FBIS Daily Report*, SOV-97-296, October 27, 1997; Tashkent Uzbek Television First Program Network, October 24, 1997, in *FBIS Daily Report*, SOV-97-297, October 28, 1997; *Interfax*, October 24, 1997, in *FBIS Daily Report*, SOV-97-297, October 27, 1997; and *Jamestown Monitor*, vol. 3, no. 202, October 29, 1997.

[56] As cited by Yelena Kornysheva, *ITAR-TASS*, March 6, 1998.

[57] During Berezovsky's ten months as executive secretary, he visited all CIS capitals, several of them repeatedly. He also paid visits to various Russian autonomous regions, as well as to Georgia's separatist Abkhazia region. He engaged in numerous one-on-one meetings with CIS leaders, attended CIS conferences, and participated in meetings of international organizations outside the CIS region.

[58] Yurii Chubchenko, "Karimov ustupil Berezovskomu, " *Kommersant-Daily*, January 27, 1999.

[59] *Interfax*, October 21, 1998, in *FBIS Daily Report*, SOV-98-295, October 23, 1998.

[60] Azerbaijani President Heydar Aliyev and Georgian President Eduard Shevardnadze in particular protested that Yeltsin could not unilaterally make such a decision without consulting with other CIS leaders. *RFE/RL Newsline*, March 5, 1999.

2
CIS Economic Integration[1]

Issues of state building were paramount when the Commonwealth of Independent States was formed, despite the horrendous condition of the late Soviet economy. Top politicians were preoccupied with the political, systemic, and financial crises of their new states, and thus gave little thought to how the economy of the CIS might function. What thought there was about economics had to be addressed to immediate concerns. Production was plummeting; state fixing of prices was causing pervasive shortages; monetary emission was out of control; there was no incentive within the system to produce anything. While much of the population was standing in lines in front of empty shops, others were turning themselves into traders—making fortunes by buying goods at low state-controlled prices and selling them on free markets, or by borrowing money at minimal interest and letting high inflation devour the repayments. Larger issues, such as how the Soviet economic system might become a market economy or how it might be privatized were widely understood to be questions for the future.

The fact that the new leaders put off dealing with economic questions did not mean, however, that they were unaware that they faced them. Eight of the Soviet republics had attempted even before the breakup to create a banking union, but were stymied by the refusal of four others (Ukraine, Azerbaijan, Georgia, and Moldova) to participate. The breakup magnified the need for such coordination, as the Russian, Belarusian, and Ukrainian leaders recognized. Among the CIS founding documents issued on December 8, 1991, was the Declaration on the Coordination of Economic Policy, which set out an agenda for subsequent negotiations toward extensive coordination. This declaration was nonbinding, however, which meant that the actual economic functions of the CIS remained unclear for some time to come.

This chapter describes first the conditions in which the CIS began, then examines the demise of state trade in the years 1992–1994. Next it analyzes the parallel collapse of the ruble zone and the emergence of a new currency and payments system. The energy trade is discussed separately. While free trade had begun to emerge in 1995–1996, it was disrupted by rising protectionism, starting in late 1996. The chapter then examines the development of intra-CIS trade, showing how much it changed with the Russian financial crisis in 1998, which has harmed all CIS economies and has provoked severe protectionism. Finally, it assesses the prospects for economic integration in the CIS.

THE FORMATION OF THE CIS ECONOMIC SYSTEM

Three contradictory models shaped the development of the CIS economic system. The first was that of the Soviet-era Council for Mutual Economic Assistance (CMEA),[2] which had regulated trade within the Soviet bloc. The tenets of this model were that state trading should continue, and that all CIS countries should stay in the ruble zone.

This model has exerted powerful influence on the development of the CIS, because a disproportionate number of CIS bureaucrats are Russians from the old State Planning Committee (Gosplan). The first CIS state trading system was inspired by Gosplan, so it seemed only natural that Gosplan officials should deal with CIS relations, particularly since the CIS states were still part of a single currency system that was controlled by Russian institutions, not by those of the CIS. In Russia, Gosplan's main suborgan, the State Committee for Technical and Material Supplies (Gossnab), was transformed into Roskontrakt, which became the Russian state trading organization for CIS countries.

It was not only the retread bureaucrats who wished to have the CIS resemble the old system as closely as possible; a host of powerful economic and political forces within Russia and some other CIS states also pressed for continued Soviet-type integration. Most prominent were the old industrial lobby and the military-industrial complex, composed of noncompetitive big state enterprises (mostly manufacturing companies) that were now divided among several countries. Not surprisingly, this lobby opposed restructuring enterprises and so wished to preserve strong cross-national organizational linkages.

The second model was a market vision of free trade between countries with independent and freely convertible currencies. The Baltic states in general, and Estonia in particular, were the main proponents of this model. None of the Baltic countries joined the CIS, and all left the ruble zone in 1992, but their experience offered a clear alternative that had supporters in several other countries, especially in Russia and in Kyrgyzstan.

The ruble zone was also an issue for those attracted to this second model. Some economic reformers, especially in Russia, wanted to end the lax monetary policies and Russian subsidies to other CIS countries permitted by the ruble zone to facilitate macroeconomic stabilization. Reformers in other CIS countries had mixed feelings about the ruble zone. Some realized that the unregulated credit-flows in the ruble zone made monetary stabilization impossible, but others saw the flow of cheap Russian credits and energy as a substantial resource for all members of the ruble zone, though it benefited primarily industrialists, commodity traders, and bankers throughout the CIS. Any country that left the ruble zone would have to introduce its own currency and program of macroeconomic stabilization, which few were ready to do.

A lobby of commodity producers, commodity traders, and new bankers, many of whom had arisen from the old system, swiftly exploited the many economic distortions of the new circumstances. These people wanted a market economy of sorts, with economic regulations for others but freedom for themselves. Indeed, commodity traders in various CIS countries were the main beneficiaries of the CIS trading system as it actually developed, exploiting all the loopholes and distortions that the system offered. In Ukraine, for example, businessmen who imported natural gas from Russia made the greatest fortunes.[3] This lobby wished to keep the CIS trading system distinct from the rest of the foreign trade system, because they were arbitraging between regulated and free prices.

The third model was that of the European Union (EU), which exerted a powerful influence on the formation of the CIS. Not only does the EU seem a natural compromise between the other two models, but it is geographically adjacent to the CIS and exhibits all the attributes of modernity. Official CIS communiqués have tended to adopt the phraseology of the EU, launching initiatives such as an economic union or a customs union. This use of EU language is frequently misleading, as was the case when EU attempts to introduce a common currency became a strong argument for maintaining the ruble zone; similarly, the example of the European Payments Union, which existed in Western Europe from 1950 until 1958, inspired those in the CIS who did not want full convertibility to propose a similar union. The EU has a customs union to govern trade relations, but some other West European countries belong to the European Free Trade Association (EFTA), offering the option of a free trade area.

Given the contradictory nature of these models and the relative strengths of the various lobbies that supported them, it is not surprising that the design of the CIS and its attempts at economic integration have been haphazard at best. The end purpose of the organization was never articulated clearly, and the actual development of the CIS has been characterized more by rhetoric than by deed, more by trial and error than by policy and plan. From the beginning, CIS members developed a tradition of making statements and decisions that were unrealistic and not meant to be implemented. This was in part due to Russia's push for deeper integration than the other CIS states generally desired and to efforts that were in turn countered by other members weakening or ignoring the measures they did not like, rather than risking open opposition to Russia.

The impulses and imperatives of sovereignty played a large role in this process, as the new nations moved to define their states. Baltic nationalists saw economic deregulation and the redirection of their trade toward the West as part of their national liberalization, prompting them to break all nonmarket links with Russia early on, even at great cost. Ukraine, Moldova, Azerbaijan, Turkmenistan, and Uzbekistan saw their interests as more mixed, for they wanted simultaneously to reduce their links with Russia and to continue to enjoy the benefits of cheap credits and energy as long as possible. Other states had a genuine interest in tight links with Russia, either because Russia was so close that there seemed to be no other choice, as was true of Belarus and Kazakhstan, or because it was so far away that it promised only benefits, not threats, as was true of Armenia, Kyrgyzstan, and Tajikistan.

Curiously enough, the nature of the economic systems that member states are trying to establish has not been predictive of the states' attitudes toward the CIS. In the beginning both Belarus and Ukraine pursued similar policies of minimalist economic reform, but their policies toward the CIS are almost polar opposites. More recently, Belarus, Turkmenistan and Uzbekistan have stood out as countries without serious market reform, but Belarus wants close integration with Russia, while Turkmenistan and Uzbekistan keep Russia at a distance. By contrast, Georgia and Kyrgyzstan have been perhaps the most reformist countries in the CIS, but Kyrgyzstan has opted for closer economic cooperation with Russia and the CIS, while Georgia has kept as far away as it can.

A much better indicator is the degree to which member states are dependent upon Russia and, to a lesser extent, the other CIS countries. In the beginning all of the new states were still closely tied to Russia economically, not just as a source of currency, but also for energy and other raw materials. Moreover, Russia could cut off supplies to other CIS countries, but it was hard for them to do so to Russia. Virtually all oil and gas pipelines, the main east-west highway, the railroad systems, and the power grid went through or were situated in Russia. With the exception of Belarus, Ukraine, and Moldova, all exports from the CIS to Europe also had to pass through Russia.

This conflicting and self-contradictory mixture of models, interests, and motivations is reflected in the efforts to create an institutional structure for the CIS, which has essentially proven fruitless, as the preceding chapter demonstrated. In 1992 economic trade and cooperation among CIS states was based on Soviet-style bilateral intergovernmental agreements, for reasons that are detailed below. The first step toward establishing a more multilateral framework was the adoption at the September 1993 meeting of the Heads of Government of an Economic Union Treaty, which was meant to lead to a full economic union like the EU. The treaty did not actually create a union, but merely sketched its outline, comprising a free trade area, a customs union, a payments union and a monetary union. Even so, the Georgian prime minister did not even attend the meeting, and only nine of the CIS members signed the agreement; Turkmenistan joined later, in December 1993, and Ukraine eventually became an associate member. More importantly, the ruble zone had effectively collapsed two months earlier, which already limited the utility of this framework. This treaty was supplemented by an

Agreement on the Creation of a Free Trade Zone at the April 1994 Heads of State meeting, but to date it has only been ratified by six countries.[4]

Despite this weak beginning, it was on the basis of that treaty that the Council of Heads of Government created the Inter-State Economic Committee at their meeting in September 1994, and the committee's creation was ratified by the CIS summit in October 1994. This committee was supposed to have executive and managerial powers over transnational systems such as power grids, natural gas and oil pipelines, and other shared transportation and communication systems, and was to develop a payments union and to administer the free trade zone in the CIS. Eventually, it was meant to manage a full economic union. Russia was to provide 50 percent of the capital and possess 50 percent of the votes, with the voting strength of other member states to be determined by the capital donated.

Very little of this actually happened. The lack of movement toward CIS economic integration is underscored by the January 1995 decision of Kazakhstan, Belarus, and Russia to create a separate customs union. This trilateral initiative was described as a basis for a customs union of all the CIS states, but it has been formalized and expanded reluctantly; Kyrgyzstan was accepted as a member in March 1996, while poor and war-torn Tajikistan, eager to participate from the beginning, was not invited to do so until 1998, and its application was not ratified by the other members of the Customs Union until February 1999.

The limited functionality of the enabling treaties did not stop the development of an extensive CIS apparatus. Most of the sixty institutions that have been set up within the CIS for intergovernmental coordination deal with economic issues, in ways that recall the functioning of Soviet branch ministries in both the description and their mostly bureaucratic style; the CIS Inter-State Economic Committee and its many subcommittees hold periodic meetings, issue reports, and promulgate guidelines for further integration. Nonetheless, while the CIS administration has elaborated close to a thousand multilateral agreements, almost none have come into force.[5]

THE END OF STATE TRADE

The financial collapse and acute shortage of goods that all of the new states suffered at independence meant that the first desire of producers was to obtain whatever supplies they could, while that of exporters was to export whatever they could. Preoccupied with state building and facing multiple emergencies, governments were engaged in short-term crisis management, with no time for long-term strategy or economic rationality.

These conditions suited the old-style bureaucrats who dealt with intra-CIS relations in the various member countries. From their perspective, trade should continue to be driven by the specific needs of production, as defined by the existing producers. They wanted intra-CIS trade to be governed by compulsory intergovernmental agreements, to which end extensive bilateral trade agreements were hastily concluded among the CIS members for 1992. The existing patterns of trade, however, had largely been erected on political grounds, with little consideration for transportation costs or demand. The Soviet republics had traded far too much with one another and far too little with the outside world; in addition, much of the old trade was inefficiently organized and no longer economically justified, as was the case for the extensive production of arms.

These first CIS trade agreements were reminiscent of old Soviet foreign trade agreements within the CMEA. They divided merchandise into three groups: the first, which comprised the bulk of the trade, consisted of about 100 commodities, essentially raw materials and energy, which were subject to compulsory deliveries, quotas, and licenses, but not to trade taxes; the second, of about 1,500 items, mainly machinery, equipment, and foods, that were traded on the basis of interenterprise contracts in accordance with targets set by the state; and the remainder, mainly consumer goods, could be freely traded, but these accounted for only a small share of total trade.

Intra-CIS trade was thus essentially ruled by the old Gosplan system, with planned deliveries, in specified quantities, regardless of whether these were economically rational. This system made the producers happy because they found little or no demand elsewhere for their products, while the CIS state trading system provided them not only with a steady demand, but also with reliable payment. Roskontrakt, which handled CIS trade for Russia and its partners in the other CIS countries, most of which were formerly republic branches of Gossnab, also appreciated these rigid planning procedures. Both customers and suppliers benefited from the nontransparent Roskontrakt system, which offered ample subsidies. The large volumes of underpriced, valuable raw materials and extensive state financing that characterized this system made it a rich breeding ground for economic crime in the CIS.

Roskontrakt only received payment for 30 percent of the goods ordered by its customers, with the difference made up by the Russian federal budget. This practice became exceedingly expensive for the Russian government. Reformers there balked at the mounting cost, but other sectors of the Russian government began to use the growing debts of partner nations as a means by which to extract political or military advantages from other CIS members.

Formally, the prices in the intra-CIS trade were supposed to be freely negotiated. In reality, however, for any commodity with a price regulated by Russia, the Russian export price to a CIS country was higher than the domestic Russian price but still far below the world market price. These underpriced Russian export commodities were primarily oil, natural gas, and metals. In the first half of 1992, for example, the state-controlled price of Russian oil exported to CIS countries was about 5 percent of the world market price, while the domestic Russian price was 1 percent of the world price. Such pricing led to extensive re-exporting of underpriced commodities and made vast personal fortunes for those involved in these activities. Although Estonia produces no non-ferrous metals, it became a major exporter of such metals in 1992–1993, when it was shipping metals out of Russia. Similarly, in 1992 Ukraine angered Russia by re-exporting millions of tons of oil, some of which had originated from compulsory CIS deliveries. In April 1992 the Russian government tried to introduce a system of export controls to stop this re-exporting, but it changed almost nothing. The more state-directed CIS economies, such as those of Ukraine, Belarus, and the Central Asian countries, all established regulated foreign trade systems with comprehensive export controls, including quotas and licenses; all of these controls bred corruption.

Over time, most commodity prices in Russia have moved toward world market levels, although the long overland hauls necessary to bring oil and natural gas to customers have kept their prices below those of the world market. Russia has also continued to link pricing to politics, particularly for natural gas. Countries that have agreed to closer political relationships with Russia have received gas at lower prices. Thus the Baltic countries faced an immediate jump to world market prices when they departed from the ruble zone in 1992. Georgia, too, was originally denied such sweetheart pricing, because it refused to join the CIS, as was Azerbaijan after it tried to withdraw. The rest of the CIS countries continued to be charged lower prices for some time. Belarus, which is seeking a union with Russia, even now enjoys low prices for its natural gas imports from Russia, and to the extent it pays at all, it is allowed favorable barter payments.

Most of the price benefits that other CIS members received from Russia were discontinued by the end of 1994, which in turn gave them little further incentive to remain within the regulated trade system. The consequences of this are demonstrated by the share of intra-CIS trade that was handled by Roskontrakt: in 1993 it handled 13.2 percent of CIS trade turnover; 11.5 percent in 1994; and less than 4 percent in 1995.[6] In 1995 compulsory deliveries were largely abolished, and several countries, including Kazakhstan and Uzbekistan, did not conclude intra-CIS agreements. The only price privileges that Russia offered after 1995 were limited to Belarus, Kazakhstan, and, from 1996 on, Kyrgyzstan—all fellow members of the Customs Union. The benefits to these last two states were all but insignificant, however, because of monopolistic pricing by the Russian oil and gas complex. Bilateral Russian subsidies on natural gas to Belarus, however, remain substantial.

Efforts to establish a Soviet-type trading system within the CIS failed after three years. Mutual trading plummeted by more than two-thirds from 1991 to 1994.[7] Much of the reduction of intra-CIS trade was undoubtedly desirable, since the original trade had been generated by political decisions rather than by market economic forces. Estimations based on the gravity model[8] suggest that the republics that became CIS countries had traded more with one another than was economically rational because of the extreme protectionism of the USSR.[9] No effective restructuring of this mutual trade took place after the USSR was disolved, however, and so CIS countries continued to ship virtually unsalable goods to one another. Once Russia was no longer prepared to subsidize the other CIS countries with low prices on energy or with substantial trade credits, the old trade dried up, and almost no new trade arose to take its place.

The demise of state trading was also connected with the transformation of the domestic economic systems of the three dominant countries in the CIS trading system, Russia, Kazakhstan, and Ukraine. Russia could be viewed as a market economy from the beginning of 1994, when it ended price controls on the most important commodities. Kazakhstan began major market reforms in 1994, and Ukraine established a market-based foreign trade system in late 1994. After these three countries had taken decisive steps in the direction of a market economy, all in the course of a single year, the rest of the CIS had no choice but to follow, even though the economies of other relatively important CIS states, such as Uzbekistan, Turkmenistan, and Belarus, remained highly regulated.

THE ESTABLISHMENT OF NEW CURRENCIES AND A NEW PAYMENTS SYSTEM

The development of a new trade system also required a new payments system. The old Soviet mindset understood a payments system to mean clearing. In the CMEA, bilateral clearing had prevailed in reality, but the unit of account for bilateral deliveries was a fictitious currency called a "transferable ruble," which thus provided an illusion of multilateral clearing. That illusion might have enticed the CIS to opt for multilateral rather than bilateral clearing. Another idea that was discussed was to develop a payments union, along the lines of the European Payments Union. A few reformers argued that market exchange rates between convertible currencies should prevail. Before any of that was possible, however, it was necessary to determine how many currencies the CIS was going to have.

A well-functioning payments system requires credit lines. In the old Soviet trading system there was no attempt to balance trade flows within the Soviet Union. In 1991, even at old, low Soviet prices, Russia had a trade surplus toward the other republics of approximately $25 billion; price liberalization would have improved Russia's terms of trade dramatically, since a large volume of Russia's exports were commodities being sold at low fixed prices. This trade imbalance made it seem inevitable that Russia would have to provide most of the other CIS states with trade credits, at least temporarily.

The cost for Russia was staggering, though, prompting discussion of the need to nationalize the Russian ruble as early as the summer of 1991. Several of the other new republics considered introducing their own currencies to confirm their independence and also to control inflation, but they were reluctant to abandon the subsidies that Russia offered. The issue of trade credits was obviously exacerbated by the persistence of the ruble zone. At the end of 1991 there were fifteen republican central banks, each independent of the others, all of which were issuing ruble credits. The more credits one central bank issued, the greater the share of the common GDP that country received, which naturally stimulated a destabilizing competition to issue credits. One result was that, in 1993, ten of the twelve CIS members suffered hyperinflation, meaning inflation of at least 50 percent per month.

At first, Russia continued to finance the rest of the CIS, but the burden quickly became too heavy for the country's strained financial resources. According to IMF estimates, the level of Russia's financial support for most former Soviet republics was truly extraordinary. At the top was Tajikistan, which received financing corresponding to 91 percent of its GDP from Russia in 1992, followed by Uzbekistan, which obtained financing equal to 70 percent of its GDP.[10] Since those transfers tended to disappear among the middlemen, the recipient countries did not necessarily benefit from Russia's largesse.

The financial situation that resulted was impossible: hyperinflation prevailed; most CIS currencies had multiple exchange rates, with official rates deviating from market rates; the rubles of various countries had different values and could not be exchanged; Russia gave big state credits, but they were automatic, not subject to any credit decisions, since they arose from trade deficits.

The CIS took two years to escape from this monetary morass. Although the preference of most CIS member states was to keep the ruble zone alive, they could find no institutional mechanism by which to do so, as the other republics were not prepared to give Russia a majority share in a common central bank, while Russia could not afford to allow the large credit outflow to continue. Gradually, the Russian government established credit limits for the other CIS countries. In July 1992 Russia separated the Russian account ruble from those of other CIS countries, at which point the unregulated market value of several other kinds of CIS rubles nose-dived. Russia's efforts to limit access to ruble banknotes and credits prompted other states to issue quasi-currencies and, eventually, real national currencies. In May 1993, as part of a major reform effort, Kyrgyzstan became the first CIS country to abandon the ruble zone.

In July 1993, after the Central Bank of Russia suddenly declared the old Soviet ruble banknotes to be invalid, Russia tightened its terms for those wishing to remain in the ruble zone. Ukraine, Moldova, Georgia, Turkmenistan, and Azerbaijan were unwilling to accept Russia's terms and so left the ruble zone, but in September 1993, Armenia, Belarus, Kazakhstan, Tajikistan, and Uzbekistan agreed to coordinate fully their financial policies with those of Russia to stay in the ruble zone. In the next few weeks it became clear, however, that to Russia "full coordination" meant that member states could not maintain their own gold or other hard-currency reserves, a requirement that was unacceptable to gold producers like Uzbekistan and Kazakhstan, and both left the ruble zone by late November. Thus in 1993 virtually all the other CIS countries established their own currencies, and inflation soon started falling throughout the region.[11]

Sensing the approaching failure of the ruble zone, Russia advocated the formation of a payments union, for which purpose an Inter-State Bank was proposed and subsequently endorsed by seven states at the January 1993 Minsk CIS summit. Due to the resistance of Russian reformers, however, the Inter-State Bank was not formally established until December 1993, by ten member states.[12]

Meanwhile, a market for currencies of limited convertibility was gradually developing. In 1993 Latvia's leading exchange bank Parex advertised throughout the CIS: "We buy all currencies and we ask no questions." The Russian ruble, Ukrainian coupons, and Kazakh *tenge* were being traded as early as 1993, and by 1995, an inter-bank market had developed for all essential CIS currencies, as the commercial banks took over currency exchange from the central banks. Commercial banks trading these soft currencies have been holding regular meetings among themselves since 1994. At the beginning of 1995 an inter-bank clearing union was created by about thirty commercial banks in Russia, Belarus, Ukraine, Kazakhstan, and Azerbaijan. By contrast, the CIS Inter-State Bank never developed a function, as was underscored by agreements made at the September 1994 meeting of the CIS Heads of State and Government, which acknowledged that it made little sense to maintain bilateral clearing through the central banks.

The Inter-State Bank was formally abandoned at the May 1995 summit in favor of the bilateral settlement of CIS interstate payments

Table 2.1
Types of Interstate Payments in the CIS
(percent of total payments)

Types of Payments	1993	1994	1995 (estimate)
Bilateral interstate clearing	50	30	15
Payments through correspondent accounts of the national Central Banks	20	15	5
Payments in national currencies through correspondent accounts of commercial banks	15	35	55
Non-governmental barter, clearing, and other kinds of non-currency payments	10	10	10
Payments in hard currencies	5	10	15
Total	100	100	100

Source: *Finansovye Izvestiya*, June 20, 1995; *Delovoy Mir*, September 5, 1995.

in dollars. The CIS currencies at best are convertible in cash and on current account, but not on capital account, and the market for CIS currencies in practice services only trade. Capital-flows among CIS countries have remained negligible.

Changes in the means of payment over time illustrate the systemic evolution of trade between CIS countries. Table 2.1 shows the approximate development of the different types of payments from 1993 through 1995. Bilateral clearing accounted for roughly half the intra-CIS trade in 1993, but by 1995, its share had fallen to about 15 percent. Centralized payments through correspondent accounts of central banks also declined sharply, from about 20 percent in 1993 to some 5 percent in 1995. Barter and similar decentralized nonmonetary payments accounted steadily for one-tenth of all payments, primarily representing payments to Russia's natural gas monopoly, Gazprom. By contrast, payments in national currencies or in hard currency have risen steadily. Payments in hard currency expanded from a 5 percent share in 1993 to 15 percent in 1995, but then fell

Table 2.2
Barter Trade of Selected CIS Countries, 1995–1997
(percent of total barter)

	Barter Exports			Barter Imports		
	1995	1996	1997	1995	1996	1997
Azerbaijan	25.3	31.2	13.9	17.3	12.4	11.8
Belarus	—	—	28.1	—	—	30.1
Georgia	21.6	11.6	5.9	3.0	2.1	0.9
Kazakhstan	19.9	6.9	2.1	15.3	4.1	2.4
Kyrgyzstan	18.6	10.4	2.8	9.8	6.3	2.9
Moldova	25.7	19.6	14.3	18.4	15.5	10.9
Russia	—	—	5.8	—	—	8.2
Turkmenistan	7.9	8.6	8.3	10.7	10.6	7.3
Ukraine	33.3	21.8	10.4	21.4	11.9	9.4

Source: UN Economic Commission for Europe, *Economic Survey of Europe 1998*, No. 3 (Geneva: United Nations, 1998), p. 102.

again, as national currencies stabilized and gained degrees of convertibility. The share of payments in national currencies increased from 15 percent of all intra-CIS trade in 1993 to 55 percent in 1995, and has continued to increase since.

Table 2.2, which provides more detailed information, deals with barter. The share of foreign trade settlements made by CIS countries in barter has fallen from 1995 to 1997, with the exception of Belarus, where barter accounted for almost 30 percent of its foreign trade payments in 1997; the amount of barter in its important trade with Russia doubled in 1998.[13] On average, barter accounted for less than 10 percent of all foreign trade of CIS countries in 1997. A number of countries have prohibited barter, viewing it as a means of distorting prices and avoiding taxes.[14] The barter that remains in intra-CIS trade is concentrated in a few major commodities, notably natural gas. In Russia and Ukraine most interenterprise payments are made by barter, while barter is much less common in the Caucasus and Central Asia. Primarily pursued by big old Soviet enterprises, barter thrives on close contacts and physical proximity; it is impractical for enterprises physically remote from one another, which probably explains the surprisingly small share of barter in interstate trade.

These two tables lead to four important conclusions about the systemic development of intra-CIS trade. First, there has been a steady development of a market-oriented system. Bilateral clearing and centralized accounts have generally given way to payments in national currencies, most of which are now reasonably convertible. Second, this gradual transformation has been guided by market forces and not by CIS institutions. Third, multiple forms of payments have developed throughout the CIS, even where national regulations—such as restrictions on hard currency payments—complicate the process. Fourth, intra-CIS barter payments are quite limited and clearly are not increasing, with the exception of Belarusian trade with Russia.

By 1995 the CIS governments had realized that markets had become more important for regulating intra-CIS trade than were either national or CIS institutions. They started accommodating to the market, modifying their payments practices to promote an uninterrupted flow of trade. In that year, the governments and central banks of Russia, Belarus, Kazakhstan, Kyrgyzstan, Uzbekistan, and Turkmenistan concluded agreements about the mutual convertibility of their national currencies. Since then, interstate payments in the CIS have differed little from international payments in the West. The dominance of payments in the members' national currencies within their mutual trade has become firmly established.

Economic reformers throughout the CIS had advocated such a solution since the collapse of the USSR, but it took three years to achieve. This transformation could not be accomplished earlier for several reasons. First, exchange rates had to be unified. While the exchange rate of the Russian ruble was essentially unified by July 1992, Ukraine had multiple exchange rates until the end of 1994, and the Uzbek *som* and the Belarusian ruble still do. Second, financial markets in most CIS countries remain poorly developed and lack depth. Until recently, a few state banks arising out of the old specialized Soviet state banks have dominated most CIS countries. While state bonds exist almost everywhere, not all countries trade stocks, and markets for enterprise bonds have scarcely developed. Financial markets throughout the entire CIS have been devastated by the Russian financial crash of August 1998, and it will take years before they become significant again. Finally, once most exchange rates were unified and adjusted to the market value of the currencies, the financing of settlement in dollars or other hard currency became too expensive, creating strong incentives to settle trade in CIS currencies.

Thus, by 1995 a market-based trade and payments system had been established within the CIS. Financing, however, remained a problem. Russia had curbed its large export credits to other CIS countries, and no other state financing of CIS trade emerged. The various governments minimized their export credits and so little credit was available, apart from some very short-term commercial credits that could be obtained from banks in the region. In 1996 the big Russian commercial banks started developing their functions, including payments and limited export credits designed to benefit Russian export companies, but the credit volumes have remained minute.

THE NATURE OF ENERGY TRADE WITHIN THE CIS

Energy trade stands out as an exception in this general move toward market principles. This is especially true of trade in natural gas, whose export is dominated by Gazprom, Russia's natural gas monopoly. Russia represents 50 percent of all intra-CIS exports, and more than half of that is in mineral resources, primarily natural gas and oil.[15] Trade in electricity is less significant, but its characteristics are similar to those of gas. Uzbekistan is the only state that has substantially increased its oil and gas production since gaining independence, and in 1995 it ceased being a net oil importer. Kazakhstan is also a significant oil exporter. By international standards, Azerbaijan currently exports little oil, but its economy is small enough to be dominated by oil; all its exports go outside of the CIS. Turkmenistan is a major natural gas producer, but a minor exporter. At the end of 1997, however, Turkmenistan started exporting gas to Iran. Uzbekistan is also a natural gas exporter, supplying southern Kyrgyzstan, southern Kazakhstan, and Tajikistan.[16]

The outstanding peculiarity of energy trade, particularly in natural gas, is a far-reaching monopolization because of the oil and gas pipelines and the power grid that constitute its transportation network. These transportation systems were built as centralized Soviet networks, which have left Russia in control of most of them because of its central location, although the parts located in other republics became the property of those new states at the time of the Soviet collapse. Russia thus controls the ability of the Central Asian countries to export gas and oil through the old Soviet pipeline system.

The problems of the energy trade are those of natural monopolies but, from a purely technical point of view, these are compounded in a variety of ways. Pipeline investments are long-term, and tariffs are to a large extent determined by capital costs. The old Soviet pipelines represent a sunk cost, however, making it impossible to assess what would be a proper tariff. Moreover, there is no world market price for natural gas; all prices are local, depending on extraction and transportation costs and, in some cases, competition.

Russia has used its monopoly control of the pipeline system ruthlessly. Its big companies, such as Gazprom and Transneft, the state-owned oil pipeline company, have largely dictated the country's energy policy. Until the end of 1997, Russia was the only CIS country to export natural gas outside of the CIS. Turkmenistan had no outlet for its gas exports other than the Russian pipeline system, and Russia would only allow it to export to Ukraine, Georgia, and Armenia, three CIS states with long histories of nonpayments. For over a year in 1997–1998, Turkmenistan's exports of gas to Ukraine were halted because of a pricing dispute with Gazprom, causing Turkmenistan's exports to CIS countries to fall by an astounding 61 percent in 1997 and its GDP to drop by 26 percent.[17] It was only at the end of 1997 that Turkmenistan found a way out of Russia's stranglehold, with the completion of a minor gas pipeline to Iran. In early 1999 Gazprom changed its policies to allow Turkmenistan to export gas through its pipelines, but the transportation prices which Gazprom charges are so high that Turkmenistan can barely make money on these exports.[18]

Russia has allowed Kazakhstan restricted oil exports through the Russian pipeline system. The official Russian excuse has been the limited capacity of the pipeline system, but nothing has been done to increase it. Russia also argues that oil from Kazakhstan is so sulphurous that it would degrade the pipelines. Unlike natural gas, however, oil can be transported by rail, so Kazakhstan has circumvented the Russian pipeline embargo by extensive, though expensive, rail transportation through Russia. In early 1999 Russia reversed itself, offering Kazakhstan more exports through its pipeline system. This may be explained by Kazakhstan's interest in building a pipeline across the Caspian Sea, which, if completed, would damage the

Russian pipeline monopoly. Eventually this monopoly will be broken.

Russia is also using its monopoly position for price discrimination, as has already been mentioned. The prices paid by various CIS countries reflect both Russia's monopoly power and its political agenda. Such discrimination is particularly true of gas pricing, since the existence of alternative means of transportation means that oil pricing is more subject to market forces. This price discrimination is also compounded by the extensive use of barter payments for gas, of which Gazprom is the main sponsor. In some cases, barter appears a natural and unobjectionable means of payment, as when Belarus, Moldova, and Ukraine are paid in natural gas for Gazprom's use of their portions of the pipelines for exports to the West. Gazprom, however, is equally, but more inexplicably, eager to receive barter in return for its gas. Belarus pays for about 80 percent of the natural gas it imports from Russia in goods and services. It is not clear why Gazprom is so enthusiastic about barter. One possible explanation is the price discrimination that barter permits, while another is that barter reduces Gazprom's tax liabilities in Russia. Barter in general remains popular in Russia, still accounting for about half of all payments made there.[19]

Another peculiarity of Gazprom's trade with other CIS countries is that it allows customers to run up substantial debts. In the past few years, most of Russia's new claims on other CIS countries have been accumulated arrears to Gazprom. The company has developed a strategy of debt-equity swaps, by which Gazprom tries to seize the gas pipeline systems of other countries. Belarus, Moldova, and Georgia have given up much of the ownership of their domestic pipeline systems to Gazprom, and Ukraine is under considerable pressure to do the same with its pipelines and gas reservoirs. Other countries deal with such large payment arrears by halting gas deliveries, as is evidenced by the 1998 decision by Uzbekistan to stop supplying Kyrgyzstan and Kazakhstan.

Another explanation for Gazprom's behavior is that it produces more gas than it can sell. Although GDP across the former Soviet expanse has fallen by about half from 1991 to 1997, Gazprom's exports of gas to CIS countries fell by only 13 percent in the same period. The explanation for this comparatively limited decline is that Gazprom managed to increase its exports of gas to countries

Table 2.3
Russia's Natural Gas Production and Exports, 1991–1997
(billion cubic meters)

	1991	1992	1993	1994	1995	1996	1997
Gas production	642.9	640.4	617.6	606.8	595.4	601.5	571.1
Gas consumption (total)	468.7	454.7	452.9	424.4	408.2	409.5	384.9
Gas exports	173.0	195.3	171.3	184.4	190.6	196.5	188.8
Foreign	90.0	88.9	92.7	105.8	117.4	123.5	116.7
Other republics	83.0	106.4	78.6	78.6	73.2	73.0	72.1

Source: *PlanEcon Energy Outlook for Eastern Europe and the Former Soviet Republics* (October 1998), p. 101. Reproduced with permission of PlanEcon, Inc.

outside the CIS by only 30 percent (see table 2.3). The falling energy prices of 1998 and the Russian financial crisis made Gazprom record a substantial loss that year, which must be the first in its history. The contrast with Russia's oil exports could hardly be greater. Its oil exports to CIS countries plummeted by 82 percent from 1991 to 1997, as the oil was diverted to non-CIS countries, to which Russian oil exports surged by no less than 87 percent in these years, even though, unlike gas production, Russian oil production contracted sharply (see table 2.4). This decline in its fortunes has led Gazprom to reconsider its very expensive investments in new gas extraction in northern Russia, and may also be an additional reason for its softer attitude toward Turkmenistan.

In the end, the peculiarities of Russia's energy trade with the CIS countries seem more a product of Gazprom policy than of Russian government policy. Gazprom's preference for barter runs against the interests of the Russian government, for it greatly complicates tax collection. Nevertheless, the old Soviet pipeline system and the power grid give Russian energy companies extraordinary monopoly powers over the other CIS countries, regardless of whether they are energy producers or consumers. Russia and its companies use their monopoly powers with little compunction.

Table 2.4
Russia's Oil Production and Exports, 1991–1997
(million metric tons)

	1991	1992	1993	1994	1995	1996	1997
Production							
Crude oil production	461.1	395.8	343.8	315.7	306.7	301.2	305.6
Refinery throughput	286.5	257.1	217.1	182.3	178.8	172.2	175.4
Exports							
Crude oil	173.9	141.7	127.6	126.8	122.3	125.6	126.8
Foreign	56.5	66.2	79.8	89.0	91.3	103.0	105.6
Other republics	117.4	75.5	47.8	37.8	31.0	22.6	21.3
Refined products	63.6	43.0	44.8	43.4	45.4	56.6	60.6
Foreign	41.6	25.3	34.3	38.0	42.1	55.0	58.4
Other republics	22.0	17.6	10.5	5.4	3.3	1.6	2.2

Source: *PlanEcon Energy Outlook for Eastern Europe and the Former Soviet Republics* (October 1998), p. 83. Reproduced with permission of PlanEcon, Inc.

RISING PROTECTIONISM INSTEAD OF ECONOMIC INTEGRATION

When the CIS presidents signed the Economic Union Treaty at their September 1993 summit, they envisioned the free flow of commodities, services, capital, and work force within the CIS.[20] This goal, however, could not be reconciled with the old state trade system. By 1995 and 1996, most of the old regulations had vanished and no customs tariffs applied within the CIS, which made many of the goals of the 1993 treaty theoretically reachable. A number of other restrictions, though, such as the poor payments systems and difficulties of financing, continued to hamper trade. Before any of these problems could be addressed, however, Russia, Belarus, and Kazakhstan formed a customs union in 1995, to which Kyrgyzstan and Tajikistan were later admitted (in 1996 and 1999, respectively).

A paradoxical situation thus developed. Technically, the members of the CIS had already taken steps to establish a free trade area among themselves, similar to those of the European Free Trade Association (EFTA), the Central European Free Trade Agreement (CEFTA), or the North American Free Trade Agreement (NAFTA). By definition, such an arrangement implied intra-FTA duty free imports. The next possible step is to create a customs union, such as the European Union, that is based on a common foreign trade regime with respect to the outside world. The Customs Union, however, is not a real customs union, for to date no serious attempt has been made to establish such a regime among its members. Rather, each country has in effect been pursuing its own unilateral foreign trade policy, intermittently imposing tariffs and quotas on trade with other members of the Customs Union. In addition, four of the five members of the Union have applied for membership in the World Trade Organization (WTO) as individual states, rather than as a customs union.

Other bureaucratic impediments to intra-CIS trade began to proliferate in 1996 and 1997. As protectionism mounted, the CIS market potential shrank, and trade regulations throughout the CIS became increasingly erratic, both in the Economic Union and in the Customs Union. In May 1996 Russia raised import tariffs unilaterally and without prior agreement by the other members of the Customs Union. Even after joining the Customs Union, Kyrgyzstan was forced to continue buying grain on the world market, because Kazakhstan, its neighbor and putative fellow union member, applied a 20 percent export tariff. Kyrgyzstan has had to buy oil from China rather than from Kazakhstan for the same reason. Belarus offers an example of the reverse, because it has refused to introduce the same high import tariffs on cars that Russia has. As a consequence, a substantial trade has developed in used cars bought or stolen in Western Europe, then exported to Belarus; there they are sold to Russians who can then take them into Russia without paying the import tariff that would have been imposed if the cars were imported to Russia directly.

The Economic Union has proven to be even less a free trade area than has the Customs Union, in large part because of problems arising from the value-added tax system. In 1992 Russia and other CIS states adopted the odd practice of applying VAT to goods shipped to other CIS countries, but not to exports outside of the CIS. This practice is not used anywhere else in the world, so, on the advice of the IMF, one country after another has altered its tax systems. The asymmetry of tax schemes caused particular strife between Russia and Ukraine, after Ukraine changed its system in 1996, because trade between the two states frequently resulted in double VAT charges. This conflict seriously hampered mutual trade until it was resolved in February 1998.

Until 1995 the CIS countries had primarily been concerned with limiting exports of commodities that were subject to domestic price controls, but as domestic prices of export commodities approached those of the world market, this was no longer perceived as a concern. Instead, companies became disturbed by import competition and so began to demand various protectionist measures. In 1996, for example, Russia introduced prohibitive excise taxes on Ukrainian metal, and Ukraine introduced VAT on steel imports. Russia put severe import quotas on alcoholic beverages and sugar, while Ukraine imposed export quotas on cattle. Part of this impulse toward protectionism was caused by the fact that the two big oil exporters, Russia and Kazakhstan, had higher price levels because of their substantial commodity exports, and so were more interested in keeping a stable exchange rate and low inflation than they were in a competitive exchange rate. As their exchange rates became increasingly overvalued, their protectionist tendencies became more pronounced.

It is standard world practice that new protectionist measures are usually introduced as unilateral surprises, and that trade disputes are usually dealt with in bilateral negotiations. In the case of disputes between CIS members, the CIS has played no mediating role. The WTO has also not had any direct role in influencing the foreign trade relations of the CIS states, for none save Kyrgyzstan has managed to become a member. The IMF and the World Bank seem to have had the greatest effect in mediation; acting in consort they have put specific conditions on trade liberalization in their loan agreements with member states, even though trade regulation is not part of their primary function.

DEVELOPMENT OF INTRA-CIS TRADE, 1992–1997

Trade data are poor, in particular for the beginning of the post-Soviet period. The situation in 1991 cannot be reconstructed accurately, for the Soviet Union was still one country, and trade in the same goods was pursued at highly varied prices, which all need to be converted into dollars. In 1992, prices of the same goods varied greatly, high inflation raged, trade statistics were poorly gathered, and multiple exchange rates were the norm (as they remained until 1994–1995).

Nevertheless, an approximate statistical picture can be assembled for the first full year of the CIS. Since then, statistics have improved year by year, because inflation has fallen, price homogeneity has increased, statistical routines have been strengthened, and differences between various sources of statistics have diminished. The basic sources are the national statistical offices and the Inter-State Statistical Committee of the CIS; various international organs have elaborated upon these statistics to make them more credible and consistent.

As tables 2.5–2.8 show,[21] the main developments in intra-CIS trade in these years have been dramatic. Intra-CIS trade fell sharply from 1991 until 1994, by approximately 70 percent. Table 2.5 shows that from 1994 until 1996, trade recovered 27 percent, but there was a significant decline of 3 percent in 1997, and 1998 saw a drastic drop in the wake of the Russian financial crisis.

The most obvious explanation for this pattern is that output fell sharply throughout the region in the years 1991–1994 because of the massive financial destabilization. The largely Soviet-type trade system that lingered on until 1994 failed to preserve the old interrepublic trade but also prevented new trade from developing.

The rebound in intra-CIS trade in 1995 and 1996 was not caused by overall economic growth; decline continued across the region, although the rate of decline had slowed significantly. The main explanation for this increase in interstate trade seems to have been that domestic financial stabilization occurred in most CIS countries, which thus pushed enterprises to intensify their efforts to export. The more market-oriented system and low tariffs thus stimulated some new trade.

Total foreign trade of the CIS countries contracted sharply in 1991 and 1992, but has increased in all other years, except 1998, even though total output fell continuously until 1997 (see table 2.6). In the first half of 1998, total foreign trade by the CIS countries plummeted by 12 percent. In every year the volume of trade of the CIS countries with the outside world has increased significantly faster than has their trade with one another. There is a strong positive correlation between the development of total trade and that of intra-CIS trade, however, suggesting that the CIS countries were not able to switch their trade to the outside world in the short term.

As a consequence of trade with the outside world rising faster than it has within the CIS, the share of intra-CIS trade has fallen

Table 2.5
Intra-CIS Trade of CIS Countries, 1992–1997
(US$ millions)

	1992		1993		1994		1995		1996		1997	
	Exports	Imports	Exports	Imports	Exports	Imports	Exports	Imports	Exports	Imports	Exports	Imports
Armenia	—	—	127	168	158	206	167	334	113	282	84	305
Azerbaijan	730	607	374	309	274	486	285	228	290	340	378	351
Belarus	1,709	1,878	1,026	1,372	1,478	2,091	2,931	3,677	3,764	4,570	5,379	5,817
Georgia	77	159	175	165	117	268	97	154	161	187	172	233
Kazakhstan	3,315	7,315	—	—	2,109	3,104	3,378	4,375	3,796	4,630	3,331	3,834
Kyrgyzstan	209	326	223	382	223	210	269	354	405	495	333	398
Moldova	211	336	305	444	406	476	467	569	546	664	613	612
Russia	38,300	24,800	19,300	14,300	15,700	12,500	17,000	17,200	17,200	18,300	17,600	17,700
Tajikistan	74	107	119	199	156	172	201	315	267	252	313	505
Turkmenistan	624	416	1,869	1,635	1,651	686	930	745	1,142	389	—	—
Ukraine	17,600	22,100	9,300	12,300	7,800	11,400	7,700	11,000	8,800	12,900	6,800	11,800
Uzbekistan	554	731	1,515	1,202	1,660	1,401	1,283	1,259	1,051	1,516	1,509	1,268
Totals	63,403	58,775	34,333	32,476	31,732	33,000	34,708	40,210	37,535	44,525	36,512	42,823
Total Trade	122,178		66,809		64,732		74,918		82,060		79,335	
Annual Increase (%)			-45.3		-3.1		15.7		9.5		-3.3	

Source: *PlanEcon Review and Outlook for the Former Soviet Republics* (October 1998), pp. 24, 42, 114, 134, 148, 159, 173, 188, 201, 213, 227, 240.

Table 2.6
Total Trade for CIS Countries, 1992–1997
(US$ millions)

	1992		1993		1994		1995		1996		1997	
	Exports	Imports	Exports	Imports	Exports	Imports	Exports	Imports	Exports	Imports	Exports	Imports
Armenia	26	50	156	254	216	394	271	674	290	856	233	893
Azerbaijan	1,484	940	725	629	637	778	637	668	631	961	781	794
Belarus	2,903	2,721	1,970	2,539	2,510	3,066	4,707	5,563	5,463	6,939	7,147	8,644
Georgia	87	176	227	239	156	327	154	379	372	686	512	942
Kazakhstan	4,769	7,885	3,277	3,887	3,542	3,561	5,913	3,807	6,720	4,241	7,051	4,275
Kyrgyzstan	285	396	335	494	340	436	409	522	531	783	609	636
Moldova	368	506	483	628	565	659	746	841	802	1,079	880	1,172
Russia	80,700	61,800	63,600	47,100	64,900	48,500	80,700	60,300	86,500	65,200	87,200	69,900
Tajikistan	185	240	382	573	452	594	707	691	707	557	782	805
Turkmenistan	1,533	446	2,918	2,136	2,145	1,468	1,881	1,364	1,693	1,313	751	1,228
Ukraine	21,400	24,300	12,500	15,000	13,900	16,500	14,200	16,900	15,500	19,800	15,400	19,600
Uzbekistan	1,424	1,654	2,434	2,183	2,690	2,610	3,110	2,893	4,591	4,721	4,388	4,523
Totals	115,164	101,114	89,007	75,662	92,053	78,893	113,435	94,602	123,800	107,136	125,734	113,412
Total Trade	216,278		164,669		170,946		208,037		230,936		239,146	
Annual Increase (%)			-23.9		3.8		21.7		11.0		3.6	

Source: *PlanEcon Review and Outlook for the Former Soviet Republics* (October 1998), pp. 24, 42, 114, 134, 148, 159, 173, 188, 201, 213, 227, 240.

Table 2.7
Intra-CIS Trade, 1992–1997
(percent of total trade)

	1992	1993	1994	1995	1996	1997
Armenia	—	72	60	53	34	35
Azerbaijan	55	50	54	39	40	46
Belarus	64	53	64	64	67	71
Georgia	90	73	80	47	33	28
Kazakhstan	84	—	73	80	77	63
Kyrgyzstan	79	73	56	67	68	59
Moldova	63	67	72	65	64	60
Russia	44	30	25	24	23	22
Tajikistan	43	33	31	37	41	52
Turkmenistan	53	69	65	52	51	—
Ukraine	87	79	63	60	61	53
Uzbekistan	42	59	58	42	28	20
Total Intra-CIS Trade	57	41	38	36	36	33

Source: Author's calculations based on *PlanEcon Review and Outlook for the Former Soviet Republics* (October 1998), pp. 24, 42, 114, 134, 148, 159, 173, 188, 201, 213, 227, 240.

continuously, from 57 percent of all foreign trade by CIS countries in 1992 to 33 percent in 1997 (see table 2.7). The expansion of intra-CIS trade in 1995 and 1996 meant only that the decline of its share of total trade slowed down. The degree to which member states now depend upon intra-CIS trade varies greatly, but the CIS countries may be divided roughly into three groups. Belarus, Kazakhstan, Moldova, and Kyrgyzstan pursue almost two-thirds of their total trade within the CIS; these shares have not decreased much, and in the case of Belarus, have actually increased. Members of a second group, consisting of Ukraine, Azerbaijan, Turkmenistan, and Tajikistan, now have about half of their trade within the CIS. For Ukraine, this represents a sharp reduction in the share of total trade, while for Tajikistan the same percentage represents an increase in its share of trade. Finally, those of a third group—Russia, Uzbekistan, Georgia, and Armenia—have from 20 percent to 35 percent of their total trade with CIS countries.

Geography means a lot to trade, as the gravity model emphasizes (see endnote 8). Soviet protectionism and a politicized pattern of trade clearly caused all of the republics to trade too much with one another when they were still parts of the Soviet Union and immediately thereafter. By that model, the reduction of intra-CIS trade for Ukraine, Armenia, Georgia, Kazakhstan, Kyrgyzstan, and Uzbekistan would appear to be a healthy market development, while it is also natural that countries that are deeply imbedded in the CIS, such as Ukraine, Kazakhstan, and Kyrgyzstan, should still have a large share of their trade with CIS countries.

Nonetheless, there are several anomalies, based on what theory might predict. The most striking is Moldova, which pursued as much as 60 percent of its trade with the CIS in 1997. The explanation is that European protectionism has made Moldova heavily dependent on Russia's market for its wine and fruit exports; it is also dependent on gas imports from Russia. Another anomaly is Belarus, whose intra-CIS trade rose to 71 percent in 1997; the explanation for this is that Belarus embraces Russia for subsidies, but it should also be noted that the value of these Belarusian exports to Russia is exaggerated, since much of this trade is pursued in barter. Tajikistan has also seen its trade with Russia rise, but this increase is artificial, as the country relies on Russian aid. Azerbaijan and Turkmenistan are both on the southern frontier of the CIS and so should not have half their trade within the CIS, but both states lack alternative means for moving their major commodities to other markets, because of a dearth of alternative pipelines. Both these countries would presumably benefit from less trade with the CIS. Russia has less intra-CIS trade than does any other member country except Uzbekistan; only 22 percent of Russia's trade is with CIS countries. Presumably this is because market forces have influenced trade more in Russia than in other CIS countries, and because Russia is less restricted by geography and transportation problems.

As intra-CIS trade has contracted, its commodity structure has changed radically. Initially, the trade consisted of two to three times more manufactured goods than energy. Many of these manufactured goods, however, were substandard and noncompetitive at almost

Table 2.8
Intra-CIS Trade Balances, 1992–1997
(US$ millions)

	1992	1993	1994	1995	1996	1997
Armenia	—	-42	-48	-167	-169	-221
Azerbaijan	123	65	-212	56	-50	27
Belarus	-168	-346	-613	-746	-806	-438
Georgia	-82	10	-151	-57	-26	-61
Kazakhstan	-4,000	—	-995	-997	-834	-503
Kyrgyzstan	-117	-159	13	-84	-90	-65
Moldova	-125	-139	-71	-102	-118	1
Russia	13,500	5,000	3,200	-200	-1,100	-100
Tajikistan	-33	-80	-16	-15	15	-192
Turkmenistan	208	234	965	184	753	—
Ukraine	-4,500	-3,000	-3,600	-3,300	-4,100	-5,000
Uzbekistan	-176	313	259	24	-464	240
Total	4,630	1,856	-1,269	-5,503	-6,989	-6,313

Source: *PlanEcon Review and Outlook for the Former Soviet Republics* (October 1998), pp. 24, 42, 114, 134, 148, 159, 173, 188, 201, 213, 227, 240.

any price, and no real customers would pay for them. Demand for energy remained more constant, because there was no effort to restructure production to make it more energy efficient. Intra-CIS trade in primary goods also changed dramatically. Trade in natural gas was maintained at a high level, while trade in oil and metals fell about as much as did intra-CIS trade as a whole. This is because oil and metals were in demand on world markets, while Gazprom had an oversupply of gas and a shortage of customers.

The intra-CIS trade balance has undergone substantial changes (see table 2.8). For the region as a whole, mutual trade has become approximately balanced, reflecting the absence of significant external financing. During the first three years following independence, Russia financed substantial trade surpluses. Russia's trade balance with the CIS deteriorated each year from 1991 to 1996, however, reflecting the shifting balance of power in the Russian government. In 1991 Russia effectively ran a trade surplus of at least $25 billion, meaning that it was financing purchases from Russia by other states to that amount. In 1992 Yegor Gaidar's reform government tried to reduce the imbalance, but it encountered stiff resistance. Under the comparatively lax leadership of Prime Minister Viktor Chernomyrdin, Russia's trade financing was allowed to swell. As Russia launched its successful stabilization in 1995, however, its trade financing was reduced, and it has declined further since. Yet, even when trade financing was available it did not stimulate trade, as is evident from the sharply falling mutual trade. Nor did that financing benefit the recipients, as the case of Ukraine illustrates; it obtained trade credits of $3.5 billion from Russia in 1993, but it lapsed into a hyperinflation of 10,200 percent.[22]

These figures allow the experience of the years since independence to be divided into three periods. From 1991 to 1994 the old state trade regime prevailed in intra-CIS trade, causing mutual trade to plummet. In 1995 and 1996 a new market economy and free trade seemed to be developing, which led to some revival and development of new trade within the region. New protectionism and the contraction of trade emerged in 1997; the problems they created were further exacerbated by the Russian financial collapse of 1998.

IMPACT OF THE RUSSIAN FINANCIAL CRISIS IN 1998

In 1996 and 1997, Russia received large foreign portfolio investments, and its bond and stock markets flourished. The boom never reached the real economy, however, which in the peak year of 1997 recorded a humble growth of 0.8 percent. By the end of October 1997, the effects of the financial crisis in East Asia hit all emerging markets in the world, deterring foreign investors. The Russian stock market plummeted, and foreign bond investors retreated from the CIS countries as well as from other emerging markets.

By late May 1998 the financial crisis had turned distinctly Russian. In spite of a large IMF-led financial package of $22.6 billion offered in July, the Russian budget deficit and short-term debt were too large to sustain the confidence of bond investors. On August 17, 1998, Russia devalued the ruble, defaulted on its domestic government debt, and declared a moratorium on its foreign debt service.

The Russian financial crisis has had numerous effects on the other CIS members. Russian capital began to be repatriated from other CIS countries by the spring of 1998, but the effects were limited, as Russian capital flows to the other CIS countries had been minuscule, and there had been a minimum of foreign direct investment (FDI). The level of total FDI has been incredibly low in all CIS countries, apart from the oil and gas states of Azerbaijan, Kazakhstan, and Turkmenistan. From 1992 to 1997, Estonia attracted almost $600 per capita in foreign investment, while the eight CIS countries that have no oil had attracted only $12 to $48 per capita; even oil-rich Azerbaijan and Kazakhstan managed to attract only $280 per capita. In this period, total foreign direct investment in the CIS countries was measured as $23.6 billion, of which $13.4 billion went to Russia.[23] Altogether intra-CIS FDI has probably been as small as a few hundred million dollars.

After the crash, foreign investors were reluctant to invest not only in Russia but also in any CIS country. Large-scale privatizations slowed across the whole region, because it was almost impossible to attract serious foreign investors, and CIS governments could no longer sell Eurobonds or domestic treasury bills to foreign investors. The other CIS countries had never attracted much foreign portfolio investment, so the withdrawal of foreign investors hurt them much less than it did Russia.[24] The absence of foreign portfolio investment, however, forced all of the CIS governments to introduce more rigorous fiscal policies, because most of them suffered declining international reserves at a time when they should have been rising.

The major blow for the entire region, however, was when Russia's market collapsed. Total CIS exports had already plummeted by 12 percent in the first half of 1998,[25] while the drop in their exports to Russia in the second half were 30 percent, since the Russian GDP is likely to fall by almost half from 1997 to 1999, in dollar terms, because of the falling exchange rate. In 1998, on average, exports to CIS countries by their CIS counterparts fell by 18 percent (see table 2.9). Moldova, Azerbaijan, Tajikistan, Kyrgyzstan, Kazakhstan, and Ukraine were the worst hit, because they are most dependent on sales to Russia; all saw their exports to Russia collapse in the second half of 1998.

Ukraine was hurt in all ways. The Russian financial crisis stopped its previously significant inflow of foreign capital. The Russian market for its exports dried up, and foreign food aid will effectively crowd out potential Ukrainian food exports to Russia. At the same time, Russian producers started undercutting their Ukrainian competitors in metals, which constitute Ukraine's main exports. Ukraine

Table 2.9
Decline in Intra-CIS Trade, 1998
(percent change from previous year)

	Exports to CIS Countries	Imports from CIS Countries
Armenia	-14	-26
Azerbaijan	-39	15
Belarus	-5	-5
Georgia	-24	11
Kazakhstan	-26	-13
Kyrgyzstan	-28	1
Moldova	-29	-27
Russia	-18	-21
Tajikistan	-24	5
Turkmenistan	—	—
Ukraine	-25	-20
Uzbekistan	—	—
Weighted Average	**-18**	**-15.5**

Source: Interstate Statistical Committee of the Commonwealth of Independent States (http://www.unece.org/), April, 1999.

had also benefited greatly from remittances by Ukrainian guest-workers in Russia, who are now effectively earning a quarter of what they did before the collapse, if they have kept their jobs at all.

This combination of plummeting exports to Russia and the end of private international finance has had a substantial effect on the other CIS countries. First, the balance of payments and capital accounts of all the CIS countries are under pressure. Second, this hurts their international reserves, which have fallen in most CIS countries in 1998. Third, Belarus, Ukraine, Moldova, Georgia, Kyrgyzstan, Armenia, and Kazakhstan have all been forced, one after another, to devalue their currencies, so far on the order of 10 percent to 50 percent (Russian devaluation in the same period has been 75 percent). While financial outflows have been small, these are mostly small economies with little monetization and little available financing, so that even minor outflows can cause depreciation. Fourth, devaluations have boosted inflation, although less than might have been expected. (While Russia recorded inflation of 84 percent in 1998, Ukraine ended the year with inflation of only 18 percent). Finally, the reduction in exports is having a direct negative impact on output. Most countries saw their GDP growth decline in 1998 in comparison with 1997 by several percentage units, a decline that can largely be ascribed to the Russian financial crisis.

Currency devaluations have been among the most damaging effects of the Russian crisis on the CIS countries; these have come one after the other, greatly upsetting relative price levels, which has meant that protectionism has grown far worse in most CIS countries. The starkest contrast has been between Russia and Kazakhstan. While the Russian ruble fell from 6 rubles per dollar in July 1998 to 27 rubles per dollar in late March 1999, the Kazakh tenge had been barely devalued. Even considering differing inflation, this meant that the price level in Russia declined by more than half when measured in tenge. Most of the other CIS countries have followed Russia in devaluing, although Uzbekistan and Belarus have allowed the difference between their official and black market exchange rates to rise. As a result, Kazakhstan found itself with the highest relative wages in the CIS, pricing it out of most markets. To maintain a market for locally produced goods at home, the government of Kazakhstan responded by introducing severe protectionist measures, such as highly disruptive import quotas and import tariffs of up to 200 percent on certain foods imported from Kyrgyzstan and Uzbekistan. Ultimately, Kazakhstan had no choice but to do as the other states had done; in early April 1999, the tenge dropped 25 percent at the official exchange rate, and even more at unofficial rates.[26]

Although it was a crippling blow to the entire CIS, the organization had no response to the Russian financial crisis of 1998; indeed, the heads of government convened only twice in that period (April 29 and November 25), as compared with the 27 meetings they had convened in the six years before. This was the period when Boris Berezovsky was trying energetically to revive the CIS (with proposals that are discussed below); neither meeting refuted Berezovsky's ideas outright, but they also were unable to make any decisions of significance.[27] The CIS Heads of State met in April 1998 and in April 1999, but the Russian financial crash, which was devastating trade among member states, was not even perceived to be an issue for their consideration at the April 1999 meeting.

What the crisis seems to have taught the members of the CIS is that the less trade a country has with Russia and with other CIS members, the better off it is. Belarus, Uzbekistan, and Turkmenistan, which had never opted for a market economy, went back to Soviet-like systems with multiple exchange rates, state orders, and regulated prices, making free trade impossible. Russia, Ukraine, Kazakhstan, and Moldova also undertook various protectionist measures. Some were meant to reinforce these states' fiscal revenues, while others were designed to protect domestic industries. Kyrgyzstan, Georgia, and Armenia responded by intensifying their efforts to become members of the WTO, distancing themselves from the more protectionist CIS members. In October 1998 Kyrgyzstan became the first CIS state to be invited to join the WTO, and it formally became a member in December 1998. All CIS countries turned to international institutions for financial support, since Russian support was no longer an option. Nobody perceived the CIS to be a plausible part of any solution, and almost nobody called for joint CIS action to face the crisis. Rather the CIS countries met Russia's financial crisis with a sense of desperation, and the desire to flee from one another.

PROSPECTS FOR ECONOMIC INTEGRATION

Intra-CIS trade has been contracting year after year. Since the economies of key CIS countries, including Russia, Ukraine, and Kazakhstan, remain stagnant, the potential for CIS trade integration is declining. Each year Russia is less prepared to provide any financing for the other CIS countries, which reduces any attraction that the CIS may hold for these states. As it has become increasingly evident that CIS cooperation is not advancing, criticism of the body has increased, and the CIS summits have become ever more infrequent and acrimonious.

At the CIS summit in Moscow in March 1997, President Yeltsin declared bluntly: "everybody is dissatisfied with the state of affairs in the CIS." In 1998 Boris Berezovsky, the new CIS executive secretary, concluded that "instead of seven years of integration, we have in effect had seven years of disintegration." He even spoke of integration within the CIS as being a "virtual reality."[28] The March 1997 summit adopted one of the last substantial CIS documents, "The Conception of the Development of Economic Integration," which Berezovsky described as "a very weak document, over which the 'spirit of Gosplan' hangs. It is written in the language of five-year plans or CMEA complex programs, in complete contrast to the reality of a market economy."[29]

Berezovsky struggled energetically in 1998 to streamline and reinvigorate the CIS. Although he was convinced that the CIS should have the profound integration of the EU as its ultimate goal, Berezovsky saw the most important immediate task of the CIS to be making itself more of a multilateral free trade zone.[30] It is an eloquent illustration of the contradictory impulses that drive the CIS that members were reluctant to approve Berezovsky's ideas until the man himself was removed as executive secretary in March 1999, thereby reducing the threat that the CIS administration might become an effective body.

The heads of state adopted Berezovsky's proposals to build up the CIS as a free trade zone, but it is difficult to see how this might be turned into reality. International trade theory questions the usefulness of a free trade zone among countries at an intermediary level of development, arguing that it may cause more trade diversion than stimulation.[31] In current conditions, however, the question appears moot. Neither Belarus, Uzbekistan, nor Turkmenistan have market economies, but instead strictly regulate prices and trade; Belarus and Uzbekistan also have multiple exchange rates with big disparities, thus making free trade with any of the three impossible. Ukraine has reduced the convertibility of its *hryvnia*. Most CIS members have introduced an array of import tariffs, export tariffs, excise taxes, and quotas, trying to satisfy the demands of various pressure groups within their respective countries. Even if it wished to do so, the CIS is too weak to counteract those strong internal interests, nor does it have the ability to resolve on its own all the legal and technical problems that a modern trade system would generate.

Even the smaller Customs Union of Belarus, Russia, Kazakhstan, Kyrgyzstan, and Tajikistan is beginning to look moribund. The three original members established a working group to harmonize tariffs within the Customs Union, but by the end of 1998, the working group had reached agreement on common import tariffs for only about 5,000 goods, a small portion of their total trade. It is not clear when this group's proposals will be adopted as law, or whether they will have any practical implication.[32] Kyrgyzstan has conformed its policies to those of the World Trade Organization, because it understood membership in the WTO to be a more important advantage than membership in the still-inoperative Customs Union. Tajikistan, the newest member of the Customs Union, has taken no part in the working group.

ALTERNATIVES TO FAILURE

The effect of the CIS on economic integration is largely negative. Initially, the CIS helped to delay necessary economic adjustments, which aggravated the economic and social costs of postcommunist transition in the member states. The persistence of the ruble zone prolonged and exacerbated macroeconomic instability. Continuing state trade and artificial pricing led to massive rent seeking, while also blocking the development of new trade. The economic success of the Baltic countries was driven by the resoluteness with which they distanced themselves from the CIS.

The years 1995–1996 might be seen as a period of economic success for the CIS, since reasonably free trade allowed for some generation of new trade. After late 1996, however, the CIS came to abound with unilateral protectionist acts, prompting mutual trade to fall. Russia's financial crisis in 1998 dealt a devastating blow to all CIS countries and aggravated this protectionist trend, leaving the tiny economies of Kyrgyzstan, Armenia, and Georgia as the only remaining convinced free traders. Work continues on creating a free trade zone and a customs union, but neither has yet been formed, nor is there anything to suggest that either would help solve the economic problems of the region if they were created.

Unfortunately, no other plausible solutions seem to be at hand either. The absence of a framework of economic integration for the CIS countries is likely to have dire consequences for these economies, of which the international economic community should take note. Trade growth requires some sort of foreign trade system and a certain standardization, but the CIS countries are moving away from any system, instead developing their own idiosyncratic regulations, which are disrupting trade even further. Increasingly the mutual trade system of the CIS is coming to resemble the unilateral protectionism that characterized world trade in the 1930s or interstate trade in Africa today. With each passing year the CIS looks less like the European Union and more like the British Commonwealth, a post imperial structure that may still have important cultural, historical, and even political purposes, but no economic function.

The World Trade Organization would seem an obvious body that might take up the economic functions at which the CIS has failed, but few of the countries are making progress toward membership; indeed, most have weakened their candidacy by introducing unilateral protectionist measures in response to the Russian financial crisis in 1998. The CIS states can be divided into three broad groups in their movement toward WTO membership.[33] The first group consists of Russia, Ukraine, Moldova, Azerbaijan, and Kazakhstan, all of which have been working toward WTO membership for years; even before 1998 those states needed to undertake significant trade liberalization to become eligible, so that the even more protectionist measures that they introduced after the Russian financial crisis effectively brought their efforts to join the WTO to a halt. The second group, by contrast, has maintained liberal trade policies; one of these, Kyrgyzstan, is already a member of the WTO, while Armenia and Georgia hope to be admitted in late 1999. The third group is made up of Belarus, Tajikistan, Turkmenistan, and Uzbekistan, none of which could become members without a complete reversal of their current economic policies; indeed, neither Tajikistan nor Turkmenistan has even applied for membership in the WTO.

NOTES

[1] This chapter draws on a commissioned paper by Vladimir R. Yevstegneyev, "Spetsifika mekhanizma mezhdunarodnoi ekonomicheskoi integratsii v SNG," (Moscow: unpublished manuscript, 1997). The authors wish to thank Constantine Michalopoulos and David Tarr for substantial and useful comments on a previous draft of this chapter.

[2] The foreign trade organization of the Soviet bloc, which essentially supported bilateral state trade agreements specified in commodities rather than money. The CMEA was established in Moscow in 1949. Over the course of its existence, its members included Bulgaria, Czechoslovakia, Hungary, Poland, Romania, the Soviet Union, East Germany, Mongolia, Cuba, and Vietnam. It was dissolved in 1991.

3 V. Viktor Timoshenko, "Vse bogatye lyudi Ukrainy zarabotali svoi kapitaly na rossiiskom gaze," *Nezavisimaia gazeta*, October 16, 1998.

4 These are Moldova, Kazakhstan, Uzbekistan, Kyrgyzstan, Azerbaijan, and Tajikistan.

5 As of June 1998, CIS members had signed 880 agreements. See A. Shurubovich, "Major Trends, Problems, and Prospects for Economic Cooperation Within the CIS," *Foreign Trade*, July–September 1998.

6 Yuri V. Shishkov and Vladimir R. Evstigneev, *Reintegratsiia postsovetskogo ekonomicheskogo prostranstva i opyt Zapadnoi Evropy*, (Moscow: IMEMO, 1994), pp. 35–6.

7 No exact number is available, as statistics were poor during the disruption of the USSR, and all prices changed. Therefore, the numbers for 1991 are highly uncertain. However, from 1992 to 1993, intra-CIS trade fell by at least 44 percent. See table 2.5.

8 The essence of the gravity model is that trade flows can be reasonably predicted on the basis of only two parameters: gross domestic product (GDP) and distance (usually measured as distance between capitals), implying that countries tend to trade the most with rich countries in their neighborhood. See, Jeffrey A. Frankel, *Regional Trading Blocs in the World Economic System* (Washington, D.C.: Institute for International Economics, 1997), p. 229.

9 Oleh Havrylyshyn and Hassan Al-Atrash, "Opening up and Geographic Diversification of Trade in Transition Economies," *IMF Working Paper No. 98/22*, (Washington, D.C.: International Monetary Fund, 1998).

10 Other CIS countries also received substantial financing from Russia: Turkmenistan, 53 percent of its GDP; Georgia, 52 percent; Armenia, 49 percent; Azerbaijan, 26 percent; Kazakhstan, 26 percent; Kyrgyzstan, 23 percent; Ukraine, 22 percent; Moldova, 11 percent; and Belarus, 11 percent. International Monetary Fund, *Economic Review: Financial Relations Among Countries of the Former Soviet Union* (Washington, D.C.: IMF, 1994), p. 26.

11 Anders Åslund, *How Russia Became a Market Economy* (Washington, D.C.: Brookings Institution, 1995), pp. 109–36.

12 Those states were: Armenia, Belarus, Kazakhstan, Kyrgyzstan, Moldova, Russia, Tajikistan, Turkmenistan, Uzbekistan, and Ukraine.

[13] Personal communication from Petr Prokopovich, chairman of the Central Bank of Belarus, February 1, 1999. Barter prices are patently inflated, usually twice as high as prices paid in money, and this artificially boosts both Belarus's exports and its GDP.

[14] In 1994 the government of Moldova banned barter except for transactions involving energy resources, raw materials, machinery, and medicine; in May 1996 the Turkmen authorities banned barter for cotton, wool, oil, and oil products, while Uzbekistan prohibited barter transactions for the export of 49 products. UN Economic Commission for Europe, *Economic Survey of Europe, no. 3, 1998*, (New York: United Nations, 1998), pp. 101–3.

[15] Ibid., p. 99.

[16] This section draws on data from *PlanEcon Energy Outlook* (Washington, D.C.: Planecon, Inc., October 1998).

[17] UN Economic Commission for Europe, *Economic Survey of Europe, no. 3, 1998* (New York: United Nations, 1998), pp. 96, 99.

[18] As pipelines are huge long-term investments, with fares highly dependent on the capital costs, it is virtually impossible to assess what would be a fair price for pipeline transportation, given that the investments are sunk costs from the Soviet period. This lack of a market economic standard contributes to the great problems of reaching any agreement on transfer tariffs.

[19] Sergei Aukutsionek, "Barter v rossiiskoi promyshlennosti," *Voprosy ekonomiki*, vol. 70, (February 1998), pp. 51–60; Clifford G. Gaddy and Barry W. Ickes, "Russia's Virtual Economy," *Foreign Affairs*, vol. 77, no. 5 (September/October: 1998), pp. 53–67.

[20] This section draws on Constantine Michalopoulos and David Tarr, "The Economics of Customs Unions in the Commonwealth of Independent States," *Post-Soviet Geography and Economics*, vol. 38, no. 3 (1997), pp. 125-143.

[21] *PlanEcon Review and Outlook*, (Washington, D.C.: Planecon, Inc., October 1998.) These CIS figures are assembled from the Washington consulting firm PlanEcon, as its numbers are well considered, comprehensive and cover our needs. The figures are somewhat less dramatic than similar World Bank statistics. See Michalopoulos and Tarr, "The Economics of Customs Unions in the Commonwealth of Independent States," p. 126.

[22] From this, Ukraine's positive service balance, which exceeded $1 billion, should be deducted.

23. Luis M. Valdivieso, "Macroeconomic Developments in the Baltics, Russia, and Other Countries of the Former Soviet Union, 1992–97," *IMF Occasional Paper No. 175* (Washington, D.C.: International Monetary Fund, 1998), p. 28.

24. Ibid., pp. 27–8.

25. UN Economic Commission for Europe, *Economic Survey of Europe, no. 3, 1998* (New York: United Nations, 1998), p. 50.

26. The *tenge* has continued to drop and in July 1999 was at 132 *tenge* per dollar. By contrast, the value of the ruble has held relatively firm, between 24 and 25 rubles to the dollar.

27. Fedor Olegov, "V Moskve proshel forum SNG," *Nezavisimaia gazeta,* November 24, 1998; Natalia Pulina and Ekaterina Tesemnikova, "Effektivnost dolzhna vozrastat," *Nezavisimaia gazeta,* November 26, 1998.

28. Boris A. Berezovsky, "SNG: ot razvala k sotrudnichestvu," *Nezavisimaia gazeta,* November 13, 1998.

29. Ibid.

30. Ibid.

31. Frankel, *Regional Trading Blocs in the World Economic System,* p. 229.

32. Personal communication from officials of the government of Kyrgyzstan in January 1999.

33. UN Economic Commission for Europe, *Economic Survey of Europe, no. 3, 1998* (New York: United Nations, 1998), pp. 103–5.

3
The Failure to Establish an Integrated Security Structure

From the very beginning of the CIS, security preoccupations were at the heart of Russia's conviction that the former USSR had to be integrated economically, politically, and militarily; naturally, Russia saw itself as the driving force in this process. While many of the new states wanted some sort of security assistance or coordinating mechanism, it was Russia that took the lead in defining the basic CIS security structures that emerged, in part because Russia also had the most ambitious picture of what the CIS security structures should become. Since the Soviet collapse, Russia has been the most interventionist state in conflicts on the territory of the former USSR. Russian political and military leaders have been at the forefront in fashioning bilateral and regional security arrangements designed to compensate for the shortcomings of the CIS. An evaluation of the development of CIS and related security mechanisms on the territory of the former USSR is inseparable from an analysis of Russian security interests and ambitions. Many Western analysts in fact have viewed CIS security initiatives, and the bilateral and regional relationships that have emerged, as essentially Russian efforts to reassert control over the former USSR.

Just as was the case with economic integration, however, the security arrangements that have actually emerged have been shaped as much by the interests and constraints of the other CIS states as they have by Russia's desires. Indeed, the combination of these other states' concerns and Russia's weakness has resulted in a post-Soviet security environment that is far more fragmented and pluralistic than most observers in late 1991 would have imagined possible. A core group of CIS states has sought from the beginning to minimize its dependence on Russian and CIS security instruments, but even those states that seek Russian help and support do so because of their own local and regional problems and interests, rather than on behalf of a unified former USSR, as is clearly demonstrated by the history of the development of Russia's bilateral security relations.

The CIS founding documents and other statements of general principle are the only examples of CIS security arrangements involving the whole of the CIS. In every concrete instance, some of the CIS countries have taken observer status or have simply refused to participate. Even those states that participate have done so in lackluster fashion, limited by their inadequate financial resources and their concerns over sovereignty. Most states have preferred to put what meager security resources they have into the creation of national militaries and border guards. Even that process, though, is barely underway in most CIS states. These states generally lack real military assets, having inherited their current forces from Soviet units and infrastructure that were already in decline in the late 1980s. Some states have also had to compete for those Soviet assets against local paramilitary and secessionist forces. None of the CIS states, not even Russia, has adequately financed, trained, or exercised its military.

Senior Russian officials frequently complain about the lack of follow-through shown by the CIS partners, yet the Russian military budget is stretched paper thin, making Russia unable to finance basic projects in border protection, air defense, or collective security. Russia's own economic and political troubles have also frequently distracted it from sustained attention to the details of CIS security policy. Perhaps most important of all, the CIS has had as little success in achieving an understanding of basic security interests, threats, and shared responsibilities as it has had in the realms of economic or political integration. Most of the CIS member states both need and want Russian security support, yet they are suspicious of Russian motives and fear surrendering control of important national assets to Moscow. While the rhetoric of CIS security discussions may focus on possible threats to member states from nonmember states, in reality the greatest challenges to security since the breakup of the USSR have come from within the CIS itself, either within a single member state or between two member states. Given this contradictory mass of aims and interests, which is further complicated by the unavoidable reality of inadequate financing, it is little wonder that the CIS has failed to coalesce as a serious security organization.

This chapter surveys the attempt to establish integrated security arrangements within the CIS, first by providing an assessment of Russian interests and how these shaped the initial efforts to establish a comprehensive CIS security structure. It then examines the actual results of those efforts in key areas such as the formation of a unified political and military structure, the integrated control of military assets, the establishment of a common defense space, and the management of conflicts on CIS territory. The chapter then examines why Russia and the CIS have failed to create an integrated security structure, and concludes with an examination of the three major bilateral security arrangements that Russia has been able to conclude—those with Kazakhstan, Belarus, and Armenia.

RUSSIAN INTERESTS AND INTENTIONS FOR CIS SECURITY INTEGRATION

There are thousands of Russian decrees, leadership statements, interviews, and articles in the Russian press about the necessity of CIS security integration,[1] but perhaps the most straightforward statement of Russia's perceived interests in relation to such integration is Russian President Yeltsin's 1995 decree, "On Affirming the Strategic Course of the Russian Federation with the Member States of the Commonwealth of Independent States." This decree states that Russian "vital interests" are at stake in the CIS and that Russia's CIS policies are inextricably linked to Russia's effort to see itself included in "world political and economic structures."[2]

While not always stated so clearly, double principles have guided Russian policy on defense and security issues in the CIS from the beginning, as Russia sought to create a unified security space and a defense alliance. Such an alliance would not only unite CIS states in pursuit of what Russia saw as positive security goals, but would also, as that 1995 decree puts it, keep wavering states "from participating in alliances and blocs directed against any of the other CIS members."[3] The outer CIS borders, essentially those of the USSR, would be secured by joint CIS border guards, led by Russian forces. In the Russian view, the inner international boundaries, those between former Soviet republics, should have a different and more elastic status. Yeltsin's decree accepts the possibility of cooperation with the United Nations and the Organization for Security and Cooperation in Europe (OSCE) for peacekeeping and conflict regulation on the territory of the CIS, but stipulates that such cooperation must include the "understanding from their side that this region is first of all a zone of Russian interests."[4]

For purposes of assessing the current state of security integration in the CIS, Russia's original intentions may be grouped into four kinds of goals: first, the creation of a unified security structure under Russian leadership, designed to encompass the senior political and military leadership of the CIS member states in a formal structure; second, the actual control of the basic assets of the Soviet military, especially the strategic weapons and key power projection capabilities control, whether through this unified structure or unilaterally; third, the stationing of Russian military units throughout the CIS and the creation of a single common defense space, with integrated structures for defending common borders and air space; and, fourth, the creation of an integrated mechanism to manage conflicts on the territory of the former USSR.

As has been noted already in this book, the CIS has been most successful in its creation of formal administrative structures; those concerning security have been no exception. Both the original Minsk (or Belovezh Forest) agreement and the subsequent Almaty declaration of 1991 created a basis for a common security policy, while the first CIS summit in Minsk on December 30, 1991, set up a basic security infrastructure.

The Council of Heads of State was given the right to devise strategy, to approve conceptual documents, to grant mandates to peacekeeping missions, and to introduce martial law throughout the Commonwealth in the case of aggression. This council governs the border guards and appoints the commander in chief of border troops. The council was to make decisions by consensus. The Council of Heads of Government was given the tasks of drafting the budget, dealing with procurement and conscription, and coordinating military-economic activity.

These two bodies together were to implement policy based on work done by the Council of Defense Ministers, which was to look at issues of joint defense, military development and cooperation, and the prevention of military conflicts. The General Headquarters of the Joint Armed Forces of the CIS and the Council of Commanders of Border Guards were also established, subsidiary to the Council of Heads of State and reporting to it.

The efforts to create an integrated political-military structure unraveled almost immediately. A Minsk summit in February 1992 failed to move discussions much beyond earlier agreements; for example, the summit's agreement on the status of strategic forces did not specify their composition, and Ukraine, Azerbaijan, Armenia, Kazakhstan, and Kyrgyzstan all appended various reservations to the document. Similarly, only eight states signed the General Purpose Forces Agreement, and Azerbaijan and Ukraine refused to sign the Agreement on Defense Budget, even though it assigned most of the financial burden to Russia.

Another treaty, the Tashkent Collective Security Treaty, signed in May 1992, established the Heads of State as a Collective Security Council, the highest political body responsible for implementing the security treaty, in consultation with the councils of Foreign and Defense Ministers. Since only six CIS members originally signed the Tashkent Treaty, and were later joined by only three more, this essentially created parallel security structures for member states, and so was folded into the Council of Defense Ministers in 1993.[5]

Perhaps as crippling was the fact that CIS members were developing the same tradition of making unrealistic and impractical statements and decisions about security questions as they were about economics. For example, Article 4 of the strategic forces agreement states: "Military command bodies of the Commonwealth's strategic forces carry out their activity in cooperation with the state bodies, enterprises, and organizations of the Commonwealth member states." The reality at the time, however, was that Russia, with the support of the major world powers, including the United States, was unilaterally trying to maintain exclusive control over the Soviet nuclear arsenal, thus turning statements about shared responsibility for control or use of the strategic arsenal into nothing more than words.

There were two separate and simultaneous efforts, one through the CIS and the other through the Tashkent Treaty, to establish a unified command of all or most of the armed forces of the CIS. The CIS established a General Headquarters of Joint Armed Forces of the CIS in late 1991, with Russia's Marshal Yevgeny Shaposhnikov as commander in chief. The Russian-Ukrainian dispute over the Black Sea Fleet and Russia's efforts to become the sole heir to Soviet nuclear weapons, however, immediately doomed this effort. In 1993 Shaposhnikov was appointed to the Russian Security Council and the General Headquarters was replaced by the Staff for Coordination of Military Cooperation of the CIS, making clear that there would be no unified CIS armed forces.

Although formally separate from the CIS, the Tashkent Collective Security Treaty of 1992 seemed at first a more serious attempt, by a more willing group of CIS members, to establish a system of collective security. The Tashkent Treaty was signed during a meeting of the Council of Heads of States;[6] the original signatories were Russia, Kazakhstan, Kyrgyzstan, Tajikistan, Armenia, and Uzbekistan, while Azerbaijan, Belarus, and Georgia signed later.[7] The treaty purports to create a full-fledged defense alliance. It obligates signatories to refrain from joining any military alliances or groupings directed against other members (Article One). Member countries are to consult immediately when a threat to one or more signatories appears (Article Two). Aggression against one member is regarded as an act of aggression against all (Article Four). As noted above, the treaty also established a Collective Security Council (Article Five).

For all its apparent specificity, the Tashkent Treaty is little more than a declaration of intent. Key questions of military organization, such as the stationing of forces, are only hinted at or are left out entirely. An even bigger problem is that the treaty is designed to deal with a common external threat to the CIS states, which none of the signatories except Russia perceived to exist. In 1994 Azerbaijan attempted to invoke the treaty to resolve its dispute with Armenia over Karabakh, highlighting the extent to which divisions within the CIS were more important to the emerging security environment than were threats from outside the former USSR.[8] Russia responded to this attempt by insisting that the Tashkent Treaty only applied to external threats. It was already clear by this time, however, that only Russia and states facing an immediate and direct security threat had any interest in collective security, and for most non-Russian states there was no shared direct threat to unite them.[9] Belarus's ratification of the treaty, for example, included the stipulation that its forces could not be sent into conflict areas. Even though it supported a common security system, the Belarusian leadership saw little reason to involve itself in the Caucasus or Central Asia.

Formed with so many inherent divisions and inefficiencies, the treaty has not brought Russia or any of the other signatories any real security benefits. Azerbaijan, Georgia, and Uzbekistan formally withdrew from the Tashkent Treaty in April 1999, putting its further survival in serious doubt.

NATIONAL ARMIES NOT INTEGRATION

With the exception of border cooperation, air defense, and peace-keeping, which are all discussed separately below, efforts to create and retain CIS strategic and general-purpose forces quickly came to nothing. In spite of the initial impulse to create the General Head-quarters of the Joint Armed Forces, all of the CIS countries, including Russia, found the drive for sovereignty and independence led inexo-rably to the creation of national armed forces. All of these national forces were formed on the basis of existing Soviet assets. Here the CIS was clearly beneficial, helping to bring some order to the disinte-gration of what had been one army, dividing its assets, and, where possible, settling conflicting claims. Most of this coordination, how-ever, was ad hoc and post factum, since the transfer of existing assets to national armies—and even more so to opposition forces, as occurred in Karabakh or the Transdniestr region of Moldova—was largely spontaneous. At the Tashkent meeting those CIS states that were also members of the Treaty on Conventional Armed Forces in Europe (CFE) divided existing assets and entitlements under that treaty's formulae for the Atlantic-to-the-Urals zone.[10] Later, when Russia tried to alter that treaty's flank limitations, Georgia, Ukraine, Azerbaijan, and Moldova actively opposed Russia's proposals, which prompted them to form the GUUAM group (discussed more fully in chapter 5).

All the CIS states, including Russia, had established national mili-tary structures by the end of 1992. Belarus and Ukraine received the lion's share of those Soviet assets that were not retained by Russia. Figures from the CFE Treaty show, for example, that in 1993 Ukraine and Belarus had 6,052 and 3,457 main battle tanks, respectively.[11] Other states got lesser amounts, and only the Baltic states refused a share of Soviet equipment. Limits imposed by the CFE Treaty prevented Russia from hoarding equipment because of the strict overall and regional ceilings within the Atlantic-to-the-Urals zone. It was also cheaper to transfer equipment than to destroy it, as the treaty would have required.

The simple possession of weaponry does not make an army. The organization of their new forces more than absorbed the small defense budgets of most CIS states, leaving no surplus for shared security tasks. Many CIS member states saw Russian or CIS help as a way to support their own militaries and expected Moscow to pay for necessary infrastructure and training. Even states that were most enthusiastic about military integration, such as Armenia or Belarus, saw collective structures as a supplement and not a substitute for their national military forces.

Russia has also faced new geographic and strategic realities that required massive readjustments. The breakup of the USSR left only eight of the sixteen Soviet military districts within Russia. Nearly the entire first strategic echelon of defense—the Soviet elite forces— were stationed outside Russia; this included thirteen armies and corps, four tank armies, two rocket armies, three antimissile armies, five air armies, a significant collection of organizations and units of various types, and huge stocks of weapons, supplies and material.[12] Even before the breakup of the Soviet Union, the collapse of the Warsaw Pact created an enormous troop withdrawal problem for the Soviet General Staff. After 1991 what was now the Russian General Staff faced the further burden of trying to oversee the apportioning of Soviet army assets among eleven other new states.

This withdrawal of Soviet and Russian forces was one of the largest in history. In the late Soviet period, large numbers of tanks and other equipment were hurriedly sent east of the Urals. Some were integrated into existing units in the Far East, but nearly 11,000 tanks were left at sites in Siberia, Kazakhstan, and Uzbekistan.[13] In 1993 alone, Russia brought 30,000 tanks and armored vehicles, 9,000 artillery pieces, 4,000 planes and helicopters, 46 divisions and 64 brigades—more than 640,000 military servicemen—back home from the countries of eastern Europe and the former USSR.[14] Managing this unprecedented peacetime withdrawal and relocation placed huge strains on the financial, logistical, and management structures of the Russian Ministry of Defense. These withdrawn forces and equipment quickly overloaded sites in Russia that were unprepared to receive them, such as those in Kaliningrad, the Leningrad Military District, and the North Caucasus; in this last instance pre-existing interethnic disturbances made the resettlement particularly controversial.

Despite this backdrop of massive relocation, Russia attempted to work with willing CIS partners to build some semblance of a forward deployed military force. Bilateral agreements established programs of joint military planning, exercises, and military education. These agreements also legitimized the stationing of Russian forces in CIS member states, as well as granting Russia access to important military infrastructure in the event of crisis. Russia's intention, as expressed in a decree by President Yeltsin in April 1994, was to have a string of Russian military bases across the former USSR, including Latvia.[15] Publication of this decree caused a furor in some of the CIS countries and abroad.[16]

As of mid-1999, the reality of Russian deployment still falls far short of those stated intentions. Russia has no operational military forces stationed in the Baltic states, Belarus, Azerbaijan, Kazakhstan, Kyrgyzstan, Uzbekistan or Turkmenistan,[17] and has negotiated the withdrawal of its forces from Moldova, although considerable controversy remains about when this withdrawal will take place. The effort to create combined Russian-Turkmen armed forces appears to have fallen apart. Nonetheless, Russia still has troops of various sorts stationed in about half the CIS countries. In addition to Kazakhstan, Belarus, and Armenia, states with which it has been able to conclude strong bilateral military cooperation agreements (discussed below), Russia also has a military presence in Georgia, Moldova, Tajikistan, and Ukraine.

Russia now has 9,200 military personnel at three bases in Georgia (Batumi, Akhalkalaki, and Vaziani). These forces represent brigade-sized units at the first two sites and a regiment at the third, and possess 140 T-72 tanks and around 500 armored combat vehicles. The Russian Air Force also deploys a composite regiment of 35 transport aircraft and helicopters at a separate site. A limited number of artillery and armored combat vehicles are deployed in Abkhazia. An additional Russian infantry battalion is deployed in Georgia in peacekeeping operations, under February 1994 and February 1995 bilateral agreements on CFE Agreement flank-allotments between indigenous Georgian and Russian stationed forces. A process of indigenization has also shaped the Russian forces stationed in the Caucasus. As one leading commentator has argued, "While formally the basing arrangements for the Transcaucasus group of forces are quite stable, in fact the Russian divisions stationed in Armenia and Adjaria are becoming indigenized to such a degree that their control for Moscow is now only symbolic."[18] The adjoining North Caucasian Military District in Russia, was also redrawn under the CFE Agreement to permit Russia to station increased forces in the region. Russian deployments in Georgia cannot be considered either settled or stable. Georgia has insisted that its long-term military concessions to Russia are linked to a satisfactory outcome of the Abkhazia dispute, where Russia has assumed the role of both peacekeeper and formal mediator. In January 1998 Georgia also negotiated the handover of ten military sites from Russia. These sites include small-scale defense and military holdings not covered by the 1995 basing agreement.[19]

In Moldova the original Soviet Fourteenth Army has slowly been reduced from around 5,000 personnel to a 2,500-strong operational group. Russian infantry battalions (around 500 personnel) are also deployed in Transdniestr peacekeeping operations. A Moldovan-Russian Agreement signed in October 1994 envisions the withdrawal of Russian forces entirely from Moldova, but, as noted, the continuing dispute between Moldova and its Transdniestr region has delayed its implementation. Moldovan authorities are concerned that the withdrawal of Russian forces will leave key pieces of equipment and ammunition stores in the hands of the Transdniestrian rebels.

The Russian deployments in Tajikistan are a holdover from the Soviet 201st Motorized Rifle Division; it now numbers 8,200 personnel and has three main bases, in Dushanbe and the Kulyab and Kurgan-Tyube regions. Five thousand of the 5,500 CIS peacekeeping forces in the country are also deployed by Russia. A high proportion of the rank and file of the 201st and of the Russian border guards stationed in the country, however, are ethnic Tajik.[20]

Ironically, Russia's largest foreign deployment is on Ukrainian territory, the country most opposed to an integrated CIS security structure. The Black Sea Fleet is the reason for this anomaly. In May 1997 a Ukrainian-Russian Agreement settled the longstanding dispute over the division and basing of this Soviet-era fleet. Russia and Ukraine agreed to divide the fleet and its assets equally, after which Ukraine sold back a portion of its entitlement to Russia. The agreement also permits Russia to deploy its portion of the fleet in the Crimea, at Sevastopol and Karatinnaya, for twenty years. The Russian and Ukrainian navies must share a third site on the peninsula at Streletskaya Bay.

Both Russian and Ukrainian elements of this fleet are now in serious decline. Russia deploys only ten submarines and eight principal surface combat ships there, even though a large number of smaller craft (perhaps as many as 800) were part of the original package over which Russia and Ukraine argued in 1992. Russia also deploys seventeen combat aircraft with the fleet. In the early 1990s, this fleet and supporting coastal defense units numbered more than 30,000 personnel, but these units have been withdrawn or reduced substantially.

This pattern of forward deployment demonstrates that Russia has succeeded in maintaining a presence in key locations throughout the CIS. There is far more retrenchment than forward deployment, however, and Russia has not been able to secure deployment in greatly desired sites, such as in Azerbaijan and in the Baltic states. The withdrawal from the Baltic states left only a single strategic radar site in Latvia under Russian control, and this site is now being dismantled.[21] Current Russian deployments are all based on pre-existing Soviet deployments. Russia has constructed no new facilities or deployed new units, although it has introduced reinforcements to the 201st Motorized Rifle Division in Tajikistan and augmented other units through consolidation. Severe resource constraints suggest that exploiting these pre-existing deployments is probably all that Russia can currently manage.[22] Indeed, the variety of local pressures that Russia faces in these deployments, including the pronounced tendency toward the indigenization of ostensibly Russian soldiers, suggests that Russia's foreign deployment is even less extensive than it may appear.

BORDER GUARDS, AIR DEFENSE, AND PEACEKEEPING

States that wished to strengthen the CIS sought to create a common security and defense space that would be more defined by its common external boundaries with the non-CIS world than it would by its internal borders. Creation of such a space was partly a matter of security, but it also suited the political preferences of many in Russia and elsewhere who wanted to prevent, or at least to slow, the transformation of the Soviet-era interrepublic boundaries into true international borders. Integrated border guards and a common air defense system were key elements of that common space. However, while there have been some successes in creating bilateral border and air defense arrangements, the common security and defense space as originally envisioned does not exist.

Russia has pushed the hardest for the integration of border guard units, whether through the CIS or through bilateral agreements. Russian policy for its own national border troops explicitly states that its main objectives do not stop at the Russian Federation state border but also extend to the external borders of the CIS member states.[23] Not surprisingly, many CIS states have viewed Russia's efforts to create an integrated border guard force for the common external CIS boundaries with skepticism and dissent. Only Armenia, Kazakhstan, Kyrgyzstan, the Russian Federation, Belarus, Uzbekistan, and Tajikistan signed the original CIS Agreement on Guarding of Borders in December 1991. Armenia, Kazakhstan, Kyrgyzstan, Belarus, Tajikistan, and Russia signed further agreements in 1995 and 1996, but Uzbekistan by that time was no longer interested. The delineation of duties between CIS border guards and national border guards has also remained contentious, despite the many concept statements that have been published on the question.

In general, there are three basic patterns of border cooperation within the CIS: states that have no special border defense arrangements at all; states that have agreed to close border cooperation with Russia, including technical assistance and the deployment of Russian experts to the country concerned, but which will not use joint forces to patrol the external CIS border; and states that actively pursue a joint border defense with Russia.

For the first group—Azerbaijan, Moldova, Ukraine and Uzbekistan—there is little difference between the agreements that they make with Russia or other CIS states and those that they make with neighbors not in the CIS. Ukraine in particular has worked to achieve the legal recognition of its borders by all its neighbors, including Russia, and Ukrainian diplomats have been prominent in denouncing Russia's desire to distinguish between internal and external CIS borders.[24] Russia has tried assiduously to change Azerbaijan's policy to promote what General Andrei Nikolaev, then chief of the Russian

Border Guards, called in a January 1994 visit to Baku "Russia's strategic interest in protecting Azerbaijan's external borders."[25] A September 1993 bilateral agreement suggested that cooperation on external borders might be possible, but the Russia-Azerbaijan Treaty of Friendship of 1997 used such bland formulae about border cooperation that little seems likely to happen.

Kazakhstan and Belarus illustrate the second pattern of active cooperation without joint patrols. A set of bilateral agreements establish the parameters for Russian-Kazakh border cooperation. The first, in February 1993, only outlined the basic principles for mutual cooperation. A September 1994 agreement gave Russia the right to transport border guards and material through Kazakhstan to support ongoing deployments in Central Asia. The October 1994 agreement, "On Cooperation in Protecting External Borders," established the ground rules for joint training, education, and intelligence sharing. It also formed a Consultative Control Council, headed by the Chiefs of Border Guards of both countries. In 1995 Kazakhstan agreed to set up joint Russian-Kazakh forces, but national forces guard Kazakhstan's borders. A small, operational group of Russian border troops has been deployed in Kazakhstan, but it provides administrative rather than operational assistance.

Russia and Belarus also have a range of special arrangements for close cooperation on border security, including a March 1994 bilateral agreement on border cooperation and a February 1995 "Agreement on Mutual Efforts to Protect the State Borders of Belarus." The two countries share the financial responsibility of maintaining Belarus's Latvian and Lithuanian borders. Russia provides help for training and equipping Belarusian border guards. There is a joint Belarusian-Russian operational group in Minsk, to support technical aid and joint training. However, Russian forces do not guard Belarus's external borders.[26]

Armenia, Georgia, Tajikistan, Turkmenistan, and Kyrgyzstan all have outer boundaries that are actively patrolled by joint border troops. For some of these states, this bilateral relationship with Russia has deepened and solidified, but in the case of Georgia, Kyrgyzstan, and Turkmenistan it has decidedly weakened.

As early as the CIS Kyiv Summit in March 1992, Tajikistan agreed that Russian border guards would patrol its 2,000-kilometer border because of concerns over instability in neighboring Afghanistan and the flow of drugs and guns across the Tajik-Afghan border. Russian border troops are deployed in Murgab, Ishkashmi, Khorog, Kalai-khumb, Moskovskiy, and Pyandzh. The size of the contingent in what is the largest joint border operation has fluctuated between 16,000 and 18,000 troops. As many as two-thirds of these are ethnic Tajiks, who are comparatively better paid in the Russian service.[27]

Armenia has sought Russian help in guarding its borders with Turkey primarily for reasons of its own security. The border guards are part of a wider bilateral defense relationship that was further upgraded by the August 1997 Russian-Armenian Treaty, discussed below.

Russian-Turkmen border cooperation initially seemed promising. In August 1992 a bilateral agreement sanctioned Russia's assumption of responsibility for guarding Turkmenistan's 2,300-kilometer border with Iran and Afghanistan. The agreement established a joint border guard force that was to be indigenized. By 1994 Turkmenistan was paying the cost of guarding the border. In 1995 an operational group of Russian Border Troops in Turkmenistan was created to supplement Turkmen deployments. By 1999, though, only Russian advisors remained.

Russian-Georgian border cooperation began in late 1993 and into 1994, when the state of Georgia was nearing collapse in large part because of Russian military assistance to break-away Abkhazia and aid to rebels in western Georgia. Georgian President Eduard Shevardnadze was forced to accede to Russian demands and to enter the CIS in exchange for Russian security guarantees. Russian border forces grew to 8,000–10,000 troops, deployed along the Russian-Abkhaz border and along the Psou River border with Turkey.[28] In December 1997 Russian border guards used force against fifty young Georgian demonstrators who were protesting Russia's unilateral decision to move a Russian frontier post one kilometer into Georgian territory. This incident showed the strain in the relations and led to the readjustment of the Russian border in favor of Georgia.

The two sides have agreed to a withdrawal of Russian border guards that was to have happened by July 1, 1999.[29] The first stages of this withdrawal took place in December 1998, with the handover to Georgian border guards of a major section of the Georgian-Turkish border in the Akhalkalaki region,[30] and Georgia took responsibility for its maritime border in August 1998. Tellingly, Georgia has turned to NATO and Ukraine for help in securing the training and equipment necessary to handle these tasks. Georgia also signed a border cooperation agreement with its partners in GUUAM in September 1998.

Russian-Kyrgyz border cooperation seems to be following the same pattern, although with less rancor. An October 1992 Russian-Kyrgyz Treaty establishes Russian responsibility for guarding Kyrgyzstan's external border. Joint Kyrgyz-Russian border forces were quickly established, under the command of Russian officers. Moscow paid 80 percent of the costs of these units. Large numbers of these Russian units were in fact ethnic Kyrgyz recruits. This arrangement seemed to work for a time, but there is clear evidence of Kyrgyz restiveness; when Russia's budgetary problems presented the opportunity to do so, in August 1998, the Kyrgyz government announced that it would form its own border service to replace the Russian force.[31] Russia ended its funding of Kyrgyz border guards on January 1, 1999, but will keep an operational group of Russian advisors in place, making its border cooperation with Kyrgyzstan similar to its arrangements with Kazakhstan.

CIS air defense arrangements show a similar pattern of security fragmentation. The CIS Unified Air Defense Agreement of 1995 called for the collective guarding of air space and warnings of missile and airborne attacks; however, most CIS member states did not participate. Ukraine did initial early agreements on the proposal when Ukrainian Defense Minister Valerii Shmarov was in office, but, as noted, this show of interest had less to do with security concerns than with the prospect that the agreement might channel funds to Ukraine's decaying military infrastructure and, perhaps, to its languishing defense plants. Such hopes quickly ran aground on the realities of the Russian defense budget, for which reason Ukraine ultimately refused to participate in any collective air defense arrangement.

Russia has taken the leading role in the air security arrangements that have emerged, flying joint air patrols on external CIS borders with Kazakhstan, Georgia, and Belarus since 1996.[32] In late 1998, Kyrgyzstan announced its willingness to participate in joint air patrols as well. For all practical purposes, the Russian and Armenian air defenses have merged.[33] Elsewhere there is no real air defense at all. The loss of key strategic radar sites is a related problem; the large gaps in the old Soviet system create serious challenges for Russia and its nuclear forces. Five of the Soviet Union's eight large phased-array radars ended up outside of Russia. The site in Lyaki, Azerbaijan, is not accessible to the Russians; Russian use of the radar at Skrunda, Latvia, ended in August 1998 and the facility is being dismantled. Its replacement, in Baranovichi, Belarus, is unfinished. More significantly, Russia's air warning system as a whole is in steep decline, as sites within Russia are suffering from defense cutbacks and the inability to modernize.

Peacekeeping operations have probably been the most controversial aspect of CIS security policy and are widely viewed in the West and in some neighboring countries as essentially Russian operations that are pursued for Russian national interests. In some cases there is little question that Russian diplomacy took advantage of local troubles and of the leverage that Russian military intervention might provide to win concessions, as it did in Georgia and Moldova. However, the conflicts that have occurred have been real enough, and Russian political and military leaders complain that their role in controlling and mediating them has not been appreciated. One reason for continued suspicion of Russia's role in peacekeeping, as even those who favor the types of interventions that have occurred will admit, is that none of them has been truly multilateral. Russian-led peacekeeping operations have also proven controversial for strictly operational reasons; they have included contingents from the warring parties in the peacekeeping force, and they have been quick to use force, or the threat of force, as key elements in maintaining order.[34]

Russia has tried from the beginning to create an integrated CIS approach to peacekeeping, one that grants Russia a leading role; it has also been willing to act unilaterally. In March 1993 President Yeltsin asked the United Nations to recognize that, in his words, "stopping all armed conflicts on the territory of the former USSR is Russia's vital interest," for which reason he wanted "distinguished international organizations, including the United Nations, to grant Russia special powers as guarantor of peace and stability in the regions of the former USSR."[35] Not only did the United Nations and other international organizations refuse to grant Russia this sanction, but international fears about how Russia might abuse its role as a peacekeeper prompted the United Nations and the OSCE to send observers to monitor Russian missions in Transdniestr, Abkhazia, South Ossetia, and Tajikistan.

The history of conflict management in the former USSR demonstrates that the role of the CIS has been at best an afterthought. Of the four main conflicts affecting CIS countries, only the civil war in Tajikistan has generated a truly multilateral CIS effort at resolution, and that was overwhelmingly Russian in concept and funding. In the two breakaway regions of Georgia, South Ossetia, and Abkhazia, the peacekeeping missions grew out of Russian interventions, not CIS mandates. Bilateral agreements between Georgia and Russia in June and July 1992 established a joint Georgia-Ossetian-Russian force to implement a cease-fire agreement. The Abkhazia mission, while officially the product of an October 1994 CIS conference, came after Russia had already been conducting unilateral missions in the area for four months.

The conflict in Transdniestr, a self-declared autonomous region of eastern Moldova, has also been managed essentially by Russia, with no CIS peacekeeping forces involved at all. In 1997 both Transdniestr and Moldova requested that Ukraine mediate their conflict, but that intervention was intended to reduce the formal role of the CIS, not to enlarge it.[36]

The deployment in Tajikistan is the best example of CIS military cooperation, as well as the most extensive attempt to settle a CIS conflict. In 1992 the defense ministers of Russia, Kazakhstan, Uzbekistan, Kyrgyzstan, and CIS commander in chief Shaposhnikov created a multilateral peacekeeping force for Tajikistan. In August 1993 those ministers met with the Tajik government to discuss the deployment of that force, which was placed under the command of a Russian general, Boris Pyankov. The force's main base of supply was placed in Dushanbe, with a second site in Khorog, a city in the Gorno-Badakhshan region of Tajikistan. Each contributing country was to finance its own forces. Russia was to take on 50 percent of the cost of sustaining the operation, with the rest shared by the four Central Asian participants.[37] While this arrangement seems a genuine effort at multilateral intervention, in practice, Russian troops have been its strongest and largest contingent. Kazakhstan, Kyrgyzstan, and Uzbekistan have each contributed battalions, while Russia has more than 20,000 military and border guard personnel on the ground.[38]

Whatever Russia's initial motivations, its involvement has helped to bring cease-fires in Transdniestr and South Ossetia (since 1992), Abkhazia (since 1994), and Tajikistan (since 1996). These conflicts have been frozen in place, however, because Russia is unable or unwilling to exert its influence to resolve them. Early Russian assumptions about the ability of its military to be an effective instrument of policy have clearly been shaken by actual experience in the field, especially in the Chechnya War. Russia is increasingly interested in seeking greater CIS and international involvement in regional conflicts, if for no other reason than to relieve Russia of the financial and military burdens it has tried to bear. Russia's willingness to bring Ukraine into the Transdniestr process in 1997 may reflect a growing realism about Russia's own limitations in managing violence in the former USSR.

Whatever their limitations, the structures of the CIS have encouraged Russia and other concerned CIS states to consult about conflicts in and along the borders of the former USSR, most notably about the chaos and violence in Tajikistan and Afghanistan. However unbalanced, the multilateral deployments in Tajikistan were the result of intense discussions between Russia, Tajikistan, and its three closest Central Asian neighbors. In October 1996 these five states agreed to form an operational group to monitor events in Afghanistan, although they emphatically insisted that no additional troop deployments were required.[39] The March 1997 CIS Summit also agreed to establish a Committee on Conflict Situations, which has had little direct impact on encouraging cooperation in conflict resolution.[40]

Russia may be willing to cede more initiative to its CIS partners, but it is not willing to delegate to the international community issues in which it feels it has crucial foreign or defense interests; to be sure, the international community has also not demonstrated any willingness to accept such delegation. However, Russia's stretched resources and the continued likelihood that conflict management and peacekeeping operations will remain necessary in the former USSR make it possible that Russia may rethink its current approach.

WHY CIS SECURITY MECHANISMS HAVE FAILED

The CIS is a failure as a security organization, whether measured against the exalted standard of proclaimed Russian ambitions or the more modest standard of what has in fact been accomplished. The reasons for this failure are the same as they have been for every other aspect of the CIS, that Russian analysts and political leaders greatly overestimated what President Yeltsin once called "the tremendous blood relationship" between the states of the former USSR,[41] and greatly underestimated the enormous geopolitical shift that had in fact taken place with the collapse of the USSR.

The other new states did not reject security cooperation or Russian help, but they were deeply suspicious of Russian motives; as has already been discussed, Russia's use of the Abkhaz crisis to maneuver Georgia into the CIS in 1993, or, even more so, its war in Chechnya, did nothing to persuade Russia's partners in the CIS that Russia might have the interest of other regional actors at heart.

Russia is the only new state that is large enough, economically or geographically, to continue to view the former USSR as a single space. Inevitably, the other CIS states seek more regional benefits in their relations with Russia. Its closest partners in Central Asia want Russia to stabilize Tajikistan and to halt the spillover of instability and violence from Afghanistan, and they want help in balancing China's growing influence. Armenia wants Russian support against Azerbaijan and Turkey. Belarus sees Russia as a key market for its declining military industries and as a partner in defense against what it sees as the encroaching West. Indeed, each of the states seeking Russia's support wants financial and infrastructure support for its own industries and militaries. Each of the other CIS states wants particular and regionally specific benefits from Russia because none of them perceive a threat from the CIS.

Perhaps the most important cause for the failure of the CIS to create a shared security environment, however, is that all of the post-Soviet states, including Russia, are too weak, distracted, and poor to be able to integrate. This is demonstrated dramatically by the inability of the CIS to cope with such security threats as do exist, all of which have been caused by regional tensions among weak states, and by poorly guarded borders that invite narcotics trafficking, gun-running, and refugees. Talk of integration has been the means by which the other CIS states try to get Russia to pay for actions, policies, or programs that they desire, but cannot afford themselves, while Russia uses such discussions to try to secure control of infrastructure and other assets that now belong to other states.

As a result, even the few common undertakings to which the CIS states have been able to agree have either been carried out shoddily or not at all, because neither Russia nor the other CIS states have the money to pay for them. Even within Russia, opposition to various integrationist schemes, such as the Russian-Belarusian union, has been growing, on the grounds that Russia simply cannot afford them.[42]

Within the CIS is a patchwork of relationships; some states are leaning toward Russia by choice (Armenia, Belarus, Tajikistan, Kazakhstan, and Kyrgyzstan), and others are trying to keep much distance (Ukraine, Azerbaijan, Uzbekistan, Georgia, and Moldova). The security fragmentation is deep and continuing. The real question facing Russia, its neighbors, and the outside world is whether this new configuration can be made stable. Russia and its neighbors have a key role to play in answering this question. The CIS does not.

TRYING TO COMPENSATE BILATERALLY FOR CIS FAILURE

As Russia has come to understand that it is unlikely to achieve the security arrangements it desires through the CIS, it has turned to bilateral relations with specific states to accomplish piecemeal what it could not achieve through an umbrella organization. In general, Russia has pursued such negotiations with a double intention, to secure the specific security arrangements it requires and to try to set up models that might be widened into the multilateral security arrangements. Russia's three most comprehensive bilateral agreements are with Kazakhstan, Belarus, and Armenia.

Kazakhstan and Russia

Kazakhstan is Russia's key strategic ally in Central Asia. Agreements between the two states have given Russia continued access to key military facilities, provided right of transit and support for other Central Asian deployments, and delegated to Russia a leading role in training and equipping Kazakh forces. As significant as the Russian military presence may be in Kazakhstan, though, it falls short of conditions that Russia has sought, and of what Russia has described as crucial to its national security. Agreements on deep military integration not withstanding, Kazakhstan has kept Russian forces and border guards out of any operational deployments in the country.

The Russians remain key advisors and control military sites in Kazakhstan, but they are not an operational presence there.

The foundation for Russian-Kazakh military cooperation was laid by the 1992 Treaty on Friendship, Cooperation, and Mutual Assistance, which guarantees Russian help in creating the Kazakhstan armed forces.[43] The treaty legalizes the continued presence of Russian military personnel in Kazakhstan, envisions the stationing of more Russian forces there, and permits their unimpeded transportation through Kazakhstan for deployments to the south. The treaty refers to the thornier issue of whether Russia would be allowed use of strategically important Soviet-built test ranges and other military facilities in Kazakhstan, but does not attempt to resolve it.

In August 1992 the two countries further agreed on the basic principles governing the transfer of officers from one army to another. Former Soviet military officers had already begun to migrate to their national armies in late 1991, a process that was hastened when the CIS general purposes forces failed to become a reality. Kazakhstan feared a wholesale exodus of ethnic Russian officers because few Kazakhs had been able to rise through the Soviet military structures to become officers. The March 1994 Treaty on Military Cooperation established the principle of joint use of Caspian Sea naval forces. A January 1995 agreement spelled out the status of Russian military personnel in Kazakhstan, including making Russian soldiers in Kazakhstan subject to Russian laws, restricting the political activity of deployed military personnel, and establishing a mechanism for the supervision and implementation of these provisions.

Among the most important questions that the two states had to resolve was the status of the Soviet-era space center at Baikonur, as well as that of other Soviet sites such as the Balkhash missile attack early warning center, the Emba test range, Sary Shagan, and many other test sites and military ranges. Now on Kazakhstan's territory, these sites were of strategic significance to Russia and, equally important, were de facto in Russian control. Kazakhstan asserted its sovereignty over those sites, closing four testing ranges in December 1992. During the Minsk CIS Summit in January 1993, the two sides worked out a set of principles that would allow Russia to continue to use the remaining sites, and a March 1994 agreement further established the principle that one side might lease facilities to the other. Detailed agreements on the Emba, Sary Shagan, and other aircraft and military test ranges were not reached until December 1994 and January 1995. These agreements were similar in form, lasting for ten years and automatically renewed for another ten years if there were no objections from either side. Russia also agreed to pay rent for these sites, but the two sides differed on the amount.[44]

Another category of concerns has been to build up Kazakhstan's own military capabilities. In August 1992 the two countries signed an agreement to train large numbers of Kazakhs in Russia, which Russia agreed to undertake without compensation; that financial arrangement has not been repeated with other CIS states. A January 1993 agreement provides for mutual military assistance, most of which flows from Russia to Kazakhstan, but Kazakhstan is able to reciprocate to some degree, because it inherited Soviet-era factories that produce items essential to the Russian Navy. Subsequent agreements provide for joint planning and training, coordination of military intelligence, and preservation of military industrial ties, including cooperation on arms sales to third countries.

Although the agreements that the two sides have reached make an impressive list, neither side is fully satisfied with the result; as one Russian critic has put it, most of these agreements "remain on paper."[45] Russian military presence in general, and the test sites which Russia wishes to use in particular, are extremely unpopular in Kazakhstan, so that the Kazakh leadership faces continued pressure to restrict Russian use of the test sites or to close them entirely. For their part, the Russians complain that the Kazakhs frequently do not pay their obligations. Russian military officials have also complained openly about how poorly the non-Russian units, the Kazakhs among them, have performed in Tajikistan.

A more serious problem, however, from Russia's point of view, has been Kazakhstan's desire to broaden its security base beyond the bilateral relationship into which Russia would like to bind it. Russia remains Kazakhstan's major security partner, but Kazakhstan has also cultivated good relations with China and has been a driving force behind the creation of the Central Asian peacekeeping battalion, which does not include Russian forces. President Nazarbayev has also expanded Kazakhstan's military and defense cooperation with the United States and NATO.

Belarus and Russia

Belarus has proven to be Russia's most faithful security partner. The two countries began cooperation almost immediately after independence, when Belarus found itself with 250,000 soldiers, more than

4,000 tanks, and two key Soviet strategic missile bases, the arsenals of which included nuclear warheads. The two states signed an "Agreement on Military Cooperation" in July 1992, which was designed to allow them to cooperate during a transitional period when, as Article 2 of that agreement states, they would be "taking decisions about their own armed forces."[46] Other articles of this agreement pledged the two sides to mutual consultations in the event of the threat of attack and attempted to provide a foundation for continued military industrial cooperation.

It is characteristic of the relations that developed between the two states that this and subsequent bilateral agreements postulated deep cooperation, but do not constitute a formal military alliance. Belarus originally declared a policy of neutrality and organized its national armed forces to defend it. The Belarusian version of neutrality tilts vigorously in the direction of Russia, but Belarus also has strictures against the stationing of foreign troops in Belarus or the deployment of Belarusian forces abroad. These stipulations have remained a part of Belarusian military doctrine no matter who is the country's leader.

Even President Lukashenko—whose regular outbursts against NATO enlargement show a pronounced hostility toward the West, and who is actively pursuing union with Russia—has nevertheless been careful to reiterate that unless Belarusian security is directly threatened, Belarus will permit no foreign deployments on its soil and will send no troops abroad. Lukashenko has stressed repeatedly that he would not send Belarusian troops to defend CIS borders in Central Asia, although he would be prepared to defend CIS interests "in the western direction, from Kyiv to Riga."[47] Belarus has never wanted its enthusiasm for bilateral and CIS-wide integration to be understood in Moscow as a sign that Minsk is prepared to carry out over-border military missions far from home. Belarus's belated decision to sign the Tashkent Treaty in January 1994,[48] for example, set off an extended debate about how the commitments of that treaty could be made compatible with neutrality.[49]

In negotiating Russian access Belarus was careful to place clear limits and to prevent small Russian deployments at important Belarusian facilities from becoming large ones. In September 1993, for example, the two sides agreed on the basic status and procedures to be applied to Russian Strategic Forces temporarily stationed on Belarusian territory. The purpose of the agreement was to establish procedures for governing these forces until their missiles and war-heads were withdrawn in December 1996 and the last supporting units left in May 1997.

Agreements reached in March 1994 and January 1995 to give Russia long-term access to a strategic early warning radar facility at Baranovichi and a low frequency communications facility at Vileyka show a similar determination to control the size and scope of Russia's military presence. These agreements are favorable to Russia—they are for twenty-five years and do not require the payment of rent[50]—but they also explicitly state that these sites may not be considered military bases, and strictly limit the numbers of Russians who may be stationed at each to 1,200 and 250, respectively. Similarly, Belarus has also limited border cooperation with Russia, accepting financial and technical assistance and the stationing of a Russian operational group in Minsk, but not allowing Russians to patrol Belarusian borders.

The fitful but apparently persistent movement toward a Belaru-sian-Russian political and economic union is paralleled by a string of agreements on military and security issues. The two countries signed an agreement in January 1995 to set up joint air defense and military industrial cooperation, and another in April 1996, to join Belarusian and Russian air space for the purposes of air defense, to be secured by joint patrols. The movement toward political union prompted Ministry of Defense officials from both states to begin discussing how to reach a common defense policy. Such efforts will presumably grow more urgent if the momentum toward union continues; however, both states are seriously short of funds, making it difficult to begin or sustain new security efforts. Despite their shared hostility to NATO expansion, especially into Poland, neither Russia nor Belarus will be able, in the short run at least, to contemplate any forward deployments of Russian forces, both for financial reasons and for the alarms that this might trigger internationally. Thus, presuming the impulse toward unification continues, Russia and Belarus are likely to increase their efforts to coordinate training and planning, and may even expand Russian influence over the Belarusian officer corps itself, but they will not become a full military union until—and unless—the two states themselves unite.

Armenia and Russia

Armenia has been an enthusiastic supporter of CIS security initiatives, taking part in Russian-led common border and air defense cooperation and becoming a founding member of the Tashkent Treaty. It has also repeatedly been willing to supplement these collective measures with special bilateral arrangements with Russia. The Armenian leadership has consistently seen Russia as a key supporter in a complex region, which is defined for Yerevan by an ongoing conflict with Azerbaijan over Karabakh and historical enmity with Turkey. Armenia signed a mutual defense pact with Russia in May 1992, at the same time that it signed the multilateral Tashkent Treaty; however, this bilateral agreement was never ratified by Russia. Much of Armenia's participation in the CIS border and air defense initiatives has a virtually bilateral character; Russian border guards work with Armenia to guard the external borders, and Russia and Armenia fly joint air patrols.

Armenia has welcomed the continued presence of Russian soldiers. The 127th Motorized Rifle Division, stationed at Gyumri, includes 4,100 personnel and 74 main battle tanks.[51] Russia also has long deployed a squadron of MiG-23s in Armenia, to which it added five of the more modern MiG-29s in December 1998. A significant percentage of these Russian forces are ethnic Armenians—some estimates range as high as 70 percent—which suggests that Russia's actual military presence may be smaller than it seems. Ethnic Armenians also form a majority of Russian forces stationed in Akhalkalaki in Georgia. Russia has provided substantial diplomatic support to Armenia, taking a leading role in addressing the Nagorno-Karabakh conflict through unilateral diplomatic efforts and as a joint effort with the United States and France under the OSCE-sponsored Minsk Group.[52]

Russia has also provided substantial direct aid to Armenia's regular and irregular military forces. Beginning in 1990 and continuing into 1992, Armenians seized weapons from Soviet depots. For example, the disintegration of the 366th Regiment in Karabakh in early 1992 provided the Armenian side with a variety of light and heavy weapons.[53] But Armenian-Russian arms cooperation went well beyond a pattern of seizures common throughout the Caucasus. From 1993 to 1996 there was a widespread and covert transfer of weapons and military equipment from Russian forces in the Transcaucasus to Armenia, which included air defense missile systems, T-72 tanks, howitzers, and small arms.[54]

The 1997 Russian-Armenian Friendship Treaty formalizes and substantially expands Russian-Armenian security cooperation. The treaty obligates the two countries to consult immediately in the event of an armed attack against either and commits them to consultations to secure cooperation and military mutual assistance, including reciprocal use of military facilities in the event of an attack. The treaty encourages joint military technical policies and production-sharing as well as joint protection of Armenia's borders with non-CIS states. In its entirety, this agreement creates a substantial legal foundation both for the current level of security cooperation and for future expansion.[55]

At the same time, though, the tendency toward deep Russian-Armenian security is clearly stalled by each state's poverty as well as by Russia's desire not to alienate Azerbaijan. As is true in the other two bilateral relationships detailed above, Armenia's needs and interests with respect to Russia are more focused than are Russia's with respect to Armenia. The substantial coincidence of interests has made Armenia cooperative, even enthusiastic, about establishing a bilateral relationship with Russia, but Armenia will place its own security interests above those of multilateral and even bilateral agreements, if it perceives a conflict between the two sets of obligations. Even more assiduously than Russia's other two partners, Armenia has used relations with Russia to secure what is sees as its vital national interests.

NOTES

[1] For a consideration of Russia's policy toward integration and its unraveling, see Sherman W. Garnett, "The Integrationist Temptation," *Washington Quarterly*, vol. 18, no. 2, (Spring 1995), pp. 35–44 and "Russia's Illusory Ambitions," *Foreign Affairs*, vol. 76, no. 2, (March–April 1997), pp. 61–76.

[2] Yeltsin's decree was published in *Rossiiskaia gazeta*, September 23, 1995, p. 4, and translated in *FBIS Daily Report: Central Eurasia*, September 28, 1995.

[3] Ibid.

[4] *Rossiiskaia gazeta*, September 23, 1995, p. 4, in *FBIS Daily Report: Central Eurasia*, September 28, 1995.

[5] By far the best article on the political-military institutional arrangement of the CIS and related structures is Andrei Zagorski, "Regional Structures of Security Policy within the CIS," in Roy

Allison and Christoph Bluth, eds., *Security Dilemmas in Russia and Eurasia* (London: Royal Institute for International Affairs, 1998), pp. 281–300.

6 The text of the Tashkent Treaty on Collective Security can be found in *Rossiiskaia gazeta*, May 23, 1992, and was translated in *FBIS Daily Report*, May 26, 1993.

7 Azerbaijan signed on November 6, 1993. Georgia acceded on December 11, 1993. Stanislav Shushkevich, former speaker of the Belarusian parliament, signed the Tashkent Treaty on January 3, 1994. It was unclear whether Shushkevich's signature was needed on the agreement, which had already been ratified by the Belarusian Parliament in April 1993.

8 *Segodnia*, February 18, 1993; Zagorski, p. 286.

9 For the clearest example of this last point, see the account by Kasymzhomart Tokayev, Kazakh foreign minister, of a conversation with then Russian foreign minister Yevgeny Primakov. When pressed by Primakov to acknowledge the problems caused by NATO enlargement, Tokayev noted simply that, "the expansion of the Alliance to the East does not directly affect the interests of Kazakhstan." *Pod stiagom nezavisimosti* (Almaty: Bilim, 1997), p. 72.

10 These negotiations occurred among CIS states that were party to the CFE accords on the sidelines of the May 1992 Tashkent Treaty discussions.

11 International Institute for Strategic Studies, *The Military Balance 1993–1994* (London: International Institute for Strategic Studies, 1993).

12 Vladimir Zolotarev, *Voennaia bezopasnost otechestva* (Kulikovo Pole: Kanon-Press, 1998), pp. 171–2.

13 International Institute for Strategic Studies, *The Military Balance 1998–1999* (London: International Institute for Strategic Studies, 1998), p. 109. Some 2,680 tanks are in storage in Kazakhstan and 2,000 in Uzbekistan and are deteriorating from lack of maintenance, pp. 158, 164.

14 Pavel Grachev, *ITAR-TASS*, December 29, 1993.

15 "*Rasporiazhenie Prezidenta Rossiiskoi Federatsii*," April 5, 1994, author's copy.

16 The most vociferous outcry occured among the Baltic states whose presidents all issued denunciations of the decree and initiated a series of diplomatic protests. *RFE/RL Newsline*, April 7, 1994.

[17] The case of Russian border guards will be considered separately. Russia does have agreements that grant access to important military sites—early warning radars, test ranges, and research and development facilities. Some of these agreements will be considered in the discussion of Belarus and Kazakhstan. There are Russian military personnel located at these sites. This section's survey focuses on operationally capable deployments of ground, air, and naval forces.

[18] Pavel Baev, "Peacekeeping and Conflict Management in Eurasia," in Roy Allison and Christoph Bluth, eds., *Security Dilemmas in Russia and Eurasia* (London: Royal Institute for International Affairs, 1998), p. 223.

[19] *Interfax*, January 8, 1998.

[20] Lena Johnson, *The Tajik War: A Challenge to Russian Policy*, Discussion Paper 74 (London: Royal Institute for International Affairs, 1998).

[21] On the Russian-Baltic security relationship and the detailed agreements that govern it, see Sherman W. Garnett, "Europe's Crossroads: Russia and the West in the New Borderlands," in Michael Mandelbaum, ed., *The New Russian Foreign Policy* (New York: Council on Foreign Relations, 1998), pp. 64–99, especially pp. 77–85.

[22] For a stark assessment of Russia's failed military reform, see Dale R. Herspring, "Russia's Crumbling Military," *Current History*, October 1998, pp. 325–8.

[23] "Fundamentals of Russian Border Policy Published," *Rossiiskaia gazeta*, November 6, 1996, in *FBIS Daily Report*, SOV-96-217. The director of the Russian Federal Border Service wrote: "when we talk about our country's policy, by this we mean realization of Russia's strategic interests on the external borders of the CIS." "Nikolaev Comments on New Border Security Concept," *Rossiiskaia Gazeta*, April 11, 1995, in *FBIS Daily Report*.

[24] See, for example, the report in *OMRI Daily Digest*, January 8, 1996, that Deputy Foreign Minister Konstantyn Hryshchenko said Ukraine finds it "inadmissible" to divide its borders into "internal" and "external" ones.

[25] *Rossiiskaia gazeta*, January 15, 1994, p. 6.

[26] Author's interviews in Minsk (May and October 1997) and Almaty (November 1997). A detailed discussion of Russian-Belarusian

military relations may be found in Anàtoly Rozanov, *Belarus-Rossiia: Voennaia integratsiia*, (Moscow: Carnegie Endowment for International Peace, forthcoming).

[27] Richard Woff, *The Armed Forces of the Former Soviet Union: Evolution, Structures, and Personalities* (London: Brasseys, 1996), p. D4–8; Lena Johnson, *The Tajik War: A Challenge to Russian Policy*, Discussion Paper 74 (London: Royal Institute for International Affairs, 1998).

[28] *Nezavisimoe voennoe obozrenie*, September 26, 1996.

[29] At the time of this writing, Russian troops were in the process of withdrawing from key sectors of Georgia's borders and were due to complete their operations by August 1999. On July 9, 1999, Georgian forces took over sectors of the Turkish-Georgian border and began patrolling the Georgian coastline, including Abkhazia's. However, Russian troops are handing over control of the Abkhaz controlled portions of the border to ethnic Abkhaz secessionist forces and not to Georgian national forces. See the *Jamestown Monitor*, July 1, 1999 and July 14, 1999.

[30] *RFE-RL Daily Report*, December 21, 1998.

[31] *RFE-RL Daily Report*, August 25, 1998.

[32] Zbigniew Brzezinski and Paige Sullivan, eds., *Russia and the Commonwealth of Independent States* (London: M.E. Sharpe, 1997), p. 544.

[33] *Krasnaia zvezda*, April 12, 1997.

[34] Pavel Baev, "Peacekeeping and Conflict Management in Eurasia," in Roy Allison and Christoph Bluth, eds., *Security Dilemmas in Russia and Eurasia* (London: Royal Institute for International Affairs, 1998), pp. 209–29.

[35] *FBIS Daily Report*, SOV-93-038, March 1, 1993.

[36] Sherman W. Garnett and Rachel Lebenson, "Ukraine Joins the Fray: Will Peace Come to Trans-Dniestria," *Problems of Post-Communism*, vol. 45, no. 6, (November-December 1998), pp. 22–32.

[37] T. A. Mansurov, ed., *Kazakhstansko-rossiiskie otnosheniia, 1991–1995: Sbornik dokumentov i materialov* (Almaty and Moscow 1995), p. 303.

[38] International Institute for Strategic Studies, *The Military Balance 1998–1999* (London: International Institute for Strategic Studies, 1998), p. 163. The Uzbek contribution is more extensive and more difficult to define. Tashkent has its own security concerns about developments in Tajikistan and is conducting a largely independent policy there. It has worked closely with Russia, but the

Uzbeks have also been prepared to go their own way in supporting various factions within the current Tajik government that Moscow has discouraged.

[39] *Krasnaia zvezda*, October 8, 1996.

[40] The committee was not given a formal structure at the time of the summit. Its future was addressed at later summits and working groups, but as of early April 1999, the statute dealing with the structure, responsibilities, and authority of the committee had yet to be ratified.

[41] "Remarks of President Boris Yeltsin at the 49th General Assembly," September 26, 1994, Press Release of the Russian Federation.

[42] On Russian and Belarusian concerns about union that manifested themselves during the 1997 debate, see Garnett, "Europe's Crossroads: Russia and the West in the New Borderlands," pp. 73–7.

[43] This treaty and other key documents from the collection are published in Mansurov, *Kazakhstansko-rossiiskie otnosheniia, 1991-1995*. The best and most comprehensive discussion of Russian-Kazakh defense relations is Mikhail Alexandrov, "Military Relations between Russia and Kazakhstan in Post-Soviet Era (1992–1997)," *Central Asia Monitor*, no. 2 (1998), pp. 10–5 and no. 3 (1998), pp. 18–25.

[44] The Baikonur leasing agreement of December 1994 states that Russia would pay $115 million per year to Kazakhstan for use of the Baikonur site. Later, however, Moscow insisted that the rent it owed should be deducted from Kazakhstan's debt to Russia; thus Russia has yet to pay Kazakhstan any rent. Kazakhstan and Russia have continued to spar over the details of control of Baikonur. Their most serious disagreement was in July 1999 after the explosion of a Russian Proton rocket on July 5, 1999 that showered debris and fuel on a loosely populated part of Kazakh territory. The Kazakh government immediately banned all Russian launches from Baikonur. By July 14, 1999, Kazakhstan reopened Baikonur to Russian launches, except Proton rocket launches, but only after it had won concessions from Moscow to begin resolving its debt arrears to Kazakhstan.

[45] Alexandrov, "Military Relations between Russia and Kazakhstan in Post-Soviet Era," p. 21.

[46] Rozanov, *Belarus-Rossiia: Voennaia integratsiia*, forthcoming, p. 7.

[47] Lukashenko made the remarks on Belarusian television, August 23, 1998. They were reported in *RFE/RL Daily Report*, August 25, 1998.

[48] The original signatories—Armenia, Kazahkstan, Kyrgyzstan, Russia, Tajikistan, and Uzbekistan—signed the treaty on May 15, 1992.

[49] Ural Latypov, "Neutrality as a Factor in Belorusian Security Policy," *Conflict Studies Research Centre Occasional Paper* (Royal Military Academy, Sandhurst, U.K., February 1994). The author of this paper is now the foreign minister of Belarus.

[50] Rozanov, pp. 11–6. An additional agreement on Russian access to radar and long-range communications facilities was negotiated in May 1996.

[51] These and subsequent Russian deployment figures are taken from the International Institute for Strategic Studies, *The Military Balance 1998-99* (London: International Institute for Strategic Studies, 1998).

[52] The OSCE-sponsored Minsk Group is the leading diplomatic forum attempting to reach a settlement of the conflict. The negotiations are currently being led by a troika of mediators made up of representatives from France, Russia, and the United States along with an OSCE representative.

[53] A. Kasatov, "Sama ne svoia," *Stolitsa*, no. 48 (1992), pp. 1–4.

[54] *Sovetskaia Rossiia*, April 3, 1997.

[55] The text of the treaty was published in *Rossiiskaia gazeta*, September 13, 1997.

4
The CIS and National
Strategies for State Building

The evolution of the CIS has been governed by a set of factors far more complex than the simple desire of Russia to become a simulacrum of the USSR, and the other states' equally simple desire to avoid that at any cost. In all the member states the exigencies of state building have proven to be such that each has developed a complex set of motives for its policy towards the CIS, just as each has had to compensate for that organization's failings in its own way. No obvious indicators have emerged with which to predict whether a state will be for or against strengthening the CIS. State building is taking increasingly divergent forms across the former Soviet expanse, as some countries try earnestly to build democracies and others try as earnestly to return to the one-man, one-party regimes of the past. Most vacillate between these two extremes. Some of the dictatorships have been enthusiastic about the CIS, while states of every political inclination have been just as determined to stay away.

Nor is the type of economy that each state is trying to build an indicator of the attitude that a given state might take toward the CIS. All the CIS countries seek to maintain their access to CIS markets, infrastructures, and commodities, but they also seek to protect themselves against the financial problems of the others by diversifying their foreign trade links. All the CIS states are competing independently for foreign direct investment as a spur to economic growth. Many have decided that they require support from the international financial institutions, for which reason they have had to adopt liberal economic policies that run counter to CIS practice, and that sometimes even violate CIS rules. All of the CIS states are also having difficulty meeting obligations to their own population, which sharply diminishes their enthusiasm for incurring direct or indirect costs derived from their CIS membership.

Even in the apparently straightforward realm of security arrangements, all the member states have proven unable to achieve the ends that they desire through the CIS, yet none has found an acceptable alternative. Every country has a broad choice of international partners and organizations to which it might turn, for matters of security, as well as for economic and political assistance; however, each of these other potential partners or organizations has demonstrable limitations and drawbacks.

In short, the CIS consists of twelve new countries, each of which faces prodigious tasks of state building. Each has had to determine how to define itself—looking to its history, ethnicity, religion, and culture—to establish a national identity and to secure independence. As events since the breakup of the USSR have proven, Russia's needs are no less in this regard than are those of its partner countries in the CIS. The almost universal tendency to equate Russia with the Soviet Union, however, and the fact that Russia is the only successor state that can claim the global significance enjoyed by the USSR, has meant that most analyses (including those done by the Russians and the other members of the organization themselves) approach the CIS as if it were a surrogate for Russia or Russian interests.

This chapter examines the CIS through a different lens, by showing the various ways in which four other member countries have seen the CIS and its possibilities—or lack of them—as part of the larger task of coping with the independence that the collapse of the Soviet Union thrust upon them. Seen in this perspective, the CIS is only one element of the vastly complicated equations that each state has had to solve as it struggles to sustain independence, juggling the conflicting interests necessary to maintain good relations with Russia, with the other CIS states, and with a broader international community.

Two large, potentially rich states and two small, poor states are chosen for this discussion. Kazakhstan and Ukraine, the two large states, each have sizable Russian minorities, and both share long indefensible borders with Russia; Kazakhstan, however, is landlocked, and is dependent on Russia for access to Western goods and markets, while Ukraine has both seaports and borders with other

European states. At present, both states depend upon Russia for their energy supplies, but Kazakhstan has a much greater potential for energy independence than does Ukraine.

The two small states are Kyrgyzstan and Georgia. Both are poor and mountainous, but otherwise are quite different. Landlocked Kyrgyzstan has no common border with Russia and badly needs its trade, so it sees Russia more as an opportunity than as a threat; it also sees Russia as a useful balance against its bigger and potentially hostile neighbors, Uzbekistan and China. Georgia, an old and self-assured nation, has access to the Black Sea, but it also shares a border with Russia in a region of the Caucasus that has proven especially volatile. Unlike Kyrgyzstan, Georgia conducts relatively little trade with Russia and has few Russian residents.

Each of these states also offers different reasons for the outside world to take an interest in it. Kazakhstan has oil, gas, and other substantial mineral reserves, while Ukraine has a complex and diverse economy that offers its foreign partners the opportunity to make strategic inroads at Russia's front door to Europe. Georgia has almost no economic resources, while Kyrgyzstan has a certain amount of gold, but both have understood their willingness to make deep commitments to radical economic and political reforms as ways in which they might enlist international support and sympathy.

Each of these four states is unique, of course, but they have been chosen because each is also in several ways representative. Belarus's relationship with Russia resembles that of Kazakhstan, while Armenia and Tajikistan are both poor, weak countries far away from Russia. These two states, like Kyrgyzstan, must look to Russia for support. Ukraine's determination to stay as independent of Russia as possible is like the choices made by Uzbekistan and Moldova, while Azerbaijan and Turkmenistan resemble Georgia in trying to distance themselves from Russia more fully. Those two states share with Kazakhstan the potential, but also the problems, conferred by enormous oil and gas reserves, and the international interest they attract because of it.

KAZAKHSTAN: INTEGRATION AND STATE BUILDING

For all its natural wealth, Kazakhstan began its independent existence with the enormous disadvantage of sharing a border of more than six thousand kilometers with Russia that had been demarcated solely for Soviet administrative purposes. Fears that Russia would not accept Kazakh statehood, and a conviction that the Soviet republics were so intertwined economically that to rupture trade ties would prove fatal, made President Nazarbayev one of the last supporters of a continued Soviet Union, and, when that finally collapsed, the same beliefs made him one of the strongest proponents of post-Soviet integration. Indeed, Kazakhstan was the only one of the fifteen Soviet republics that did not declare independence until after the USSR had formally dissolved.

While a strong supporter of integration, Nazarbayev was never happy with the Russian domination implicit in the CIS, and so worked hard to replace the CIS with a more egalitarian institution of his devise, which he called the Euro-Asian Union. As noted in chapter 1, this union did not enjoy support from other CIS members; over time, however, Kazakhstan has grown more self-confident as a state, and Russia has weakened. Kazakh leaders are still concerned with maintaining good economic and security relations with their neighbor to the north, but President Nazarbayev is now less concerned with the consequences of failing to revise the CIS or in creating a successor organization for it. He still speaks positively about strengthening the Customs Union of Russia, Kazakhstan, Kyrgyzstan, and Belarus (and now Tajikistan as well), although he would prefer the emergence of a more comprehensive organization than the strengthened CIS.[1]

The foreign policy of Kazakhstan is consciously international. Since 1995, Kazakhstan has been willing to accept close guidance from the international financial community about how to restructure its economy, to which end it has received more than $2 billion in assistance from the IMF and the World Bank.[2] The government's intent is to create sufficient investor confidence to allow the rapid exploitation of Kazakhstan's vast mineral reserves, and then to use some of this income to develop a more diversified economy.

Kazakhstan's goal is to be a serious actor in the global community, to serve as a bridge between Europe and Asia, as Kazakh President Nursultan Nazarbayev is fond of saying.[3] What he also seems increasingly to believe, but is less quick to verbalize, is that Russia will not provide the avenue through which Kazakhstan can reach that goal. For that reason, in Nazarbayev's calculations, the CIS, the

Customs Union and other such formal organizations are features of the transition period.

It is difficult to predict how long Kazakhstan's transition period will last, because the Kazakhs have not yet been able to reach their economic goals. Some of the reasons for this are beyond their control; an example is the difficulty that international consortia have had in finding transit routes for oil and gas exports. Other reasons are more controllable, such as the corruption that pervades Kazakh ruling circles and society more generally; among other things corruption has made it more difficult for foreign investors to operate, particularly in the metallurgy sectors on which Kazakhstan is pinning so many of its hopes. Nor does the government always seem to be determined to achieve economic reform as its first priority. The decision to move the nation's capital from Almaty to Akmola (now renamed Astana) in a span of just three years has already cost billions of dollars and will require billions more.[4]

Such problems not withstanding, Kazakhstan still must be considered a relative success in the post-Soviet world. The country has the highest rate of foreign direct investment per capita of any post-Soviet state outside the Baltic region, having received more than $7 billion in foreign investment by 1998.[5] Per capita GNP is now second only to that of Russia, at $1,340 in 1997.[6] The high level of foreign direct investment has enabled the government to keep the standard of living from dropping as precipitously as it has elsewhere in the CIS; nevertheless, according to United Nations Development Program statistics, about half of Kazakhstan's population is living in poverty. Kazakhstan has issued a detailed thirty-year plan of development, called "Kazakhstan 2030," but it lacks detail, suggesting that the state has actually made little headway in planning how it might develop a sustainable economy.[7]

Kazakhstan remains a remarkably stable place. While anecdotal evidence suggests that poverty is becoming more widespread, as income distribution has become very uneven,[8] the country is unlikely to face major challenges to its internal cohesion until President Nazarbayev passes from the political scene. However, the presence of so large a Russian minority—roughly one-third of the country's total population—means that Kazakhstan remains potentially vulnerable to a Russian challenge to its security at any time. The Kazakh leaders have done what they can to minimize this risk by developing bilateral and multilateral security arrangements, but these do not protect them against the theoretical threat of a more nationalist and more meddlesome Russian government, if one were to come to power in the future.

Kazakhstan's leaders view maintaining ethnic harmony as the greatest challenge that Kazakhstan faces. Over time, the Kazakhs have grown increasingly confident that, while the Yeltsin government will occasionally "play the ethnic card," the present Russian leadership will not actively try to destabilize Kazakhstan, as the Kazakhs originally feared. It is generally believed, for example, that President Nazarbayev decided to move his capital to Akmola to consolidate Kazakh control over the northern, and much more heavily Russian, part of the country and thus to diminish the chances for such destabilization.

The leader's fears were not empty. Kazakhstan witnessed serious violence on December 16, 1986, when Dinmukhamad Kunaev, an ethnic Kazakh who had been Communist Party first secretary for twenty years, was unceremoniously replaced by Gennady Kolbin, a Russian with no previous ties to Kazakhstan. Official efforts to dispel quickly a small rally of young Kazakhs only made the protest grow much larger; rioting broke out, leading to injuries, property damage, and death. There is still controversy about how many people died in these riots, with numbers ranging from the original official claim of two deaths to estimates of more than 150.[9]

This demonstration has become the defining event for Kazakh statehood, which is why Nursultan Nazarbayev chose to issue the country's declaration of independence five years later on December 16, 1991, and why the date is now a national holiday. Officially interpreted to mean that the people living in Kazakhstan must control their own fates, the "Almaty Uprising," as the riot is sometimes termed, can serve as a national symbol because, although the demonstrators themselves were Kazakhs, it was not the local Russians who were the targets of their anger.[10] More importantly, Kazakhstan has not witnessed any major incidence of interethnic violence since.

That there was no such violence in the past does not wholly reassure the Kazakh government that there will be none in the future. Not only is Kazakhstan the most multiethnic of all the post-Soviet states, but, more importantly, it is the only one in which the eponymous nationality was not a majority at the time of independence, when Kazakhs constituted only about 39 percent of the population.[11] Relative to total population Kazakhstan also had the largest Russian minority of any, save the Baltic states; as noted, Russians made up some 36 percent of the country's population.

The Latvians and Estonians were determined to isolate their large Russian populations both culturally and politically, but the Kazakhs took a different tack. Although the official rhetoric of state building adopted by President Nazarbayev and his various governments claims that Kazakh statehood is hundreds of years old, lost in the nineteenth century, and then restored in 1991,[12] in reality the country's leaders view independence as an unexpected boon, which they assumed at first Russia would try to snatch away as quickly as fate had granted it.

The Kazakh elite may have expected Russian attempts to destabilize their new state, but they were not resigned to them. Seeing the example of other new states in which Russia was using the local Russian population to bend new states closer to its will—as for example in Moldova, where the Transdniestr region had become almost a state-within-a-state—the Kazakh elite set up their new state in a way that maximized their own control. The political influence of nationalism was reduced to a minimum, as the government refused to legalize nationalist groups. Some, like the Russian groups Lad (Harmony) and Edinstvo (Unity), and the Kazakh group Azat (Freedom), were refused registration as political parties but were allowed to register as civic organizations, which meant that they could not contest seats in parliamentary elections on a party basis, although their members were free to do so as individuals.[13] Others, like the Kazakh group Alash[14] and Kazakhstan's several Cossack organizations, were denied registration as legal organizations of any sort. Alash's program of radical Islam, and the Cossacks' claim that they were a separate ethnic group entitled to ethnic autonomies established where they had had their prerevolutionary headquarters,[15] were equally unacceptable to the Kazakh leadership. Many Cossack groups did later gain registration.[16]

The Kazakh leaders were also alert to a more concealed threat. Russian nationalist groups wanted the Russian ethnic enclaves of northern Kazakhstan to be able to separate from the rest of the country,[17] but they knew that to argue this position openly would make legal registration impossible, so they promoted the idea that

Kazakhstan should become a federation. That idea was unequivo-cally rejected; the 1993 Constitution firmly establishes Kazakhstan as a unitary state.

Knowing that such legalistic maneuvers would not be much pro-tection against a determined Russian effort to destabilize their state, if one were to be mounted, the Kazakh leaders also chose to become strong proponents of CIS integration. Their understanding of the CIS, however, was from the beginning that the organization should mitigate Russian domination. Some of Nazarbayev's resistance to Russian plans for the CIS was undoubtedly due to personal ambition; proposed as the Soviet Union's number two man after the August 1991 coup, either as Soviet prime minister or as Gorbachev's vice president, Nazarbayev considered himself to be Yeltsin's equal.

In the organization's first few years, however, Nazarbayev had little weight that he could throw against Yeltsin. The economies of Russia and Kazakhstan remained fully intertwined, but Kazakhstan seemed more vulnerable to potential ruptures of relations than did Russia.[18] Russia bought 100 percent of Kazakhstan's aluminum, iron ore, and chrome, and Kazakhstan got just about all of its industrial machinery and heavy equipment from Russia.

The biggest hold that Russia had over its neighbor was that Kazakh-stan was still forced to import energy from Russia, at a cost of roughly $1 million per day. In the Soviet period oil and gas pipelines and hydroelectric grids had all been set up to minimize the distance between producer and consumer, without regard to republic admin-istrative boundaries; the cost of such large-scale infrastructure made their rapid post-Soviet replacement impossible. The electric power grids supplied Kazakhstan's northern *oblasts* with electricity from southern Siberia, in Russia, while Kazakhstan's oil refineries were not linked to its major oil fields, nor did they have the technical capacity to process most of the oil that was pumped in the country even if they were. The same situation was true for natural gas; output from the giant Karachaganak field had to be sent to Orenburg in Russia to be turned into condensate, while southern Kazakhstan was dependent upon Uzbekistan for its gas.

Kazakhstan quickly accumulated an enormous debt to Russia, and a somewhat smaller one to Uzbekistan. That Russian debt in particular, and the interconnection of the two countries' economies in general, made President Nazarbayev reluctant to leave the ruble zone. He strongly believed that the economic integrity of the USSR's geopolitical expanse had to be preserved at almost any price short of surrendering the juridical independence of the individual states, for which reason he made the significant concessions of sovereignty that Russia was demanding as the price of remaining in the ruble zone.

Even after Russia's demands forced the ruble zone to collapse, Kazakhstan's debt remained a complicating factor in its relationship with Russia, shaping the government's decisions on matters such as security. This debt was an important lever in negotiations over the status of the Soviet space center at Baikonur, which was now in Kazakhstan; eventually the complex was leased to Russia for a one-time payment of more than $1 billion and a nominal yearly rent of $115 million, both of which were to be offset against what Kazakhstan owed.[19] Although the issue of Kazakhstan's debt was never raised publicly in Russia's expressions of concern about treatment of the state's Russian minority, there is anecdotal evidence to suggest that it also served as a lever in closed-door sessions to make the Kazakhs treat ethnic Russians more gingerly.[20]

In the first years of independence, President Nazarbayev sought to mollify local Russians in as many ways as he could. The constitution mandated that Kazakh would become the official state language, but Nazarbayev pushed back the deadline by which this was to be achieved, and tried also to give the Russian language a public status nearly equal to that of Kazakh.[21] Although he encouraged efforts to give both Russians and Kazakhs reasons to identify with the Kazakh state, Nazarbayev resisted the attempts of leaders in Russia to introduce formal dual citizenship for their "ethnic conationals" across the CIS. He proposed instead that citizenship be made interchangeable across the CIS, allowing people to exchange their citizenship in one member state for that of another. This proposal was not adopted by the CIS, but it was agreed to in a bilateral agreement that Yeltsin signed in 1995; this did not, however, come into force until 1997, because the Russian Duma delayed ratification of the agreement for two more years.[22]

That delay is symptomatic; in general the Kazakh leadership was willing to accept a much greater degree of integration with Russia than the Russians were with Kazakhstan, provided only that terms of the relationship defined each of the members as equal sovereign states. This was when President Nazarbayev became convinced that Russia would never allow CIS institutions to develop the kind of equality that he proposed in the aforementioned Euro-Asian Union. The EAU envisioned much more deeply integrated membership than even the CIS proposed, but it offered better protection for weaker states. Member states would share a common currency and foreign economic policies, which would be regulated through decisions made by an intergovernmental parliamentary assembly in which each member state had an equal vote, with decisions based on a four-fifths majority. EAU agreements were to be ratified by the parliaments of all the member states before they were considered binding.

As has been mentioned, there was almost no support for the idea of the EAU when Nazarbayev formally presented it to the CIS leaders at their April 1994 summit. Russia preferred a structure that it could dominate, but even the smaller states were reluctant to concede the amount of sovereignty that Nazarbayev's plan would have required, even if this surrender was to give them a stake equal to Russia's in the new body. The opportunity to make their own choices about what political and economic paths their new states would follow proved to be more attractive to the other CIS leaders than was the security that Nazarbayev's plan might have bought them.

At the same time that Nazarbayev's EAU proposal was failing, Kazakhstan's domestic problems were beginning to make economic development seem more pressing than geopolitics. Inflation was skyrocketing, while industrial production was plummeting.[23] The severity of their economic crisis encouraged the Kazakhs to turn to the international financial community for guidance, which was quickly supplied. The introduction of the national currency, the *tenge*, in November 1993 was supported by an IMF Systemic Transformation Facility. This loan, dispensed on January 1, 1994, amounted to $54 million.[24]

President Nazarbayev also brought a new reform-oriented government to power. The Soviet-era legislature was dismissed in December 1993, because President Nazarbayev deemed it a brake on economic reform. New elections were not held until March 1994 and the new parliament was convened shortly thereafter. This long hiatus was deliberate; Nazarbayev used his powers of presidential edict to install a new legal regime, one that better protected private property and could stimulate private investment. An ambitious three-stage privatization program was introduced, which, although imperfect in its execution, has led Kazakhstan to have one of the largest private sectors in the post-Soviet space.[25]

Nazarbayev also appointed governments that were more receptive to international business. Akezhan Kazhegeldin, named prime minister in October 1994, had experience in defense-related industries, while his successor, Nurlan Balgimbaev, named in October 1997, had until his appointment been the head of the Kazakh oil industry.[26] The moves toward privatization, which these governments oversaw, brought large numbers of foreign investors, including Russian companies, into Kazakhstan. The Russian company Trans World Group (TWG) gained control of a huge share of Kazakhstan's aluminum and chrome industries,[27] while the Russian state-owned oil pipeline monopoly Transneft and the largely private Russian oil company Lukoil both became partners in the Caspian Pipeline Consortium (CPC) that eventually will carry Tengiz oil.[28]

The entry of Russian private and state-owned companies into Kazakhstan's economy seems to have mitigated the Russian government's objections to Kazakhstan's plans. Although it was the Russian government's position that the Caspian Sea could not be divided into national sectors, the Kazakh government went ahead and tendered Caspian shelf reserves.[29] In July 1998 Russia and Kazakhstan reached a preliminary agreement on where the boundaries between their two sectors lay, and are planning for joint development of some reserves in the north Caspian. Russian companies have stakes in plans to exploit the giant gas field at Karachaganak,[30] and the construction of the consortium oil pipeline is moving ahead, in part because Russian groups now have an economic interest in its completion.[31]

This is not to suggest, however, that Russia is more than just one part of Kazakhstan's overall economy. Russia remains Kazakhstan's most important trade partner, but its share of Kazakhstan's market is diminishing.[32] The Kazakh government still supports the idea of strengthening the economic union with Russia, but it is also working to meet the conditions necessary for entry in the WTO,[33] even if present economic problems are forcing the government to pursue protectionist policies, as chapter 2 discusses.

Kazakhstan's leaders are also growing less fearful of the country's Russian population, which has been declining steadily since the

1980s.[34] The Russians who are staying seem to be growing more apathetic, apparently resigned to the fact that they will live out their lives in a place where they feel like second-class citizens. Some nationalist leaders have left the country;[35] others have been harassed into silence.[36] As the Kazakh government expands and refines its security apparatus, it has even become more confident that it can control the Cossack population, for which reason some of these groups were allowed limited legal registration in 1997.[37] Russian nationalist groups have also been affected by a broader closing off of opportunities for public expression of dissent that the government has orchestrated.

Ultimately, the failure of the CIS to develop as a strong multilateral regional organization seems to have been to Kazakhstan's advantage. The lack of a multilateral security apparatus has encouraged the Kazakhs to develop a cooperative bilateral security relationship with Russia, while also carving out an independent international posture. They have used their proximity to Russia, and the threat that Russia might pose to their independence, to win the assistance of Western governments in directing foreign direct investment to Kazakhstan. They have also been able to develop strong economic and political relations with China,[38] and yet have managed to remain on reasonably good terms with Russia.

KYRGYZSTAN: ATTEMPTING TO KEEP THE WAY TO THE WORLD OPEN

Kyrgyzstan possesses a number of peculiarities that condition its attitude to the CIS and the rest of the world. It is landlocked and far from any sea, so it must strive to avoid being shut away from the world. It is also a small and mountainous country, with only 4.6 million citizens, surrounded by bigger and more powerful neighbors.

It has three big neighbors—China, Uzbekistan, and Kazakhstan— which are all potential threats, while its fourth neighbor, Tajikistan, has been embroiled in civil war since before independence. Kyrgyzstan's nearest potential ally against such threats—Russia—is too far away and too weak to be of much assistance.

Kyrgyzstan's position is also complicated by ethnic issues. According to the National Statistical Committee of Kyrgyzstan, on January 1,

1997, 60.8 percent of the country's population was Kyrgyz, 15.3 percent was Russian, and 14.3 percent was Uzbek.[39] A large number of ethnic Kyrgyz live in China, but the government in Kyrgyzstan has shown little interest in their situation; the government also actively prevents the local Uighurs from supporting the nationalist aspirations of their ethnic fellows across China's border. Although the government tries to accommodate these diverse nationalities, the greatest internal threat is the Uzbek minority in southern Kyrgyzstan, where approximately a third of the population lives. In the south, Uzbeks account for 28.1 percent of the population. These groups have a history of recent violence; in summer 1990, the local authorities passed control of a state farm from Uzbeks to Kyrgyz, which set off ethnic confrontations in the southern Kyrgyz city of Osh that ultimately turned into riots in which 230 people died. While it never became clear who was responsible for the rioting, this disaster undermined the power of the communist elite and led to the ouster of Absamat Masaliyev, first secretary of the Communist Party of the Kyrgyz Republic, in October 1990.[40]

Finally, to aggravate the situation even further, Kyrgyzstan is one of the poorest countries to emerge from the former Soviet Union. In Soviet days it exported little but sheep products and some gold and ran a chronic trade deficit with its fellow Soviet republics. It also had some portions of the Soviet defense industry within its boundaries, but these seemed out of place in the local context; a particularly vivid example for a state about as far from an ocean as any country on earth was the factory that produced torpedoes. Independence left the country in desperate need of economic restructuring. Kyrgyzstan trades primarily with Russia, Kazakhstan, and Uzbekistan, in this order, because poor transportation facilities and other infrastructure problems reduce other trade partners nearly to insignificance. The country is dependent on imports of natural gas and oil from Uzbekistan and Kazakhstan, to which it exports electricity.

In short, Kyrgyzstan is a country that cannot afford enemies. Thus it has had to cultivate relations with its three big neighbors and with Russia, while also trying to attract the interest and sympathy of the outside world.

A big plus in this otherwise dire list of minuses has been Askar Akaev, who has been president of the Kyrgyz Republic since 1990.

A prominent physicist, he had been president of the Kyrgyz Academy of Sciences and, much earlier in his career, had lived for seventeen years in Leningrad, where he was part of a liberal Russian intelligentsia environment. Unlike most other rulers in Central Asia, Akaev was neither a Communist Party first secretary, nor was he appointed by Moscow. Rather he had been elected in October 1990 by an obstreperous Kyrgyz parliament, which refused to follow the pattern of other republic legislatures in transforming their party first secretaries into presidents. Moscow ignored the Kyrgyz parliament's show of independence. Akaev was reelected in popular elections in October 1991 and December 1995.[41] The second election was particularly noteworthy, since it came in the same year that Presidents Karimov and Nazarbayev of Uzbekistan and Kazakhstan, respectively, extended their own terms as presidents through popular referendum, rather than by contested election.

Akaev may have been an outsider to the party hierarchies, but he was well connected with the old Kyrgyz establishment. He was chosen president because of his reputation as a democrat, his academic background, and his long experience in Russia. Akaev understood early that Kyrgyzstan needed to nurture ties with the West, but he was also comfortable with Russian and Kazakh liberals. Although there is growing concern that President Akaev's democratic lapses are becoming dangerously frequent, Kyrgyzstan enjoys far greater pluralism and openness than does any other Central Asian country.[42]

President Akaev has been the dominant political figure in Kyrgyzstan; his policies have been the most liberal in the region and are shaped by his keen perception of the limitations imposed by *realpolitik* and Kyrgyzstan's peculiar conditions. Politically, he has tried to encourage democratic reforms and political pluralism. Economically, his choice has been radical economic reform, opting for a normal market economy based on private property. His foreign policy has aimed at opening Kyrgyzstan to the world, developing good relations with everybody, while not intimidating anybody. In general Kyrgyzstan's policies are Western-oriented, which has given the country an excellent relationship with the international financial institutions. This orientation does not lead the country into any conflict with Russia, because from Kyrgyzstan's vantage point Russia too appears to be a comparatively liberal and Western country.

Akaev has also been eager to maintain ethnic tolerance. A large part of the Russian and Russian-speaking population left the country soon after independence, causing serious shortages of certain categories of qualified workers, such as physicians. Akaev did a number of things to attempt to persuade those who had not yet emigrated to remain in Kyrgyzstan. Russian was made an official state language, equal to Kyrgyz. He encouraged the organization of various ethnic associations and formed a national assembly of all these associations to give them an official role. Bishkek became home to various private universities, several of which had international founders. One of these universities is the Kyrgyz-Russian Slavic University, which uses Russian as its language and is financed by the Russian government.[43] There are many schools in which the language of instruction is Uzbek, Russian, or some other language of Kyrgyzstan's ethnic minorities. These policies were successful; the exodus of ethnic minorities dropped sharply after 1994.

President Akaev saw radical economic reform to be one of his country's most pressing challenges, but he did not undertake it in a systematic way until May 1993, when Kyrgyzstan launched the *som* as its new independent currency, becoming the first of the CIS states to abandon the destabilizing ruble (as noted, the Baltic states had dropped the ruble in 1992). A major reason for this delay was that Kyrgyzstan did not want to antagonize the other CIS countries by leaving the ruble zone, and so waited until its move received the blessing of Boris Fedorov, the liberal Russian minister of finance.

Kyrgyzstan could not realistically have instituted a policy of full market economy any earlier; it was a desperately poor country, with no international reserves whatsoever. For that reason Akaev had to assure himself of full support from the IMF before beginning his reforms, which Kyrgyzstan continues to assure by meticulously complying with IMF conditions for its programs.

Kyrgyzstan swiftly became the favorite CIS state among the international donor community; it was peaceful and relatively democratic, its leadership was liberal and well educated, and it implemented important and beneficial reforms of all kinds. Equally important, Kyrgyzstan has needed a lot of assistance. The bulk of its international financing comes from the IMF, the World Bank, the Asian Development Bank (ADB), and the European Bank for Reconstruction and Development (EBRD), but Kyrgyzstan has also benefited from significant bilateral contributions by a number of countries, including Japan, the United States, Germany, and Switzerland.

International and domestic support has allowed Akaev to direct a significant restructuring of Kyrgyzstan's economy. Inflation was quickly brought under control. Small enterprises were swiftly privatized, after which many big and medium-size enterprises were also privatized, using a mass privatization scheme.[44] Kyrgyzstan also carried out a comprehensive land reform, which has proven all but impossible in most of the other post-Soviet states. The government was reorganized to resemble a more Western model, and a goal was set to reduce the number of bureaucrats.[45] Kyrgyzstan undertook a radical tax reform, reducing the number of taxes and lowering tax rates.

GDP plummeted by 45 percent from 1991 to 1995, but then recovered dramatically, with a growth of 6 percent in 1996 and 10 percent in 1997. However, this growth is concentrated in certain sectors. Agricultural production surged by 13 percent in 1996 and 10 percent in 1997, following the distribution of formerly collectivized agricultural land, but that increase is perceived to be a one-time adjustment. Investment and GDP figures for 1996, 1997, and 1998 were also swollen by another short-term contribution, the huge investment that the Canadian firm Cameco made to develop the country's Kumtor gold mine. Overall industrial production in Kyrgyzstan has shrunk from 32 percent of GDP in 1992 to 12 percent of GDP in 1996.[46] Industrial output in 1998 was only one-third of the 1991 level.[47]

President Akaev has understood how to turn his country's weaknesses to advantage in foreign policy. The Kyrgyz realize that they cannot defend themselves against any military threat and so try to forestall them by developing good relations as widely as they possibly can. Akaev originally considered a policy of military neutrality, but then found it prudent to accept Russian border troops and the Tashkent Treaty, as chapter 3 has explained. Kyrgyzstan took advantage of the Russian financial crisis in the summer of 1998 to begin redefining the agreement with Russia on border guards, who have gradually been replaced by Kyrgyzstan's own troops.[48]

Kyrgyzstan's border with China makes the giant neighbor a clear potential threat, so the Kyrgyz work to accommodate Chinese wishes and also to strengthen other ties, especially in commerce. Muratbek Imanaliyev, whom President Akaev appointed minister of foreign affairs on July 1, 1997, had previously served as Kyrgyzstan's ambassador to China; he is a scholar of Chinese history and speaks fluent Chinese.

Kazakhstan and Uzbekistan also have the capacity to undermine order in Kyrgyzstan. The Kyrgyz try to develop close relations with both countries, but for many reasons its relations with Kazakhstan are much closer than those with Uzbekistan. The Kazakhs and Kyrgyz are similar ethnically and culturally; both peoples were nomadic livestock breeders until the Soviet period. By contrast, the Uzbeks have tilled their land for hundreds of years, for which reason they consider themselves culturally and historically superior to both their neighbors. Kazakhstan's strategies of economic and political reform are similar to those of Kyrgyzstan, while Uzbekistan has been hesitant about both economic and political restructuring. Kazakhstan and Kyrgyzstan look toward Russia and Europe, while Uzbekistan is more hostile to Russia and less accepted as a part of Europe. As noted, Kyrgyzstan also sees the Uzbek minority that lives near its border with Uzbekistan as the country's greatest potential security threat.

Whatever the tensions among them, the three Central Asian neighbors are also dependent on one another in a number of ways, which is why they have formed the Central Asian Economic Community (discussed in chapter 5). Kyrgyzstan provides the other two with water and hydroelectricity, while Uzbekistan and Kazakhstan both export natural gas to Kyrgyzstan and Kazakhstan also ships it oil. Kyrgyzstan does not face any immediate threat from these neighbors, but it needs to manage its relations with them carefully.

Within the CIS, Kyrgyzstan has tried to align its policies with those of Russia and Kazakhstan, while also trying to sustain its complicated relationship with Uzbekistan, whose economy remains thoroughly regulated. It was an obvious choice for Kyrgyzstan to join the CIS Economic Union and the Free Trade Area, but the Customs Union (of Russia, Belarus, Kazakhstan, and, eventually, Tajikistan) presented more of a conundrum; the country had already adopted a simple, uniform import tariff of only 10 percent for trade from outside the CIS, and it enjoyed free trade inside the CIS. Membership in the Customs Union could force Kyrgyzstan to raise those tariffs to accommodate Russian protectionism, which the Kyrgyz had no interest in doing.

Characteristically, in 1996 Kyrgyzstan joined the Customs Union and simultaneously applied for membership in the World Trade Organization.[49] Although Russia had applied for membership in the

WTO three years earlier, it was free-trading Kyrgyzstan that became the first CIS country to be admitted to the WTO. Russia protested this judgment by the world's economic community and was joined by Kazakhstan in arguing that all of the members of the Customs Union should enter the WTO together.

Kyrgyzstan's economic success was badly damaged by the events of 1998. The country's growth in GDP fell from 10 percent in 1997 to barely 2 percent in 1998, for a number of reasons. Agricultural growth fell from 10 percent in 1997 to zero percent in 1998, and no significant investment took the place of Cameco's investment in the Kumtor gold mine. As noted in chapter 2, there has been little foreign direct investment across the entire CIS, and most of what there has been is concentrated in oil and gas investments. Kyrgyzstan does not have either. It also has a tiny domestic market and is far from other important markets.

The most important cause of Kyrgyzstan's falling growth rate was the Russian financial crisis. Exports, which go primarily to Russia and Kazakhstan, shrank by 22 percent. The share of Kyrgyzstan's exports going to CIS countries declined from 55 percent in 1997 to 45 percent in 1998. Because of its financial crisis, Russia sharply reduced its traditional imports from Kyrgyzstan—tobacco, wool, cotton and textiles.[50] The Russian financial crisis also ricocheted off its neighbors to hit Kyrgyzstan; Uzbekistan and Kazakhstan reduced their purchase of electricity from Kyrgyzstan in 1998, and both Kazakhstan and Russia initiated various protectionist measures. Disputes over payment also prompted Uzbekistan repeatedly to cut off gas supplies in 1998 and 1999.

The financial crisis of 1998 meant that Kyrgyzstan could no longer continue to juggle the wishes of Russia, Kazakhstan, and Uzbekistan in its foreign trade policy, as it had been diplomatically attempting to do. As noted already, the 1998 crisis forced the Kyrgyz Republic to choose between the obligations of its Customs Union with Belarus, Russia, and Kazakhstan (Tajikistan was not yet a member) and the demands of the WTO. Without hesitation, it chose the WTO and an outward trade orientation.

By 1998 Russia and Kazakhstan had become active agents of destabilization. Russia imposed tariffs on many of its exports, and in early 1999, Kazakhstan imposed severe import quotas and import tariffs of up to 200 percent, targeting particularly food imports from Kyrgyzstan and Uzbekistan. An example of the magnitude of this change is Kyrgyzstan's export of cement to Kazakhstan, the average volume of which had been about 800,000 tons each year; suddenly Kazakhstan imposed an annual import quota of 50,000 tons. Import tariffs were not renewed when they expired six months later. As was discussed in chapter 2, Kazakhstan's initial reluctance to devalue its currency as the others states had been forced to do meant that its own products could no longer compete against imports.

Kyrgyzstan has taken the lesson of the 1998 financial crisis to be that it should increase its reliance on the international financial organizations even more than it had already done. The country's foreign reserves contracted only slightly when the 1998 crisis struck, but its current account deficit remained large, so that Kyrgyzstan was forced to devalue sharply in late 1998. Knowing that neither Russia nor any of the other CIS countries had funds to contribute, Kyrgyzstan turned for assistance to the outside world; in early 1999 it received additional credit from the IMF to boost its reserves.

Kyrgyzstan has no intention of abandoning the CIS. Its commitment to the CIS has become more limited, however, since this organization cannot solve the problems the country is facing. Even though it has enjoyed the most generous possible support of international institutions, getting most of its international loans at the subsidized rate of about 0.5 percent per annum, Kyrgyzstan's total indebtedness has grown disturbingly large, now amounting to more than three-quarters of GDP. Kyrgyzstan understands that it must attract more foreign direct investment, which cannot come from any CIS country, since they all are in financial crises.

The Kyrgyz Republic remains committed to free trade, so that its primary demand of the CIS is that the organization implements in fact the free trade policies that its agreements proclaim. Kyrgyzstan seems quietly to be abandoning hopes that the Customs Union might prove to be a functioning entity, but it avoids antagonizing its putative partners in that union unnecessarily. In security concerns, Kyrgyzstan remains a member of the Tashkent Treaty, but the significance of that agreement shrank after Kyrgyzstan asked Russia to withdraw its border troops from the country.

Disappointment in the efficacy of the CIS has made Kyrgyzstan interested in all manner of alternative regional associations. It has joined the Central Asian Economic Community, the Economic Cooperation Organization (ECO), and the Transport Corridor Europe

Caucasus Asia project (TRACECA), but to date none of these organizations has amounted to much, nor do any of them seem likely to become important in the immediate future. Thus Kyrgyzstan is going to be forced to maintain its membership in the CIS, while simultaneously striving to maintain the favor of larger international organizations, such as the IMF, the World Bank, the Asian Development Bank, and the WTO. It is far from clear, however, whether Kyrgyzstan's juggling act will work. Kyrgyzstan cannot develop its economy if big, economically hostile neighbors surround it, while the international community will hardly bankroll Kyrgyzstan indefinitely.

UKRAINE: NATION BUILDING BUT LITTLE ECONOMIC REFORM

With 51 million citizens, Ukraine is the second largest country, after Russia, to emerge from the former Soviet Union. Its sense of nationhood is much stronger than is that of most other CIS states, even though it had enjoyed only a brief period of modern independence, in 1918. Ninety percent of the voters in Ukraine opted for independence in the December 1, 1991, referendum, thus setting the stage for the agreement a week later by which Russia, Ukraine, and Belarus dissolved the Soviet Union and formed the CIS.

While Ukrainian nationalism may have existed for hundreds of years, Ukraine as a nation-state is new, meaning that it has had to define itself no less than have the other post-Soviet states. The greatest challenge to that definition is posed by Russians, who tend to regard Ukrainians as if they were little brothers and are reluctant to acknowledge Ukrainian as a language separate from the Russian language, which it closely resembles; indeed, before 1917, Ukraine was officially known as "Little Russia." Ethnic Ukrainians account for 73 percent of the state's population, with Russians constituting 22 percent, and many Ukrainians speak Russian as their first language. Eastern Ukraine and the Crimea are predominantly ethnically Russian. As was discussed in chapter 3, Ukraine also found itself with important military assets on its territory at the time of independence, including a large number of nuclear arms from the Soviet Black Sea Fleet, of which Russia claimed to be the proper heir.

Ukraine's insecurity about the durability of its existence has meant that nation building has absorbed most of the new state's energy and foreign policy, with economic restructuring postponed or ignored. This preoccupation with nation building has made Ukraine's policies seem contradictory. It has constructed a thoughtful foreign policy designed to make the country a part of Europe and the Western world, but its failure to deal with economic reform and the resulting economic problems have forced Ukraine to compromise with Russia and the CIS more than it wishes.[51]

Ukraine has also had a paradoxical history, for it is situated between Poland and Russia. The eastern Ukrainians chose to ally with Russia in 1654, while western Ukraine did not come under Russian domination until 1939, when Nazi Germany and the Soviet Union divided Poland between them. The eastern Ukrainians were used to accommodating Russia, who they saw as a natural peer even if they also suffered Russian condescension, while those living in the west saw Russia as an evil that they escaped for centuries, until they were finally overwhelmed by the combined treacheries of Stalin and Hitler. The western Ukrainians understood their decades under Soviet rule to be a forced and unwanted turn toward the east, and so with independence demanded that their new state redirect itself exclusively toward the West.

These contradictory impulses were evident when Ukrainians voted for independence, because at the same time they also elected Leonid Kravchuk as their first president. Kravchuk had come from the old party apparatus, eventually rising to become second secretary of the Communist Party of Ukraine; his election helped preserve the power of the old Russian-oriented Communist Party *nomenklatura* in Ukraine, particularly since Kravchuk knew absolutely nothing about economics. Kravchuk was born in western Ukraine[52] and spoke Ukrainian as his native language, however, so his election seemed a victory for Ukrainian nationalists. The combination of old communist ways and linguistic nationalism that Kravchuk's election offered appeared to be precisely the mixture necessary to unite Ukraine.

In reality, neither of Ukraine's two tendencies prevailed in the early stage of independence. Ukraine was not able to turn either to Russia or to the West, but instead was forced in upon itself. Speaking of a "Ukrainian economic model" that would feature a great deal of state regulation and intervention, Ukraine chose not to liberalize its economy. Instead, it established foreign trade regulation of the Soviet type, based on state trading and comprehensive licensing of almost all foreign trade. Many prices remained regulated at a low level. Price subsidies ballooned, and the National Bank issued subsidized credits freely, throwing Ukraine into one of the worst hyperinflationary spirals in the CIS; in 1993, inflation reached 10,200 percent, while output and the standard of living both plummeted. Ukraine became mired in severe corruption, spreading the misery further.

By the end of 1993, the situation was so critical that the survival of Ukraine seemed in question. In addition to the economic crisis, which was making life hard everywhere, linguistic nationalism was exacerbating tensions between the eastern and western parts of the country. Separatist sentiment was also growing in Crimea, which had only become an administrative part of Ukraine in 1954, and which was overwhelmingly populated by Russians, who had been moved in to take the place of the Crimean Tatars expelled by Stalin in 1944. In January 1994, a Russian nationalist was elected president of Crimea, and the regional legislature began demanding autonomy so great as to border on independence.

Repeated strikes and protests by coal miners in eastern Ukraine eventually forced President Kravchuk to call early parliamentary and presidential elections in the spring and summer of 1994, respectively. Because parties were not permitted to contest in the parliamentary elections, the new body was badly fragmented. The biggest winner was the Left, but it fell short of a majority.[53] The corrupt "party of power" suffered the worst losses. In effect, an amorphous center became pivotal, while under heavy pressure from a communist-dominated Left.

The presidential elections demonstrated the polarization of eastern and western Ukraine. The Russified east voted for Leonid Kuchma, a former state enterprise manager, while the west, and Ukrainian nationalists everywhere, voted for Kravchuk.[54] Although Kuchma had spoken during the campaign in favor of economic reform and against corruption, his program for change was vague. The real dispute in the election was over nationalism, which those who leaned toward Russia won, when Kuchma was elected the second president of Ukraine, on July 10, 1994.[55]

Contrary to expectation, however, Kuchma did not try to bring Ukraine closer to Russia. Rather, he made economic reform the center of his policies and succeeded in ameliorating the country's desperate situation. Kuchma also made a point of improving his poor Ukrainian and would use only Ukrainian in his speeches. He soon closed the worrisome breach between east and west, while the Russian government in the Crimea collapsed under the weight of its own economic incompetence. Rather than turning to Russia, as most observers expected he would, Kuchma developed Ukraine's international relations in general and those with the West in particular.

From the first moments of independence, Ukraine's security policy has been peaceful and focused. Ukraine decided from the beginning to stay out of all collaboration on security policy in the CIS. It never considered joining the Tashkent Treaty when that was formed in 1992, and it has never revisited the issue. The CIS has played no role in its security policy, nor is it likely to do so in the future.

Ukraine originally considered the idea of neutrality, which is the reason why the decision to give up its nuclear weapons was relatively uncontentious.[56] Ukraine did not want to be left to negotiate the nuclear issues with Russia alone, however, and so asked for U.S. participation, which Washington was happy to supply. Negotiations on Ukraine's nuclear disarmament were speedy and surprisingly uncomplicated, which brought Ukraine a great deal of international good will. This process also helped consolidate Ukraine's national status, permitting the Ukrainian president to join the presidents of Russia and the United States as equals when the Trilateral Agreement was signed in Moscow in January 1994.

There were many security issues between Russia and Ukraine, however, that were necessarily bilateral. The Black Sea Fleet, the home port of which is Sevastopol, Crimea, has been a major point of contention between the two countries. Many Russians argue that Crimea as a whole, and Sevastopol in particular, does not rightfully belong to Ukraine, since the huge peninsula had been passed to Ukraine's control by Soviet Premier Nikita Khrushchev as a grandiose gift in 1954, to mark the tricentennial of the treaty that had joined eastern Ukraine to Russia. As has been discussed in chapter 3, this issue was finally resolved in May 1997, when Russia agreed to split ownership of the fleet evenly, and Ukraine agreed to lease back part of its share and granted Russia the right to continue to use facilities at Sevastopol and Karatinnaya for twenty more years.

Perhaps because of its own problems with Crimea, Ukraine has been careful to avoid getting involved in Transdniestr's attempts to separate from Moldova, even though many of the separatists are ethnic Ukrainians, and Ukraine also has historical grounds on which it might claim the breakaway region on which it borders. Ukrainians have been so successful in this regard that they were invited to serve alongside Russians as peacekeepers.[57] Ukraine showed a similar scrupulousness in moving to settle a border dispute with Romania, which it did by a bilateral treaty in June 1997.

Ukraine has consistently stayed away from any military cooperation with Russia or the CIS, but it has gradually come closer to NATO. Ukraine opposed NATO expansion at first, but then came to favor it; it has participated actively in NATO's Partnership for Peace and in joint military exercises, and has taken part in peacekeeping operations in Bosnia. Ukraine and NATO also negotiated a charter on a distinctive partnership in May 1997, which envisages consultations between Ukraine and NATO on political and security issues, conflict prevention, the control of arms exports and transfers of space technologies, and non-proliferation of weapons of mass destruction.[58] Ukraine also hopes that the fledgling GUUAM alliance will form the kernel of a security counterweight to Russia, but it is careful to keep its efforts from appearing threatening.

Ukraine's foreign economic policy has been nearly the opposite of its skillful security policy. It is possible to discern the same desire to keep a distance from Russia in economic matters as it has in security ones, but the state's economic weakness has repeatedly forced, or tempted, Ukraine to draw much closer to Russia. To be fair, Ukraine's economy was also tightly interwoven with that of Russia; more than two-thirds of Ukraine's foreign trade in 1992 was with the CIS, most of that with Russia, which meant that Ukraine could not avoid the CIS economically in the same way it could on security matters.

The complexities and contradictions of Ukraine's position were illustrated by the way in which it left the ruble zone. Many Ukrainians wanted, for nationalist reasons, to introduce a Ukrainian currency immediately upon independence. To that end, a special Ukrainian coupon was launched as a parallel currency in January 1992. This did not replace the ruble, but instead merely added to the money supply. Ukraine's National Bank continued to issue vast amounts of ruble credits, forcing the Russian government to limit the convertibility of Ukrainian rubles into Russian rubles. Ukrainian monetary policy seemed unprofessional and uninformed, but it also appeared to have the explicit intention of siphoning off as much money from Russia as possible. The inevitable consequence was the hyperinflation of 1993, for which Russia forced Ukraine out of the ruble zone. Ukraine thus gained an independent currency by default in late 1993, but it was not until September 1996 that the Ukrainian leadership felt secure enough in its control of the economy to introduce the *hryvnia* as a national currency. Ukraine's monetary policy caused a serious economic decline in Ukraine.

What made this behavior particularly odd is that Ukraine had never favored monetary union, but argued that the CIS should be a free trade area. While most politicians opposed political superstructures like the Inter-Parliamentary Assembly, there was no such resistance to signing all kinds of technical agreements that the state considered consistent with building up the CIS as a free trade area. It is for that reason that Ukraine has never shown any interest in joining the Customs Union, which it feels works against this goal.

At the same time, however, Ukraine was also establishing a Soviet-type state trade system, which drew Ukraine far deeper into the CIS state trade system economically than it desired politically. Ukraine's highly regulated foreign trade system did not allow it to trade freely with any country. Most exports were subject to quotas and licenses until a substantial liberalization occurred in late 1994, but then new regulations and restrictions began to proliferate again as early as the summer of 1995. Ukraine applied for membership in the WTO in 1994, but its regulations make membership seem a distant hope.

Another factor that drew Ukraine deeper into the CIS trading system was its large debt to Russia, most of it to Russia's Gazprom for imports of natural gas. The gas trade between the two countries involves an intricate array of monopolies and dubious practices. Gazprom insists on charging comparatively high prices for its gas, which Ukraine refuses to pay. Increasingly, the payments are being made to private gas suppliers in Ukraine who should then pay Gazprom, but these providers tend to hide behind state guarantees because of bills not paid by their public customers. Gazprom also complains that Ukrainians siphon off gas without payment, which is being piped through Ukraine for export to Europe. Both countries agree that Ukraine's arrears are large, but they differ greatly in their figures. Gazprom prefers to clear such debts through debt-for-equity swaps to gain control of Soviet-era pipelines and gas reservoirs, but Ukraine has staunchly resisted Gazprom's claims to such infrastructure on grounds of national security. Instead, over the years substantial arrears for gas have been transformed into state debt.

In 1994 Russia made clear that it was no longer prepared to bankroll Ukraine, forcing Ukraine to look abroad for financing. The first agreement with the IMF was reached in October 1994 and a standby agreement was signed in spring 1995. These agreements stabilized prices in Ukraine and also allowed Ukraine to go to the World Bank, private bond markets, the EU, Japan, and the IMF again for loan financing. The problems with gas arrears persist, but Russia's role as a lender of last resort has shrunk significantly.

As President Kuchma declared in spring 1996, Ukraine would like to become a member of the European Union. The response from the EU, however, could not have been less encouraging, an indication to Ukrainians that for the foreseeable future this was a vain aspiration. Despite a 1998 Partnership and Cooperation Agreement between Ukraine and the EU, a series of antidumping complaints brought by the EU about Ukrainian exports, particularly of steel, have further dampened Kyiv's enthusiasm for the EU.

Ukraine and Russia have also argued repeatedly over protectionism and dumping. In 1996 and 1997 Ukrainian vodka, beer, and sugar flooded the Russian market, to which Russia responded with quotas and import tariffs, hurting Ukrainian exports badly. On the advice of the IMF, Ukraine started exempting exports from VAT in 1996, while adding VAT to imports. Russia charged VAT on its exports, and as a result both countries taxed imported goods to Ukraine. This practice continued for more than a year. The dispute was settled in early 1998, but the protectionist measures and countermeasures had already caused a severe contraction in mutual trade.

In October 1997 Ukraine was hit by the Asian crisis just as Russia was. Also dependent on foreign bondholders, Ukraine pushed its interest rates even higher than those of Russia. This caused its stock market to collapse, but the market for this was too small to be of real international consequence. With private investors withdrawing their funds, the state teetered on the verge of default throughout 1998. The government was unable to comply with most of the conditions set by the IMF and the World Bank, leaving Ukraine with almost no international funding. Russia's August 1998 devaluation hit Ukraine in two ways: by shrinking demand within Russia for Ukrainian exports and also by making Ukraine's exports, especially steel, less competitive on the world market than were Russia's.

In response, the *hryvnia* was devalued roughly 50 percent in September 1998. The government responded by introducing stricter currency regulations and certain protectionist measures. Having alienated both Russia and the international financial community with its economic policies, Ukraine found itself with nowhere to turn. Ukraine's official GDP fell by 59 percent between 1991 and 1998; its present economic polices and isolation make it likely that Ukraine's economic decline will continue. Under these circumstances, the Rada (the parliament) adopted a resolution to reduce the budget deficit, a key IMF condition, and in September 1998, the IMF approved a new three-year $2.26 billion extended loan program for Ukraine. Since Kyiv did not comply with the loan requirements, however, the IMF suspended the program in November 1998. The decision to resume disbursements was made in March 1999.[59]

Despite the contradictory impulses of its security and economic policies, Ukraine's overall position on the CIS has been consistent from the moment of independence. The only function for the organization that Ukraine supports is that the CIS should be a free trade area. However, the Inter-Parliamentary Assembly of the CIS has proven a point of domestic contention. Ukrainian communists and socialists have urged strongly that Ukraine join, while Ukrainian nationalists have argued as passionately that to do so would mean surrendering Ukrainian sovereignty. Over the years the Ukrainian parliament has repeatedly voted on the question; the result was frequently close, but it was not until March 1999 that a majority voted to have Ukraine join the Inter-Parliamentary Assembly. This was a concession sufficient to persuade the Russian Duma to ratify the Russian-Ukrainian Friendship Treaty, which further secured the decisions made on the division of the Black Sea Fleet and the status of Sevastopol and was an important recognition by Russia of Ukrainian sovereignty. By itself though, membership in the Inter-Parliamentary Assembly is of little consequence; it has not aroused significant political ardor in any other CIS states, and its decisions are non-binding.

Ukraine has managed successfully to stay clear of any substantive involvement in CIS security policy. Ukraine's economic relations are seriously troubled, however, within and outside the CIS, because the country has done little to build a normal market economy, while the CIS has failed to function as a free trade area. Ukraine's security policy has been successful in theory, but Ukraine has been left with fewer friends and resources than it might have had if it had managed its economy differently.

GEORGIA: BETWEEN RUSSIA AND THE WORLD

The recent history of Georgia illustrates a common post-Soviet syndrome: that ambitions far outstrip results. Since independence, and especially since Eduard Shevardnadze took charge,[60] the country's leadership has embraced an outward-looking strategy of greater global integration as a way to create a stable, democratic, and market-oriented state. Georgia's leaders concede that they must have strong ties with Russia, but they are not content to have their country be defined by Moscow's "vital interests" or to confine their horizons to the post-Soviet space.[61] Georgia has pursued close relations with Turkey, lobbied hard for the construction of a key Caspian oil pipeline that would run through its territory, tried to secure greater international involvement in the management and resolution of conflicts in its secessionist regions of Abkhazia and South Ossetia, and has turned to NATO and the United States for assistance in building up its military.

Georgia's ability to realize these ambitions of global reach has been seriously impaired by both internal and external constraints. Georgia has faced ethnic conflict, well-armed secessionist movements, murderous internal power struggles, and floods of internal refugees. Before it was hit by the broader economic problems of 1998, Georgia's economy was just beginning to recover from the state of disarray of recent years, when the standard of living had nose-dived, wages were chronically unpaid, and even basic electricity was supplied only intermittently. Nor were any of these problems made easier to solve by Georgia's geographic location in the Caucasus, which is the most unstable region of the CIS, and of Russia as well.

The collapse of the Soviet Union has exposed the weaknesses that Georgia earned from its own more distant past as a regional imperial power. The state has not yet unified, and it is not certain that it ever will, even if the main ethnic and territorial challenges to that unity have ceased to be violent.

Georgia's ethnic conflicts may have been unavoidable, but there is no question that tensions were exacerbated enormously by the country's first president, Zviad Gamsakhurdia. A fiery Georgian nationalist, Gamsakhurdia had seemed at first to wish to accommodate the state's many ethnic minorities, but then quickly began to assert that only ethnic Georgians had a claim to the state.[62] Soon Gamsakhurdia institutionalized ethnic Georgian nationalism as the sole legitimate political force in the newly independent Georgian state. The result was a blossoming of armed factions and a civil war, which drove Gamsakhurdia from power in January 1992 and helped bring Eduard Shevardnadze to lead the country in March 1992.

Both South Ossetia and Abkhazia had been so alarmed by Georgian nationalism that these regions voted overwhelmingly in support of Gorbachev's Union Treaty,[63] and when that proved to be useless, they began to organize armed resistance, turning for help both to locally stationed Soviet forces and to sympathetic ears in Moscow.

South Ossetia was the first region to announce its intention to secede from Georgia, and to unite with the republic of North Ossetia, across the border in Russia. Soviet Ministry of Interior troops were able to contain most of the violence between Ossetians and Georgians, but it escalated as the USSR unraveled. Paramilitary units from both sides continued to fight until Russia brokered a cease-fire, signed on June 22, 1992, by Georgian and South Ossetian negotiators. Russian troops began patrolling the South Ossetia–Georgia border on July 14, 1992. Since then no serious fighting has occurred, but subsequent negotiations have failed to produce an agreement on the status of South Ossetia. At present, the Tbilisi government exercises no control over the region.

Georgia's more serious problem, though, has been the de facto secession of the Abkhazian Autonomous Republic. In August 1992 Tengiz Kitovani, then Georgian minister of defense, led a force of Georgian soldiers and tank columns into Abkhazia, capturing its capital, Sukhumi, occupying the parliament building, and tearing down symbols of Abkhazian independence. Unable to consolidate control, Georgian forces fled Abkhazia in September 1993 as Abkhaz rebels, aided by Russian hardware, military forces, and volunteers from elsewhere in the north Caucasus, reconquered Sukhumi. Gamsakhurdia loyalists in western Georgia tried to take advantage of the turmoil in Abkhazia to overthrow the Shevardnadze government. These two conflicts in concert nearly toppled the state, so that in October 1993 President Shevardnadze was forced to ask Russia for military assistance. Russia's rapid intervention allowed the Georgian army to rout Gamsakhurdia's forces and also paved the way for a Russian-brokered cease-fire in Abkhazia, under UN auspices, in June–July 1994. Russian peacekeepers have been patrolling the Abkhaz-Georgian border since June 20, 1994, and little progress has been made toward a political settlement between Abkhaz and Georgian authorities. At present, Abkhazia is also a de facto state.

The Adjar Autonomous Region, led by Aslan Abashidze,[64] has also achieved a large degree of de facto autonomy, but it has managed to do so without violence. Following the example of Tatarstan in Russia, Adjaria has created local political structures that are strong enough to challenge the central government successfully. The Adjar population considers itself to be ethnically Georgian, which has made Abashidze and his political party, the Union for Democratic Revival, serious contenders for national political power. In some ways the Adjars thus pose an even greater threat to Georgia's current leadership than do the Abkhaz or the Ossetians. There is also no guarantee, in the volatile world of Georgian politics, that Adjaria's ambitions for autonomy will continue to be met peacefully.

The Abkhaz and the South Ossetian conflicts over autonomy, especially those that turned violent, have created a tide of internal refugees that remains a serious obstacle to Georgian stability.[65] The cost of providing for the displaced Georgian refugees is a significant strain on the central government's budget, and the refugees have created political organizations that have considerable weight in Georgian domestic politics. Some of the refugees have also formed paramilitary groups which occasionally attack Russian and Abkhaz troops, and have even hit UN observers.[66] Repatriation of refugees has been one of the major hurdles in the negotiations between Georgia and Abkhazia.[67]

Beset by these and other difficulties, Georgia's GDP declined by roughly 80 percent from 1990 to 1994. Industrial production dropped 83 percent, agricultural production declined by 63 percent, and, in 1994, inflation reached 8,380 percent.[68] Coping with civil war in

South Ossetia, Abkhazia, and western Georgia, a flood of refugees, the physical destruction of infrastructure and farmland, and the necessary militarization of the civilian economy meant that in the first years of Georgia's independence there could be no orderly approach to the equally daunting task of moving the country from a Soviet to a market economy.

It was not until the end of 1994 that the country's internal situation stabilized sufficiently to allow Tbilisi to attempt a bold plan of market reform. With help from the IMF, World Bank, and EBRD, Georgia has managed to become a successful transition economy. In 1997 inflation dropped to 14.3 percent, GDP grew by 11 percent, and the new national currency, the *lari*, remained stable, as it had since its introduction in the fall of 1995.[69]

Given the abyss into which baselines for measuring changes in the Georgian economy had fallen, however, such growth figures convey a misleading impression. High levels of GDP growth over a three-year period do not prove that Georgia's economy is sufficiently viable to support a modern state. Even after economic growth resumed in 1995 and 1996, the earnings of an estimated 70 percent of the Georgian population put them below the minimum subsistence level.[70] The industrial infrastructure destroyed during the years of civil war has not been rebuilt, and most of Georgia's economy is now based on the agricultural and service sectors. Outside aid from Western countries and international relief organizations has been crucial in preventing humanitarian disaster,[71] while Georgia's inability to provide for its energy needs has resulted in widespread rationing of electricity and heat.

As was true elsewhere in the CIS, the financial collapse of 1998 exacerbated the existing problems enormously. The *lari* was devalued in early December 1998, and the government began to warn that it will have difficulty making pension and other state social payments because of revenue shortfall and a budgetary crisis, which President Shevardnadze has blamed on corruption and the inability of the state to perform basic functions such as tax collection.[72] Georgia's economy remains in a disastrous state from its early years of independence; despite the West's optimistic view of Georgia's economic reforms, it will take decades for the country to build a modern economy after its Soviet past and destructive civil wars.[73]

Georgia's principal hope for economic prosperity in the foreseeable future lies in oil transport and trade. Georgia lobbied hard for the Baku-Ceyhan routing of an oil pipeline out of the Caspian basin, because this would run through Georgia, but as world oil prices continued to deflate throughout 1998, the likelihood that it might quickly be built diminished.

The Azerbaijan International Oil Company (AIOC), a consortium of international oil companies that has the concession to ship oil from Azerbaijan's Chirag oil field, has also shown increasing reluctance to invest the billions of dollars necessary to build a pipeline along this potentially expensive route, because the oil reserves promised in the Caspian have not yet materialized. The Baku-Supsa pipeline that has just opened will provide Georgia some revenue, but not in such quantities as to be a panacea for the Georgian economy. The development of a Eurasian trade corridor offers Georgia a better chance for earning transit income.[74]

The Transport Corridor Europe Caucasus Asia project (TRA-CECA) to create a new "Great Silk Road"—which is supported by the EU, IMF, World Bank, most CIS countries and Mongolia—has the long-term potential to bring Georgia substantial trade revenue and investment. Georgia's immediate economic problems, however, are short-term and pressing. In the next few years Georgia must either strengthen itself to take control of the shadow economy, to collect taxes, and to provide a decent standard of living for its citizens, or it will become increasingly vulnerable to internal and regional forces of instability.

Georgia's foreign policy since independence has been oriented almost exclusively toward the West. Georgia refused to join the CIS when it was created in 1991, preferring to go its own way, with as much help from the West as it could get. Unlike Ukraine, however, which pursued similar goals, Georgia was prevented by its internal instability from establishing contacts with NATO and key Western nations. Georgia gained membership in the OSCE and entered the Council of Europe in March 1999, only the fourth CIS state to do so (after Moldova, Russia, and Ukraine).

Georgia's desire to distance itself from Russia and the CIS did not mean that Russia was interested in distancing itself from Georgia. While Moscow has not always pursued a consistent policy toward the Caucasus in general, Russia has been a major and a persistent influence on Georgia. Russia's interests in Georgia were several; its boundaries with NATO-member Turkey make it an important part of Russia's near-abroad, while the country's proximity to the Caspian and a possible southern route for trans-Eurasian trade give it considerable geopolitical importance for Russia. Russia has seen Georgia's independent foreign policy and its refusal to join the CIS as dangerous examples for other new states, and it wanted the right to station troops in Georgia, just as it wanted the right to do so elsewhere.

It has not always been clear in Georgia which actions are the result of Russian policy and which are the result of undisciplined decisions made by Russian troops stationed in or near Georgia. Locally stationed Russian forces clearly intervened in the civil war on the side of the Abkhazians, probably with some encouragement from persons higher up in the chain of command.[75] Local Russian commanders have also benefited personally from the flow of arms to both sides. The Russian commanders in the region have little reason to love Georgia in general, and most are actively hostile to Shevardnadze, whom they consider to have been a leading architect, along with Gorbachev, of the collapse of the USSR.[76]

Russia's use of military and economic assistance to coerce Georgia into the CIS was more deliberate. In October 1993, when Georgia was about to collapse under the combined pressure of the Abkhaz offensive and the advances in western Georgia of Gamsakhurdia's rebels, Shevardnadze had no other choice but to appeal to Russia for help. He announced immediately Georgia's intention to join the CIS, and a few months later, in February 1994, signed a comprehensive military agreement providing Russia with three military bases, the right to put Russian troops on those bases, as well as the right to station Russian peacekeepers in Abkhazia and Russian border guards on Georgia's external borders,[77] and the free transit of all of these troops and their support material through Georgian territory. Russia later added the right to have two more bases and access to other facilities. In return, Russia promised to provide economic assistance and to find a solution to the Abkhaz problem. Georgia made these military agreements conditional upon the return of refugees to Abkhazia, but as the refugee problem remains unresolved, Georgian military treaties with Russia have been initialed but have not been ratified by the Georgian parliament.

However, Russia has failed to control Abkhazian secessionists and the volatile situation in the North Caucasus more generally. It is not clear whether the persistent refugee problem represents a choice or a failure on Russia's part, but it has angered and disappointed the Georgian leadership,[78] which has begun to use this failure as grounds on which to take back some of the military advantages that Russia had wrung from them. Georgia has successfully insisted on taking back control over portions of its external border with Turkey, and as a result of negotiations in January 1998, the Russians have agreed to return ten military sites to Georgia that were not covered by earlier agreements.

Russia's fiscal and military weakness, its internal problems and many distractions elsewhere as well as President Shevardnadze's skills as a negotiator have meant that Georgia has increasingly been able to avoid being locked into a single bilateral relationship. Russia remains an important influence in Georgia, but in the past two or three years, Georgia has also been able to increase substantially its cooperation with NATO and with key Western countries on military and defense issues.[79] Russian-Georgian relations have begun to develop a pattern of periods of intense Russian pressure followed by a slackening of interest, which allows Georgia to increase its activity in other directions.

Georgia has actively pursued regional and bilateral partnerships with other CIS states and has used its position as a player in Caspian pipeline politics and the proposed Eurasian Corridor to strengthen bilateral relations, especially with Azerbaijan, Uzbekistan, Ukraine, and Moldova (all GUUAM states) as well as with some of the Western powers, particularly with Turkey and with the United States.

Georgia is benefiting from the inability of Russia's diverse set of foreign policy actors, including Russian forces stationed in Georgia, to decide what Russia's policy toward the state is to be. If Russia tries to encourage Georgia to become a more unitary state, it will destroy its ties to the separatists, which have proven valuable in the past and may also in the future; conversely, if Russia continues to stimulate the separatists, this might destabilize not only Georgia, but the entire Caucasian region. It is also possible that Russia is no longer in a position to carry out any policy, even if its leaders and foreign policy establishment were able to decide upon one.

Having the major foreign influence upon it prove so weak, however, does not make Georgia strong. Georgian foreign policy strategies are not able to compensate enough for the country's fundamental internal and external problems to be able to provide the political and economic stability and territorial integrity that Georgia needs to be able to sustain an active foreign policy well beyond its immediate region. Georgia's problems are such that it remains becalmed between traditional dependency on Moscow and a more active role in the world, with little on the horizon to suggest that it could be pushed deeper into dependency or escape it entirely. Georgians have spoken strongly of defending their independence and their territorial integrity, but limited resources have forced them to be exceedingly cautious about actions that might turn such words into deeds. Their hopes for economic transformation may also prove to be mere rhetoric, if other forces continue to make Caspian oil too expensive to be worth building pipelines through Georgia to transport it to market. This condition—of being caught partway between Russia and the outer world—is a dilemma confronting many of the CIS states.

COMMON FEATURES

As these four studies suggest, one of the most curious features of the CIS is that its failure has affected its member states equally, no matter whether they had wished the organization to become a success, as is true of Kazakhstan and Kyrgyzstan, or had viewed it as an evil that they would avoid as best they could, as is true of Ukraine and Georgia. None of the states has been able to achieve the free trade among the members that all seem to have considered a potential benefit of the CIS. Those states wishing to achieve the assurance of mutual security have been left at risk by the failure of the CIS to provide it, while those states hoping to find their security guarantees elsewhere have proven vulnerable to the destabilizing intrusions of such military capabilities as still remain in the CIS.

Even the states that have been most successful in enlisting the support of international lenders or the interest of foreign investors, such as Kyrgyzstan and Kazakhstan, respectively, have also discovered that the resources of the outside world are insufficient to solve the dizzying mountains of problems that they each face. Many of these states have also discovered that Western financial and military assistance also has a price, just like that supplied by the CIS or any of its members. Few of the CIS states have been able or willing to change their national practices enough to fully satisfy the conditions of lenders like the IMF and the World Bank, and they are beginning to understand that even the most generous loans, from the most sympathetic lenders, nevertheless accrue interest and must be repaid.

The problems that the CIS was created to solve were real, and remain so, but the impulse to solve them through an umbrella organization like the CIS was a reflex from the Soviet period, which had only just ended. For seven decades the Soviet government had not only made a fetish of unity and unanimity, but had further taught that disagreement with the "one truth" was not only an error, but a dangerous threat to the whole of society. By 1991 most of the leaders of the post-Soviet states must certainly have lost their illusions about the "one truth" that the Bolsheviks had promulgated, but their instincts probably remained that there must still be a single solution, which they all should share, no matter how different their dimensions, populations, geographical locations, histories, and aspirations.

The new states were also aware from the beginning, however, that the differences among them were real, because the nature of each of the states was unique. As this study has shown, the degree to which the leaders at independence understood the unique characteristics, and therefore the unique national interests, of their new states varied from country to country. Since independence, however, all the new states have been ascending a steep learning curve as they discover the various ways in which the CIS and the international community alike are unable to serve fully the particular needs of each. More than any other single cause, it was probably this growing self-awareness of the member states that doomed the CIS as a workable organization. At the same time, however, the process of trying to make the CIS fit has forced each of the states to understand its own needs and interests better and to seek other ways of meeting them.

NOTES

[1] For a statement by Nazarbayev on the Customs Union, see *ITAR-TASS*, September 3, 1998, as translated in *FBIS Daily Report*, SOV-98-246, September 4, 1998. For his statement in strong support of CIS integration, see *Interfax*, December 25, 1998, in *FBIS Daily Report*, SOV-98-359, December 29, 1998.

[2] Kazakhstan received $1.65 billion in World Bank loans between 1992 and 1998 and $500 million in IMF loans between 1993 and 1998. *ITAR-TASS*, June 26, 1998; *Jamestown Monitor*, June 3, 1998.

[3] Nursultan Nazarbayev, *Piat let nezavisimosti: iz dokladov, vystuplenii i statei Prezidenta Respubliki Kazakhstan* (Almaty, Kazakhstan: 1996).

[4] President Nazarbayev announced the move to Akmola in September 1995. The government moved to its new home on December 8, 1997, and a ceremonial opening for the capital was held on June 10, 1998. Nazarbayev changed the name of the city from Akmola to Astana, which means "capital" in Kazakh, in May 1998.

[5] This figure represents total foreign direct investment from 1995 through the first quarter of 1998. International Monetary Fund, *International Financial Statistics* (Washington, D.C.: International Monetary Fund, January 1999), p. 916.

[6] World Bank, *World Development Report: Knowledge for Development* (New York: Oxford University Press, 1999).

[7] Nursultan Nazarbayev, "Kazakhstan-2030: Protsvetanie, bezopasnost, i uluchshenie blagosostoianiia vsekh Kazakhstantsev," *Kazakhstanskaia Pravda*, October 11, 1997.

[8] UNDP Regional Bureau for Europe and the CIS, *Poverty in Transition?* (New York: UNDP, 1998), p. 212.

[9] Martha Brill Olcott, *The Kazakhs*, 2nd Edition (Stanford: Hoover Institution Press, 1995), pp. 252–3; *Alma-Ata 1986* (Alma-Ata: Altyn Orda, 1991).

[10] We are using Almaty instead of Alma Ata for consistency. Alma Ata was formally renamed Almaty on May 13, 1993.

[11] This figure comes from the last Soviet census in 1989, as printed in *Soiuz*, no. 32 (August 1990).

[12] See Statement of Kazakhstan's "state identity," as printed in *Kazakhstanskaia Pravda*, May 29, 1996, p. 3, and Nazarbayev, *Piat let nezavisimosti: iz dokladov, vystuplenii i statei Prezidenta Respubliki Kazakhstan*.

[13] Only political parties with broad national and ethnic support could contest seats on the basis of party lists. Martha Brill Olcott, "Democratization and the Growth of Political Participation in Kazakhstan," in Karen Dawisha and Bruce Parrott, eds., *Conflict, Cleavage, and Change in Central Asia and the Caucasus* (Cambridge, U.K.: Cambridge University Press, 1997), p. 220.

[14] The party is named after the mythic founder of the Kazakh people.

[15] Sergei Irikeev, "Ural'skoe kazachestvo v Kazakhstane: vzgliad atamana," and Aleksandr Alekseenko, "Vostochno-Kazakhstan-skaia *oblast:* novoe Kazachestvo," in Galina Vitkovskaia and Alexei Malashenko, eds., *Vozrozhdenie kazachestva: nadezhdy i opaseniia* (Moscow: Carnegie Endowment for International Peace, 1998), pp. 171–4, 175–81.

[16] By 1996 Cossacks were allowed to wear uniforms in public and to sponsor meetings and other organized activities.

[17] In eight of the nine *oblasts* along Kazakhstan's border with Russia, the population in the northern parts is almost 90 percent non-Kazakh. *Karavan,* July 22, 1994, p. 4.

[18] International Monetary Fund, *Direction of Trade Statistics Yearbook: 1998* (Washington, D.C.: International Monetary Fund, 1998), p. 276 and p. 383.

[19] Martha Brill Olcott, *Central Asia's New States: Independence, Foreign Policy, and Regional Security* (Washington, D.C.: United States Institute of Peace Press, 1996), p. 72.

[20] Author's personal communication with former Kazakh government officials.

[21] Legislation passed in 1989 made Kazakh the official language of the republic, although the law would not take effect in the most heavily Russian areas for fifteen years. A new language law was passed in 1997, extending the date by which all citizens would be expected to function in Kazakh to January 1, 2006. This law purported to put Russian on an equal footing with Kazakh through such provisions as requiring both languages to be used in the armed forces, police, and security services. Russians worry, however, about provisions of the law that allow Kazakh proficiency tests to be given to applicants for certain administrative, managerial, and service-sector posts and which require at least half of all television and radio broadcasts to be in Kazakh. For more information on the effect of these language laws, see William Fierman, "Formulation of Identity in Kazakhstan's Language Policy Documents 1987–1997," paper presented at the annual meeting of the AAASS, November 1997.

[22] This agreement streamlined procedures by which citizens of one country moving to the other country could gain citizenship in the second country. It also decided the legal status of citizens of one country who permanently reside in the other.

[23] Consumer price inflation was 90.9 percent in 1991, 15,130 percent in 1992, 1,571 percent in 1993, 1,880 percent in 1994, and 176 percent in 1995. Industrial production declined by 0.8 percent in 1991, 13.8 percent in 1992, 16 percent in 1993, 28.5 percent in 1994, and 7.9 percent in 1995. *Economist Intelligence Unit Country Reports, Kazakhstan*, November 29, 1996, August 21, 1996, and June 10, 1994. GDP decreased by 11 percent in 1991, 5.3 percent in 1992, 10.6 percent in 1993, 12.6 percent in 1994, and 8.2 percent in 1995. International Monetary Fund, *World Economic Outlook*, May 1998 (Washington, D.C.: International Monetary Fund, 1998), p. 155.

[24] Author's personal communication with an IMF official.

[25] Between the inception of the privatization program in 1992 and the third quarter of 1998, almost 85 percent of small enterprises were privatized, as were 11 percent of medium-sized enterprises and close to 5 percent of large enterprises. European Commission, *Kazakhstan Economic Trends*, Third Quarter 1998, (Brussels, Belgium: European Commission, 1998), p. 178.

[26] Balgimbaev was appointed minister of oil and gas in October 1994, and in March 1997, after the ministry was dissolved, was appointed head of the state oil company, Kazakhoil. He had earlier worked to attract Chevron's investment in Kazakhstan's huge Tengiz oil field and had even studied at Chevron headquarters in the United States.

[27] Trans World's holdings in Kazakhstan include Pavlodarskii Aluminum plant, the Soklovskii-Sarbaiskii mining-and-dressing combine, and the Kazkhrom holding company, incorporating the Donskoi mining-and-dressing combine. Beket Aubakirov and Nataliia Gotova, "Kazakh Industry Minus Comrade Mette," *RusData Dia-Line-BizEcon News*, March 16, 1996.

[28] The CPC includes Russia with 24 percent interest, Kazakhstan with 19 percent, Oman with 7 percent, Chevron with 15 percent, Mobil Oil with 7.5 percent, Oryz with 1.75 percent, Russian-American Lukarco (a partnership of Lukoil and ARCO) with 12.5 percent, Russian-British Rosneft-Shell Caspian Ventures with 7.5 percent, Agip with 2 percent, British Gas with 2 percent, and Kazakhoil-Amoco with 1.75 percent. *Interfax Petroleum Report*, March 27–April 3, 1998.

[29] In November 1997 Kazakhstan signed a production sharing agreement setting up the multinational Offshore Kazakhstan International Operating Company (OKIOC) to explore Kazakhstan's Caspian Sea shelf. The consortium included Italy's Agip, British Gas

International (including BP and Statoil), Mobil, Shell, and Total. In September 1998 Kazakhstan sold its share of the consortium to U.S.-based Phillips Petroleum and Intex of Japan. Kazakhstan will continue to profit from the consortium, however, through taxes, royalties, and bonuses.

[30] Formed in 1998, the Karachaganak Oil and Gas Production Company consortium includes British Gas with 32.5 percent and Italy's Agip with 32.5 percent, Texaco with 20 percent, and Lukoil with 15 percent. *Interfax*, "Oil & Gas Report for 12–18 February 1999," in *FBIS Daily Report*, SOV-1999-0210, February 12, 1999. An agreement was reached with Gazprom in late 1998 allowing for the modernization of the gas refinery in Orenburg, Russia, so that it could refine gas condensate from the Karachaganak field. *ITAR-TASS*, November 24, 1998, in *FBIS Daily Report*, SOV-98-328, November 30, 1998.

[31] CPC head Viktor Fedotov said in October 1998 that plans were being made to ship oil to Astrakhan through an existing pipeline, thus providing funding for a stepped up construction schedule of the CPC-sponsored pipeline from Kazakhstan to the Black Sea. The first tanker is to sail from a new port near Novorossiisk on June 30, 2001. *Interfax*, October 14, 1998. A later report cited Kazakh Prime Minister Nurlan Balgimbaev as predicting that the pipeline would be ready even earlier, by the year 2000. Reuters, "Big Kazakh Oil Projects 'Moving Fine,'" *Russia Today*, September 15, 1998.

[32] In 1992 Kazakhstan's exports to Russia equaled 71.03 percent of its total exports, and imports from Russia came to 72.42 percent of its total imports. In 1993 these figures were 69.66 percent and 70.91 percent, respectively. They came to 44.40 percent and 39.52 percent for 1994, 42.27 percent and 49.05 percent for 1995, 44.47 percent and 54.97 percent for 1996, and 33.88 percent and 45.98 percent in 1997. Figures for 1992 and 1993 from calculations based on figures in *Europa World Yearbook 1997*, Vol. II (London: Europa Publications Limited, 1997). Remaining figures from "Republic of Kazakhstan: Recent Economic Developments," IMF Staff Country Report No. 98/84 (August 1998).

[33] The WTO has established a working party to consider Kazakhstan's bid for accession, and bilateral negotiations with members are being held.

34 Net out-migration of Russians from Kazakhstan between 1992 and 1996 totaled 710,000: 923,000 Russians left the country during this period, while only 213,000 Russians moved in. Galina Vitkovskaia, "Emigratsiia netitul'novo naseleniia iz Kazakhstana, Kyrgyzstana i Uzbekistana," unpublished manuscript, p. 14.

35 Aleksandra Dokuchaeva of the Lad movement is one of the most prominent nationalists to have left Kazakhstan. She now lives in Russia.

36 Petr Svoik, leader of the Azamat Opposition Movement, was detained and arraigned in October 1998 on charges of slander, inciting national conflict, and insulting an official. *Interfax*, October 30, 1998, in *FBIS Daily Report*, SOV-98-303, November 3, 1998. Earlier that year, he, along with former prime minister and presidential hopeful Akezhan Kazhegeldin, had been charged with minor offenses connected with the two leaders' involvement in a gathering of organizations called "For Free Elections." *Interfax*, October 14, 1998, in *FBIS Daily Report*, SOV-98-287, October 15, 1998.

37 One such group was the Akmola, Karaganda, and Kokchetau Cossacks' regional organization called "Union of Cossacks of the Steppe Region." *Economist Intelligence Unit Country Reports, Kazakhstan*, February 28, 1997.

38 In 1997 the Kazakhs sold the Chinese Petroleum company a 60 percent stake in the lucrative Uzen oil field, which is second in size only to the Tengiz field. *ITAR-TASS*, September 24, 1997, in *FBIS Daily Report*, SOV-97-267, September 24, 1997.

39 In addition Kyrgyzstan's population consisted of 1.5 percent Ukrainian, 1.2 percent Tatar, 1.0 percent Dungan, and the rest consisted of nationalities that comprise less than 1 percent of the population. See Ainura Elebaeva and Nurbek Omuraliev, "Mezhetnicheskie Otnosheniia v Kyrgyzstane: Dinamika i tendentsii razuitiia," *Tsentralnaia Aziia*, no. 15, 1999.

40 Olcott, *Central Asia's New States*, pp. 42–3, 53.

41 Adrian Karatnycky, Alexander Motyl, and Charles Graybow, eds., *Nations in Transition 1998: Civil Society, Democracy and Markets in East Central Europe and the Newly Independent States* (New York: Freedom House, 1999), pp. 324–5.

42 Ibid; Olcott, *Central Asia's New States*, pp. 17–8, 91–7.

43 The university was opened on September 9, 1993, at a ceremony attended by President Akaev and the ministers of foreign affairs

and education of Russia and Kyrgyzstan. The countries assumed "dual responsibility" for the university, and it was registered with each country's Ministry of Education as a state university.

[44] By April 1997, 80.4 percent of industry had been privatized, 56.8 percent of construction, 51.2 percent of transportation, and the general level of privatization had reached 62.9 percent. As published on the Internet website of the Inter-State Statistics Committee (www.mek.ru/archive/issues/economic/1/p6.htm).

[45] According to Kabar News Agency, April 5, 1999, the staff of the office of the prime minister has been reduced by 12 percent.

[46] International Monetary Fund, "Kyrgyz Republic: Recent Economic Developments," IMF Staff Country Report No. 98/8, (Washington, D.C.: International Monetary Fund, January 1998).

[47] *RFE/RL Newsline*, January 19, 1999.

[48] On July 17, 1999, Russia and Kyrgyzstan signed agreements on cooperation in border issues, on the procedure for transferring sections of the state border that were guarded by the Russian Federal Border Service to Kyrgyzstan, and on a protocol on the conditions, procedures for acceptance, and training of servicemen of the Ministry of Defense of the Kyrgyz Republic in the higher education establishments of the Russian Federal Border Service. *BBC Summary of World Broadcasts*, "Kyrgyzstan, Russia Sign Border Agreements," July 19, 1999.

[49] Constantine Michalopoulos and David Tarr, eds., "The Economics of Customs Unions in the Commonwealth of Independent States," *Post-Soviet Geography and Economics*, vol. 38, no. 3 (1997), pp. 128–32.

[50] Mekhman Gafarly, "Kirgiziia perezhivaet daleko ne luchshie vremena," *Nezavisimaia gazeta*, February 3, 1999.

[51] Sherman W. Garnett, *Keystone in the Arch: Ukraine in the Emerging Security Environment of Central and Eastern Europe*, (Washington, D.C.: Carnegie Endowment for International Peace, 1997).

[52] He was born on January 10, 1934, in the village of Velyky Zhytyn, Rivne *oblast*.

[53] Elections were held March 27, 1994, with repeat by-elections on a continuing basis. As of August 1994, 393 deputies had been elected to the 450-member parliament. Among them 216 were independent, 91 Communists, 21 members of the Ukrainian Peasant Party, and 13 Socialists. *Interfax*, August 8, 1994.

[54] In the first round of the Ukrainian presidential election on June 26, 1994, Leonid Kravchuk captured 37.68 percent of the vote; Leonid Kuchma, 31.3 percent. In the second round on July 10, 1994, Kravchuk received 45.1 percent and Kuchma received 52.2 percent. Kuchma received on average 65.2 percent of the vote in the heavier populated eastern Ukraine, while Kravchuk received 78.0 percent of the west's vote. It is interesting to note that Kravchuk received more than 90 percent of the vote in such nationalist strongholds as Ivano-Frankivsk, Lviv, and Ternopyl *oblasts,* while Kuchma got 89.7 percent of the vote in Crimea and 91.9 percent in Sevastopol. Compiled based on data from the Internet website of the International Foundation for Electoral Systems (IFES) (http://ifes.ipri.kiev.ua/Elections94/Presidential/).

[55] The nationalist issue did not hold much political capital in the central *oblasts* of Ukraine, where neither candidate received more than 60 percent of the vote in the second round. For a discussion of the voting patterns of the central belt of eight *oblasts* that do not fit easily into the stereotypical view of either half of Ukraine, see Garnett, *Keystone in the Arch,* p. 19.

[56] There was some reluctance in Ukraine to becoming a non-nuclear state. This wavering can be attributed to Ukraine's aversion to handing its nuclear weapons over to Russia, the very country from which it had gained independence, rather than to a desire to maintain its status as a nuclear state. Ukraine preferred destroying its nuclear arsenal on site with international assistance over placing them under Russia's control. The seeming reluctance to rid his country of nuclear arms was also an expression of former Ukrainian President Kravchuk's tactic of using nuclear weapons as a bargaining point to obtain security assurances and financial compensation from the West. Ukraine signed the Trilateral Agreement in January 1994, and then the Non-Proliferation of Nuclear Weapons Treaty (NPT) in October 1994, only after the United States formally linked Ukraine's disarmament with its broader economic and security concerns. For a discussion of the negotiations leading up to Ukraine's signing of the Trilateral Agreement and NPT, see Garnett, *Keystone in the Arch,* pp. 113–24; Bohdan Nahaylo, "The Shaping of Ukrainian Attitudes on Nukes: Part II," *Ukrainian Weekly,* April 25, 1993, p. 2.

[57] In September 1997, newly elected Moldovan president Petru Lucinschi made an unofficial visit to Crimea, where he asked Kuchma

to take a more active role in settling the Transdniestr conflict. A formal decision to send Ukrainian peacekeepers was made on March 20, 1998, at an Odessa meeting of the leaders of Moldova and Transdniestr, mediated by Kuchma and former Russian Prime Minister Viktor Chernomyrdin. *Interfax*, August 26, 1998. In July 1999 Moldova and Ukraine agreed to set up a joint peacekeeping battalion in Transdniestr. *Interfax*, July 21, 1999.

[58] The document provides for NATO-Ukraine consultations to be held periodically within the framework of the North Atlantic Council, NATO committees, military partnership mechanisms, and bilateral meetings among top military leaders of NATO countries and their Ukrainian counterparts. A Ukrainian military liaison mission will be added to Ukraine's political mission to NATO. *Jamestown Monitor*, July 10, 1997.

[59] *RFE/RL Newsline*, April 28, 1999; October 9, 1998; August 31, 1998. *Interfax*, March 30, 1999.

[60] Former Georgian president Zviad Gamsakhurdia was forced to flee Georgia in January 1992 after forces led by Jaba Ioselani and Tengiz Kitovani took power in Tbilisi and declared a new government led by a Military Council. On March 10 the Military Council transferred its powers to a State Council led by Eduard Shevardnadze, who had returned to Georgia on March 7, 1992. Shevardnadze was popularly elected chairman of the State Council with a reported 95 percent of the electorate supporting him on October 11, 1992.

[61] Georgia, Kazakhstan, and Belarus have been commonly seen as the basic building blocks of Russia's CIS strategy and as states of vital interest to Russia on account of their strategic location, historical ties, and presumed common interests with Moscow. An early and influential statement of this view is found in "Strategiia dlia Rossii," a report of the Foreign and Defense Council, published in *Nezavisimaia gazeta*, August 19, 1992. See especially section 2.3.9.

[62] "Georgian Leader Insists He'll Stay Put," *Houston Chronicle*, September 18, 1991.

[63] *Europa World Year Book 1997* (London: Europa Publications Limited, 1997), p. 1384.

[64] Aslan Abashidze is immensely popular as the leader of Adjar Republic and is considered a key challenger to Shevardnadze in

the next round of presidential elections. He claims to be a descendant of an ancient and famous family of Georgian rulers and his grandfather Memed Abashidze is a national hero of Georgia recognized for being the chairman of the first Adjar parliament as well as a defender of Georgians against the Turks.

[65] Estimates vary, but during the South Ossetian conflict, thousands were killed and as many as 28,000 people became refugees. In Abkhazia, almost the entire ethnic Georgian population of the region fled from the fighting. At present, there are 270,000 ethnic Georgian refugees from the Abkhaz conflict, most of whom live in Georgia in substandard conditions. Roughly 20,000 civilians were killed in the Georgian-Abkhaz war. [Unpublished data provided by the United Nations High Commission for Refugees (UNHCR) office in Tbilisi.]

[66] Eighty-three United Nations observers from twenty-one countries are currently stationed in Georgia under the auspices of UNOMIG (UN Observer Mission). International Institute for Strategic Studies, *The Military Balance 1998–1999* (London: International Institute for Strategic Studies, 1998).

[67] As recently as late May 1998, fighting broke out in the Abkhazian Gali region between Georgian and Abkhaz forces. As a result, 30,000 ethnic Georgians fled Abkhazia after having already been repatriated. *RFE/RL Caucasus Report*, May 26, 1998, Volume 1, no. 13.

[68] Ministry of the Economy of Georgia, "Georgia: Economic and Social Challenges of the Transition," Vladimir Papava and Elene Chikovani, eds. Reprinted in edited form in *Problems of Economic Transition*, vol. 40, no. 7/8 (November/December 1997), p. 5.

[69] *EBRD Transition Report 1998* (press release). Tables 3.1, 3.3.

[70] *Europa World Yearbook 1997* (London: Europe Publications Limited, 1997), p. 1388.

[71] In 1996, foreign aid made up 7.1 percent of Georgian GDP. World Bank, *World Development Indicators 1998* (Washington, D.C.: World Bank, 1998.), p. 342.

[72] Eduard Shevardnadze, remarks broadcast on *Tbilisi Radio Network*, December 7, 1998, as translated in *FBIS Daily Report*, SOV-98-341.

[73] The EBRD predicted a 9 percent rate of GDP growth for Georgia in 1998, while the Economic Commission for Europe estimated GDP growth at roughly 8.9 percent. *Economic Commission for*

Europe, Economic Survey of Europe 1998 No.3 (New York: United Nations, 1998); *EBRD Transition Report 1998* (London: European Bank for Reconstruction and Development, 1998). These figures can be misleading; given Georgia's small size and war-torn economy, small improvements can have a sizable effect on GDP.

74 A pipeline to transport oil from the Azeri port of Baku to Turkey's Ceyhan port has long been a goal of U.S. and Turkish diplomacy, as such a route would further U.S. strategic goals by avoiding Russia and Iran as well as providing economic benefits to Turkey. The Baku-Ceyhan route has been estimated to cost anywhere from $3 billion to $4 billion, making the transport cost of oil per barrel $2.80. As a result of the cost of this route, the lack of proven reserves, and the decline in world oil prices, the future of a Baku-Ceyhan route remains in doubt. Importantly, a pipeline from Baku to Georgia's Black Sea port of Supsa with a transportation cost of only $1.90 per barrel has been renovated and became operational in the spring of 1999. This pipeline lacks the capacity of the proposed Baku-Ceyhan route, although its existence takes some of the immediacy out of the need to make a final choice over Baku-Ceyhan.

75 Dodge Billingsley, "Georgian-Abkhazian Security Issues," *Jane's Intelligence Review*, February 1996, pp. 65–8. Billingsley provides a careful review of the evidence of Russian intervention on behalf of the Abkhazians, arguing that it never reached either the coordination or the level commonly assumed on the Georgian side. On the other hand, the nature of the conflict—especially the relatively small size of the opposing forces—meant that small interventions, even by a few tanks or planes, could have an important impact.

76 Ghia Nodia, "The Conflict in Abkhazia: National Projects and Political Circumstances," in Bruno Coppieters, Ghia Nodia, and Yuri Anchabadze, eds., *Georgians and Abkhazians* (Cologne, Germany: Bundesinstitut fur ostwissenschaftliche und internationale Studien, 1998), pp. 38–40.

77 Although estimates vary, according to figures of the International Institute for Strategic Studies, in 1998 there were approximately 9,200 Russian troops and 1,500 Russian peacekeepers stationed in Georgia. Russia also maintains five military bases in Vaziani, Akhalkalaki, Akhaltsykhe, Batumi, and Gudauta. These figures do not account for the number of Russian border guards in Georgia,

although these are now being withdrawn to the Northern Caucasus.

[78] "Georgia Bridles at Russia's Heavy Hand," *International Herald Tribune,* January 14, 1997.

[79] On July 20, 1999, Georgia's parliament agreed to President Eduard Shevardnadze's plan to send a platoon of Georgian peacekeepers to Kosovo under NATO command. The twenty-man unit is Georgia's first to have been specially trained for participating in NATO-led operations. France and Turkey have both offered to include the Georgian unit in their Kosovo contingents.

5
Regional Alternatives
to the CIS

The overall failure of the CIS to coalesce as a political, economic, or security organization has led its members, including Russia, to seek both bilateral and regional ways to achieve the goals that they had hoped to achieve through the CIS but could not. As the previous chapters have shown, the enormous disproportionality between Russia and even the next biggest new state has meant that the dynamics of many of those bilateral relationships have tended to duplicate those of the CIS, as Russia and its various partners jockey to get as many advantages from one another as they can, while keeping the price that they must pay for them to a minimum.

To a certain extent this replication of the tensions of the CIS is also true of regional organizations that include Russia, as the discussion of the Customs Union that follows in this chapter will show. Nonetheless, the failure of the CIS, the recognition that several of the CIS states share regional interests, and the difficulty inherent in trying to offset the enormous disproportionate advantage that Russia enjoys, have prompted some of the CIS states to begin banding together to seek alternative ways to solve their problems that require neither the total solidarity of the CIS nor the total isolation of full neutrality. Three important organizations have emerged as a result. Two of these organizations—the Central Asian Economic Community and the GUUAM group—do not include Russia, and so implicitly serve as a counterbalance to Russia and Russian interests.

Unlike the CIS or Russia's bilateral agreements, where Russia exerts a greater influence than others, the third important organization, the Customs Union, officially treats Russia as a partner equal to the other member states. These regional initiatives are important

because they act simultaneously as a mechanism for greater cooperation and as an impetus for redefining the post-Soviet space in ways
that derive more from common needs and goals, and less from the
inertia of history. These regional groups give their member states
experience in negotiation and cooperation, while simultaneously
allowing them to articulate better their national interests than the
initial CIS structures did; that experience will presumably grow
more important as the CIS itself continues to unravel.

This chapter begins with analyses of the Central Asian Economic
Community and the GUUAM group, which are the two most extensive attempts at regional cooperation that do not include Russia. It
concludes with an analysis of the Customs Union and the Russian-
Belarusian Union, which have the most ambitious political and economic agendas of any of the post-Soviet organizations. These two
in tandem intend to create an integrated core of states that, at least
some of its participants hope, will prove to be so desirable that other
post-Soviet states would wish to join.

THE CENTRAL ASIAN ECONOMIC COMMUNITY[1]

The national communities in Central Asia have a stronger sense of
common ancestry and of shared cultural and religious heritage than
do any other peoples of the former Soviet Union, but these sensibilities have also bred competition. Each of the Central Asian presidents
dreams of being the preeminent figure in the region, and each is
able to reconstruct the history of his people in a way that furthers
such claims. Nevertheless, nearly a decade after independence, the
Central Asian states remain closely connected economically, and
diaspora populations of each of the other states' ethnic groups are
found in all the states of the region.

Much has been written in Russia and the West about the potential
instability of the states of this region.[2] The Central Asian leaders
and the people of the region share such concerns, for they are aware
of the region's many potential flashpoints, where the risk of intercommunal violence is real—in the Fergana Valley, which is shared
by Uzbekistan, Tajikistan, and Kyrgyzstan; along the Tajikistan-
Uzbekistan border; along the Amu Darya, a river shared by Turkmenistan and Uzbekistan; and near the Aral Sea, which is bordered
both by Kazakhstan and Uzbekistan. It should be noted, however,

that the Central Asians' own concerns about the potential for conflict has kept most of these flashpoints from igniting. Apart from some clashes in 1989 and 1990, Central Asia has so far managed to keep most of its potential conflicts under control. The one exception is the civil war that has ravaged Tajikistan since 1991, but self-discipline on the part of other Central Asian states has kept it from flaring into an international or multiethnic conflict.[3]

Mutual concern about the potential for conflict, as well as a sense of shared interest, prompted the Central Asian leaders to begin working together even before the Soviet Union collapsed. The republic leaders established an interrepublic working group in June 1990; the main topic for the group was the management of the region's water resources and hydroelectric system, but the meeting occurred at the same time as the violent clashes that broke out between the Uzbeks and Kyrgyz of Osh *oblast*, in the Kyrgyz Republic.[4]

It was as the CIS was failing to coalesce into a functioning multilateral organization that the Central Asian leaders began to see the growing need for an institution that would permit them to strengthen the relations between the states of the region. The idea of a Turko-Asiatic Union was first brought up at a Bishkek summit of Central Asian leaders in April 1992. In January 1993 the Central Asian states went one step further, signing a communiqué affirming the existing Soviet-era borders and agreeing to establish diplomatic relations and embassies within the region. They also agreed to pursue a policy aimed at creating a Central Asian common market, to establish an interrepublic Coordinating Council, and to exchange government representatives to coordinate joint activities.[5]

Participants agreed that this communiqué was a necessary first step, but no more than that. As the Central Asian states attempted to contain the unfolding civil war in Tajikistan, they became more dependent upon Russia, just at a time when most of the states were trying to find ways to cut Russia's influence. None of the states wished to give Russia the opportunity to take actions unilaterally. At the same time, however, each of the Central Asian states saw different degrees of urgency in such undertakings; the leaders of Kazakhstan, Uzbekistan, and Kyrgyzstan have from the beginning been more interested in finding ways to cooperate than have the leaders of the other two states.

On May 28, 1993, the presidents of Kazakhstan, Kyrgyzstan, and Uzbekistan held a ceremony at Ordobasy Hill, in Kazakhstan, to celebrate Central Asian unity. In 1726 three Kazakh elders had met on the same hill to launch a unified campaign against the invading Dzhungars. At the ceremony, Kazakh President Nazarbayev explained that his Uzbek and Kyrgyz counterparts had been invited as honored guests because Uzbek and Kyrgyz tribes had joined those three eighteenth century elders in their fight.[6]

A more substantive attempt at modern unity was begun in January 1994, when the leaders of Uzbekistan, Kazakhstan, and Kyrgyzstan agreed to make a "common economic space" of their three countries. In July 1994 they called for the creation of an interstate council (of presidents and prime ministers), a permanent executive committee to regulate affairs between council sittings, and an interstate bank: the Central Asian Bank for Cooperation and Development. They also established separate councils of presidents, foreign ministers, and defense ministers.[7]

Neither President Nazarbayev nor President Akaev intended for the Central Asian Economic Community to replace the CIS; rather they wished to create a successful model of integration among post-Soviet states that other nations might emulate. Thus, they did not see the Central Asian Economic Community as inconsistent either with the CIS or with the Customs Union of Russia and Belarus, which Kazakhstan joined in 1995, Kyrgyzstan in 1996, and Tajikistan in 1999. President Karimov's intentions for the Central Asian Economic Community were quite different; his primary interest was to manage relations within Central Asia. Although none of the presidents was anxious to link his state to Tajikistan, all three shared an interest in controlling events in Tajikistan as much as possible. Tajikistan became an observer in the Central Asian Economic Community in 1995, but became a member only in July 1998. The country's shattered economy and fractured society keep it a very junior partner. Turkmenistan has refused to join the organization in any formal capacity, claiming that this would be inconsistent with its neutral status, but representatives sometimes attend meetings as observers.

The Central Asian Economic Community provides an important forum for regional summits and has served to stimulate other forms of cooperation, especially in security relations. There are signs that the organization could develop into a more comprehensive regional organization, as seemed to be the case at the June 1999 summit held in Bishkek when Turkey, Ukraine, and Georgia were awarded observer status.[8] In the years since its formation, however, this union has failed to develop into a vehicle for serious economic cooperation. The Central Asian Bank for Cooperation and Development remains seriously underfunded and has only undertaken a handful of large projects, none of which has been commercially successful.[9] In fact, the bank almost collapsed in 1997 and was resuscitated only when the Kyrgyz opened a branch in Bishkek.[10] Kyrgyzstan was also the only country to make its mandated initial $3 million deposit in a timely fashion. In July 1997 the presidents of Kyrgyzstan, Kazakhstan, and Uzbekistan called for the Central Asian Bank to increase efforts to attract funding from international financial institutions.[11]

The Central Asian Economic Community has also failed to become a successful regional economic initiative in other ways. The region's leaders have devoted little imagination to the problem of how they might help solve each other's economic problems, whether through national specialization or by creating cooperative regional projects. The only exception is in the area of transport, where all are enthusiastically participating in the TRACECA (Transport Corridor Europe Caucasus Asia) project to create a new "Silk Road," which is described in chapter 6. Foreign investors interested in projects that straddle more than one country are confronted with the considerable trade barriers that exist between the Central Asian states. Even publicly supported operations, such as the Central Asian–American Enterprise Fund, have found it difficult to set up factories that depend upon goods from neighboring states or that target a regional market.

Although becoming a free trade zone was one of the explicit goals of the Economic Community, Central Asia shows no signs of reaching this goal in the near future. All the member states are far more concerned with their national security than they are with promoting close economic ties with their neighbors.

Despite Tajikistan's admittance to the Central Asian Economic Community, the Tajik-Uzbek border in Leninobad *oblast* (Khujand) has essentially been closed, first because the Uzbek government did not want its relatively cheaper goods to flow into Tajikistan, and then because the Tajiks did not want political opposition groups to be able to infiltrate from Uzbekistan. The February 1999 bombing in Tashkent also heightened Uzbek fears of insurgents entering from

Tajikistan.[12] The border is a porous one, putting both countries at risk. The Tajik claim that the Uzbeks have already directly intervened in their affairs. The troops of former Tajik Army Colonel Mahmud Khudoiberdiev were given safe haven in Uzbekistan, both before and after they attempted, unsuccessfully, to seize power in Khujand, in November 1998.[13] The government in Uzbekistan, for its part, objects that local Uzbeks and pro-Uzbek forces continue to be excluded from Tajikistan's government of conciliation.

Unlike their relations with Tajikistan, the three states of Kazakhstan, Kyrgyzstan, and Uzbekistan all enjoy good bilateral and multilateral relations with one another. In March 1998, at one of their frequent summits, the presidents of these states signed a symbolic agreement of "eternal friendship."[14] The Kazakhs and Kyrgyz are now even linked by marriage, after President Nazarbayev's daughter married President Akaev's son in July 1998; cultural traditions in both countries make such links nearly as important as state-to-state treaties.

The Central Asian states are also developing cooperative security arrangements. The most visible of these is the Central Asian Battalion, formed on December 15, 1995, at a meeting of the presidents of Uzbekistan, Kazakhstan, and Kyrgyzstan in what was then Jambyl (now again known as Taras) in Kazakhstan. The unit was formed under the auspices of NATO with the intention of diffusing conflicts in the region.[15] In September 1997 the battalion participated in a major multinational military exercise under the auspices of NATO's Partnership for Peace. The operation, called "Central Asian Battalion-97," took place on the territories of Kazakhstan and Uzbekistan and involved U.S., Russian, Turkish, Georgian, and Latvian troops.[16] Despite Russian unease that a NATO-sponsored exercise should be held in former Soviet territory, a similar exercise, "Central Asian Battalion-98," took place the following September in Uzbekistan and Kyrgyzstan. Also sponsored by the Partnership for Peace, this operation involved troops from Russia, the United States, Turkey, Georgia, and Azerbaijan, as well as from the three states of the Central Asian Battalion.[17] These operations have showcased U.S. military cooperation with Central Asian countries, but even more importantly, they have encouraged the Central Asian states to cooperate with one another.

The borders between Uzbekistan, Kazakhstan, and Kyrgyzstan are considerably more open than are those with either Tajikistan or

Turkmenistan, but trade restrictions nevertheless persist. These are largely the result of differences in the economic strategies pursued by these three states. Uzbekistan's currency, the *som*, is not freely convertible, and the country continues to impose price controls and to provide subsidies. The economic strategies pursued by the Kazakhs and Kyrgyz are similar, but the Kazakhs enjoy a higher standard of living, which creates substantial price differentials between the two countries. Each state has periodically become concerned about the risk of raiding by the other and has introduced tariffs and trade restrictions on certain goods.[18]

These restrictions are difficult to enforce, as the countries are closely interconnected. In the Soviet period, Osh (Kyrgyzstan) and Andijan (Uzbekistan) were close enough to be nearly twin cities, as were Talas (Kyrgyzstan) and Jambyl, while the economy of Shymkent (South Kazakhstan *oblast*) was closely linked to that of Tashkent just over the Uzbek border. The interconnections between Tajikistan and Uzbekistan were closer still; Khujand (Leninobad *oblast*) was a virtual satellite of Uzbekistan, while Uzbekistan's Surkhan Darya and Kurgan Darya regions used to be closely tied to Dushanbe. All these regions are forging new trading relationships through their nations' capitals, but there is still a great deal of illegal trade and many barter transactions.

The Uzbeks are even going so far as to build new roads. A bypass is being built on the Tashkent-Samarkand road to eliminate a small stretch of road that goes through Kazakhstan, just as a major new highway project is going forward to better link Andijan with Tashkent. This will allow the Uzbeks to travel the road through Kokand even in winter, without fear of attacks from Tajik highway marauders.

The Central Asian Economic Community members are similarly self-protective in their formal economic relationships, offering one another little or no preferential treatment in price setting. This would be less troubling if market conditions were allowed to prevail in other forms of cross-border trade. Southern Kazakhstan, including the Almaty area, is dependent upon Uzbekistan for its natural gas supply. As the price of gas rose steadily in the years following independence, Kazakhstan ran up a large debt to Uzbekistan. Disputes over this interstate debt have regularly left Kazakh households without power, heat, and cooking fuel.[19] Disagreements over the pricing and payment terms for Uzbek gas also almost led to the collapse of a major $275 million investment that the Belgian firm Tractobel was trying to make in Kazakhstan.[20]

Kyrgyzstan is also dependent upon Uzbek gas and regularly accumulates substantial debt. It is rumored that President Karimov directly links this debt to questions of how Kyrgyzstan treats the ethnic Uzbeks in southern Kyrgyzstan, where, as noted above, they account for about a third of the local population. Though far from conclusive, it is nevertheless suggestive that when the Kyrgyz government has shown that population greater solicitude in recent years, it has found it easier to negotiate energy agreements with Uzbekistan.

The Kazakhs and Kyrgyz have squabbled over the cost of hydroelectric power. In 1996 Kazakhstan refused to buy electricity from Kyrgyzstan because of disagreements over price, and Kyrgyzstan retaliated by cutting off the water supply to Kazakhstan from its Toktogul reservoir.[21] As detailed below, Kyrgyzstan also threatened to cut off Kazakhstan's water again in December 1997.[22]

Issues of water usage are particularly sensitive throughout Central Asia. At a 1994 meeting in Nukus, Uzbekistan, Central Asian leaders agreed to replace Soviet-era management structures with a new interstate body to regulate the use of water resources. As of 1997, the theoretical structure of Central Asian water management consisted of state-level ministries that reported to the Basin Water Management Organization, which in turn was responsible to a regional water management council.[23] In fact, by 1998 two organizations—the International Fund for Saving the Aral Sea and the Inter-State Council of the Central Asian Economic Community—had taken the lead in dealing with water issues in the region.[24] Periodically, leaders of various countries in the region have agreed to create additional bodies that would regulate and coordinate water resources management, including an April 8, 1999 Central Asian Heads of State summit on the problem of the Aral Sea.

In reality, however, states in the region have tended to deal with water usage issues through a series of bilateral or trilateral agreements, all of which have been marred by conflicts. These agreements usually amount to little more than controlled barter. In 1997, for example, water-rich Kyrgyzstan agreed to deliver water to neighboring Kazakhstan and Uzbekistan in return for coal from the former and gas from the latter. In late December of that year, however, Kyrgyzstan threatened to cut off water supplies to Kazakhstan, which had failed to fulfill its part of the bargain. The dispute was resolved in a few days' time with new promises from the countries in question. Barter deals such as this one must be constantly renegotiated. In March 1998, for example, Kyrgyzstan, Kazakhstan, and Uzbekistan signed an agreement that was substantially the same as the one they had signed the year before, which suggests that the cycle of barter and conflict shows no signs of slowing.

Like gas, oil, and other natural resources, fresh water is distributed unevenly throughout Central Asia. Unlike the case with other resources, however, water is supplied free to users, while the source states must pay for the maintenance of all dams, reservoirs, and other water storage facilities on their territories. The biggest water users are Turkmenistan and Uzbekistan,[25] which have an abundance of other resources, while the region's primary water suppliers are Tajikistan and Kyrgyzstan, which are poor and have few other resources. Water puts a particular burden on Kyrgyzstan, which pays for the maintenance of irrigation centers, such as the giant Toktogul dam. These facilities, constructed in the 1960s, 1970s, and 1980s, flooded 16,000 hectares of Kyrgyzstan's limited supply of arable land,[26] which makes them a double burden from the Kyrgyz point of view. The Kyrgyz would like to see the current water management regime replaced by a unified regional energy management system, in which oil, gas, electricity, and water usage were all regulated simultaneously; the other states, however, do not share this interest.

The inability of the Central Asian Economic Community to regulate economic relations between member states is not creating any immediate security risk in the region, but the inequalities created by the failure of this Community could grow more glaring with time. Much of the current cooperation is the result of the personal rapport that has developed among the region's leaders, who all rose up through the ranks of the Soviet elite. How the next group of leaders will relate to each other is another question.

There are other unresolved, yet pressing problems that the Community was formed to address. The lingering civil war in Tajikistan, with its occasional contagion from the civil war in Afghanistan, is a reminder of how fragile peace in the region is, and how difficult it is to reestablish a state once its basis for political community has been shattered. The Central Asian Economic Community was formed in part because of the war in Tajikistan, as an explicit recognition of the degree to which all states were still interconnected. In addition, there are new problems looming in the area; the most prominent of these is the narcotics business, which is feeding voraciously on the region's economic problems. The Central Asians have made some attempts at cooperation in addressing the drug trade, but without much success.

Turkmenistan's refusal to join the Central Asian Economic Community is also troubling, particularly since this is part of that state's wider lack of interest in Central Asian affairs. The Turkmen, for example, still have not exchanged ambassadors with Kyrgyz.[27] This policy of indifference seems less studied than careless, because Turkmenistan has no other choice but to be dependent upon its neighbors for water.

The biggest failure of the Central Asian Economic Community, however, is that the region's five states remain economic competitors against one another. A rise in standards of living that was more or less shared across the states of the region would make it possible for them to cooperate with one another more easily. However, a pattern of uneven development, in which neighbors grow increasingly poorer or richer in relation to one another, seems to guarantee that regional crises in Central Asia will grow more common in the future.

THE GUUAM GROUP

Formal and open cooperation between Georgia, Ukraine, Azerbaijan, and Moldova (and since April 1999, Uzbekistan) has its roots in revisions in flank limitations made to the Conventional Forces in Europe Treaty in late 1996 and the first half of 1997, when Russia complained that current flank limits did not allow it to deploy adequate forces in regions of serious security concern. Russia had already begun to deploy forces on the flanks in anticipation of a favorable outcome of the negotiations.

The leaders of Georgia, Ukraine, and Azerbaijan had already formed a consultative arrangement in late 1996. Yet all three, plus Moldova, were now alarmed that these troop level revisions would not only tilt the balance of military power further in Russia's favor, but would also legitimize the continued presence of Russian forces still stationed in Georgia, Moldova, and Ukraine, regardless of host nation consent. The effect of what became known as the GUUAM group could be felt when the treaty's changes were approved at a May 1997 OSCE meeting, but with the stipulation that forces stationed outside their national territory would require the full consent of the host nation.[28]

In October 1997 the four presidents who were then members of GUUAM met while at a Council of Europe Summit in Strasbourg and issued a communiqué formally announcing the continuation of the group. The communiqué noted the coincidence of views on key security issues of the four nations and the advantages of continued cooperation. Senior foreign ministry officials from all four countries met in Baku in late November 1997 to flesh out the substance and structure of the GUUAM group. The meeting identified a number of issues where coordination would be of mutual benefit, such as regional conflict resolution and peacekeeping, making energy supplies reliable, the creation of an Asia-Europe transit corridor, cooperation in international organizations, and the promotion of closer relations with the West. Azerbaijan even proposed holding consultations with NATO on regional security issues in a NATO-GUUAM context.[29]

Further efforts by GUUAM since November 1997 have sought to expand the realm of cooperation. In September 1998 commanders of border troops for Ukraine, Georgia, and Azerbaijan signed a cooperation agreement; the Moldovan commander was not present but agreed to participate in subsequent border guard cooperation. In October 1998 the Heads of Delegations from the GUUAM countries, meeting at the IMF in Washington, issued a joint statement stressing the familiar themes of cooperation on regional security, interest in a Europe-Asia transit corridor, and the swift development of Caspian energy. They also pledged joint efforts to minimize the impact of the Russian financial crisis.[30] At the end of 1998, the group considered creating joint peacekeeping forces for the Caspian and Black Sea regions. Ukraine had already taken a larger role in the mediation of the Transdniestr conflict in mid-1997, and Georgia, like Moldova, has long sought Ukrainian participation in peacekeeping in its several conflicts to counterbalance Russian influence. Ukrainian-Georgian military and defense cooperation has also expanded, with the

Ukrainian Ministry of Defense providing direct aid to the Georgian military in the form of patrol boats, officer training, and plans for the purchase of new equipment or the refurbishing of old Soviet equipment in Ukraine.[31] Defense ministers from Georgia, Azerbaijan, and Ukraine met in Baku in January 1999 to flesh out the idea of a joint peacekeeping force that might also guard proposed oil pipeline routes.[32] Uzbekistan's membership in GUUAM increases that organization's military potential.

While in Tbilisi in June 1999, Ukrainian Minister of Foreign Affairs Boris Tarasiuk suggested creating an institute on special representatives to coordinate joint activities. If this proposal is supported by other GUUAM members, Ukraine would be eager to host the first meeting of the organization. Irakli Menagarashvili, Georgia's minister of foreign affairs, welcomed the idea.[33]

At its formation the GUUAM group took great care to deny that it was creating a counterbalance to Russia or any other country, a stance which the member states have reiterated since; nevertheless, at least some Russian observers see GUUAM as a potential threat to their country's interests.[34] The leaders of the GUUAM states adamantly deny this, but the effect of the group has plainly been to add additional weight to the member states' views on issues of importance both inside and outside the CIS.

Most of the issues on which GUUAM has cooperated pit the interests of the five against stated Russian positions. From a broad perspective, the GUUAM group represents a direct refutation to the way in which Russia purports to view the post-Soviet space. It is a mechanism of cooperation over which Moscow has no influence. The foreign policies of all the GUUAM members are opposed to key elements of Russia's foreign policy designs. Specifically, the countries have banded together around the CFE flank limitation negotiations as a counterblock to Russia. They all support transportation and pipeline routes that are at odds with Moscow's proposals. Their recent offer to form a peacekeeping force to guard pipeline routes exacerbates Moscow's annoyance.

It would be wrong, however, to exaggerate the significance or influence of GUUAM. In addition to their common interests, the five member states also have common problems that constrain cooperation. None of them is a rich or powerful nation. Their cooperation has been most effective where little real financial support is necessary, such as in the negotiations over the CFE Treaty or in small-scale military cooperation, such as a planned GUUAM peacekeeping battalion.[35] The group's current plans for expanded defense cooperation, equipment purchases, and the formation of military units will be a real test of GUUAM's vitality in the security field, for these ventures will require serious expenditures. GUUAM might succeed in diversifying existing peacekeeping efforts in Transdniestr and Abkhazia; however, this is as much a product of Russia's interest in spreading the costs of these operations as it is in Ukraine's willingness to take on this role.[36] It is less likely that GUUAM will have influence over key energy or transportation matters. While all five want Caspian oil to flow and the East-West corridor to be created, they do not always agree on how to prioritize the development of specific East-West routes. Geography also makes Ukraine, Uzbekistan, and Moldova relatively marginal players on oil pipeline issues.

Ukraine's reluctance to assume large financial or military burdens or to risk entanglements in regional conflicts in which it has only a marginal interest limits the potential for GUUAM's influence. Although the Ukrainian leadership is actively seeking an expanded role in regional affairs, supporting GUUAM, and cooperating bilaterally with GUUAM countries (particularly Georgia and Moldova), Ukraine's own interests and resource limitations will prove to be serious constraints on the group's further development.[37] In short, Ukraine, like its GUUAM partners, welcomes the advantages of cooperation but is unprepared and unable to take on excessive burdens. This view is likely to be shared by GUUAM's other members.

A fundamental constraint on GUUAM's effectiveness is the bilateral relationship that each of its members has with Russia. Despite claims to the contrary, GUUAM's purpose and function lie in its role as a regional counterbalance to Russian influence in the CIS. Georgia, Ukraine, Uzbekistan, Azerbaijan, and Moldova, however, are each more dependent upon and vulnerable to Russia than they are committed to one another. Russia has a variety of ways in which it can pressure or buy off individual member states, which GUUAM is powerless to resist. This structural weakness is further exacerbated by a general lack of resources and an uncertain political resolve among its members, which suggests that Russia would inevitably prevail in any serious confrontation with GUUAM.

For all its inherent weaknesses, however, the GUUAM group has proved itself a useful forum for cooperation, allowing its five member states to coordinate and pool their influence on a limited set of issues of mutual concern.

THE CUSTOMS UNION

The CIS treaty of September 1993 on the "Conception of an Economic Union" envisioned a union built on several blocks, such as a free trade area, a customs union, a payments union, and a monetary union, but it did not specify when the different steps should be taken. The CIS members concluded a treaty on the formation of a free trade area in April 1994, but soon it became clear that economic integration within the CIS would not move quickly. Belarus and Russia, the two states that were most keen on broad and fast cooperation, opted to create the Russian-Belarusian Community on April 2, 1996.

Kazakhstan was also interested in more profound integration, but primarily in economic matters. As a result, Belarus, Kazakhstan, and Russia launched an initiative to form a trilateral Customs Union, which they conceived to be within the CIS framework. They reported their progress to the CIS Heads of Government in November 1995, who instructed the CIS Inter-State Economic Committee to coordinate the extension of the Customs Union to other CIS states. In January 1996 the CIS Council of Heads of State recommended a swift extension of the trilateral Customs Union to new members. Little came of this exhortation, however, as only Kyrgyzstan joined. In March 1996 Belarus, Kazakhstan, Kyrgyzstan, and Russia signed an Agreement on Increased Integration in the Economic and Humanitarian Spheres, which became the formal basis of the Customs Union. However, it was declared temporarily closed to other applicants,[38] even though Tajikistan expressed its interest in joining. It was not until 1998 that Tajikistan was allowed to begin the application process, which was not completed until February 1999.

Members of a customs union generally establish a free trade area and adapt a common foreign trade policy toward the outside world. Since trade among the CIS countries was already free in principle under the terms of the CIS Free Trade Agreement, the only remaining advantage of such a union would be to set up a common outside customs wall.

Initially Belarus, Kazakhstan, and Russia negotiated a common external tariff on the basis of Russia's tariff, but soon they all began to introduce unilateral modifications.[39] Russia raised its import tariff for cars to protect the Russian automotive industry, while Belarus, which produces no cars, lowered its tariff, thus stimulating a substantial trade in cars transiting from Europe through Belarus to Russia. Belarus has also never made its ruble convertible, and it has maintained multiple exchange rates, which complicates all international payments, including those within the Customs Union.

In spite of the variations in specific tariffs, the average Russian import tariff has been almost constant at 14 percent since 1996. When Kyrgyzstan joined the Customs Union, however, it had a uniform import tariff of 10 percent for all countries outside the CIS and free trade with CIS countries. Rather than raising its tariffs to the level of the rest of the Customs Union, Kyrgyzstan has maintained its low, uniform tariff, while the original three members have undertaken a large number of unilateral modifications. As has been discussed already, the members of the Customs Union have also all applied to join the World Trade Organization as individual members, even though a customs union is supposed to apply as a single entity.[40]

The Customs Union has not developed any real institutions, but it remains a forum for high-level meetings. Belarus, Russia, and Kazakhstan have established a working group for the harmonization of tariffs within the Customs Union, effectively trying to restore what they had disrupted in 1995, but as explained in chapter 2, by the end of 1998 this working group had reached agreement on common tariffs for only a small part of their trade. Although it chose to remain a formal member of the Customs Union, Kyrgyzstan preferred to accept membership in the WTO over whatever its obligations may have been in the Customs Union and is living up to the free trade obligations of that organization.

As noted in chapter 2, Russia and other CIS states in 1992 adopted the strange practice of applying VAT to goods shipped to other CIS countries, but not to exports outside the CIS. This system defies world practice, which is to exempt exports from VAT. International advisers urged member states to change the practice, but the states did so in an uncoordinated fashion, so that, for example, in the summer of 1997, Kazakhstan and Kyrgyzstan decided bilaterally to charge VAT on imports and not on exports, while Russia and Belarus levied VAT on exports. As a consequence, Russian and Belarusian enterprises had to pay VAT twice when exporting to Kazakhstan and Kyrgyzstan. The members of the Customs Union reached an agreement on the issue, but the problem was only partly resolved.[41] Finally, in 1999, even Belarus and Kazakhstan made a bilateral agreement that exempted exports from VAT, leaving Russia alone with its VAT system.[42]

As a matter of practical politics, the Customs Union can only achieve a common external tariff if it adopts the Russian tariff. As this is higher than the tariffs of Kyrgyzstan and Kazakhstan, its adoption would lead to a diversion of trade for these two countries. More importantly, Russian tariffs have been designed to protect Russian producers and not to benefit other countries. Thus, if it were to become a reality, the Customs Union would directly harm the economies of Kazakhstan and Kyrgyzstan. The only advantage that these two states derive from the Customs Union is that it helps to protect them against a possible Russian customs wall; fear of this prompted them to join the Union in the first place. Armenia provides a clear example of the unconventional weighing of pros and cons characteristic of the Customs Union. Armenia favors a close relationship with Russia for security reasons, but has never shown any interest in the Customs Union. Armenia's tariff, at a maximum of 10 percent, is even lower than that of Kyrgyzstan, which means that Armenia's joining the Customs Union would entail a costly trade diversion.[43]

RUSSIAN-BELARUSIAN INTEGRATION

Although the purpose of this chapter has been to examine regional alternatives both to the multilateral CIS and to bilateral relationships through which most of the states, including very prominently Russia, have attempted to compensate for the failure of the CIS, it seems nevertheless that this is the proper context in which to discuss the proposed integration of Russia and Belarus, which continues to lurch ahead in various guises. The series of agreements between Russia and Belarus has constituted the most ambitious and, perhaps, the most successful integration effort in the former USSR. As such, this union provides a clear alternative to the CIS model of post-Soviet integration, a model that that body has failed to provide.

It was widely assumed when Belarus became independent that it would seek integration with Russia. Belarusian national identity seemed weakly developed, and the new Belarusian government appeared reluctant to embrace its newfound independence or to undertake political and economic reforms. Although Minsk insisted on formal neutrality, its relationship with Russia was far more cordial than with any other country. Belarus remained economically dependent on Russian energy and subsidies, as well as upon Russia's willingness to accept barter arrangements for payment.[44]

The first moves toward closer integration came under Belarusian Prime Minister Vyacheslav Kebich, who in September 1993 concluded a major bilateral agreement that was said to create a "new kind of ruble zone," followed shortly by an agreement on monetary union in January 1994. Kebich's desire for a currency union was primarily driven by the collapse of the Belarusian economy; Belarus's need for outside assistance to prop up its economy remains one of the country's foremost motivations for integration. Russia recognizes this fact, which is the major reason why attempts at full economic integration between the two countries repeatedly begin with broad statements and far-reaching agreements, which then unravel as soon as Russia understands the price it would pay for integration. The one-to-one exchange of Belarusian for Russian rubles proposed by the 1993 agreement would have been particularly disadvantageous to Russia. Russian Prime Minister Viktor Chernomyrdin, aware that Belarus stood to gain more from Russia than it was able to give, stressed in September 1994 that monetary union was not automatic but required first that Belarus privatize and reform its economy. Despite the lack of such reforms in Belarus, Russia's perceptions about its other needs and desires influenced it to proceed with efforts to create the Customs Union described above, and to increase the bilateral security ties with Belarus that are detailed in chapter 3.

The impulse toward integration grew much stronger after Aleksandr Lukashenko was elected president of Belarus in 1994. The Belarusian president had campaigned unflaggingly for Russian-Belarusian integration, and in the process became a favorite of the political forces in Russia that most strongly desire bilateral, regional, and CIS-wide integration.

The series of bilateral agreements made before Lukashenko's election already sought to define and deepen ties between the two countries, but Lukashenko, along with a broad spectrum of senior Russian politicians, including, most prominently, Boris Yeltsin, have since 1996 negotiated an even more ambitious set of agreements. These agreements define the ultimate goal of Russian-Belarusian integration to be a "union" or a "union state." The three main accords in this process were the April 1996 agreement to create a Russian-Belarusian Commonwealth, the April 1997 agreement to upgrade this relationship to a union, and the December 1998 treaty that established equal rights and treatment for the citizens of both countries.[45] A Russian-Belarusian joint statement at the end of 1998 promised that "a treaty on the unification of Russia and Belarus in a union state" would be signed in 1999.

The April 1996 treaty creating a "Community of Sovereign States" has its origins in the Russian presidential elections, when Yeltsin's Communist and other opponents began to accuse him of having caused Russia's present troubles by signing the December 1991 agreements that ended the USSR. Wanting to seize back such national patriotic issues from his Communist opponents, Yeltsin embraced the cause of Russian-Belarusian integration, concluding an agreement in little more than a month of negotiations that included seven hours of direct bargaining between Lukashenko and Yeltsin.[46] In what was to prove a model for future negotiations, however, people in Yeltsin's government objected to the supranational "organs of cooperation" to which the two presidents had agreed, and so greatly diluted the actual text of the agreement. Even so, that agreement established a Higher Council and an Executive Committee, which were to harmonize reforms and prepare the way for a united currency.

Yeltsin's reelection campaign, as well as his severe health problems, and Lukashenko's successful drive to reshape his country's political structures and to rewrite its constitution, kept both presidents too occupied to deal any further with questions of integration until November 1996. At that time, Lukashenko made a state visit to Russia designed in part to refute the leading Russian objections against integration, especially the charge that Belarus would be an unbearable economic burden on Russia.[47]

The following January, President Yeltsin also tried to push the proposed integration ahead, by suggesting to Lukashenko that the two states should conduct a referendum to win public approval for synchronizing the broad implementation of the economic, political, and security agreements to which the two countries had already agreed. Lukashenko warmly supported Yeltsin's initiative, and the two sides worked to produce a draft treaty in time for a March 1997 summit. The agreement sought to create a formal union of the two states. Though explicitly preserving the state sovereignty of both parties, the draft treaty envisioned dual national and union citizenship and the establishment of a High Council for coordinating key issues of political, economic, and security policy. The high council, which was to consist of the presidents, prime ministers, and parliamentary leaders of both countries, would exercise basic control over the coordination of budgetary, monetary, tax, foreign trade, and security policies. The chair of this council would serve for two years and rotate between the presidents of the two states.

The proposal had strong support in Russia's Foreign Ministry, in the military, among some of Yeltsin's foreign policy advisers, and with the Communist and nationalist factions of the Duma.[48] Even so, on the eve of its signing, the treaty was substantially gutted. Russian opponents of the agreement managed to get the High Council eliminated and diluted all of the most ambitious provisions.[49] All that was left was a memorandum of agreement between the two sides outlining ways of "discovering and heeding public opinion" and "streamlining the contents of the Russian-Belarus Charter."[50]

Russian opponents of the original agreement argued that integration with a politically backward and economically depressed Belarus would entail huge costs for Russia.[51] More significantly, according to a Russian participant in the negotiations and a supporter of the agreement, opponents thought that Russia would be disadvantaged by an agreement that provided for equal treatment with Belarus.[52] Despite its much greater enthusiasm for the treaty, Belarus also had hesitations about what might happen to its sovereignty if it were more closely bound to a much larger and more powerful partner. Senior Belarusian officials have admitted that they are certain that neither Russian opponents nor supporters of integration have any concern for the fate of Belarusian sovereignty.[53] One point on which most Belarusians seem united, from ordinary citizens to President Lukashenko himself, is that any agreement that would return Belarus to the status of a province of Russia is unacceptable.[54]

A more short-term impediment to further integration appeared in fall 1997, when Belarus jailed Pavel Sheremet and Dmitri Zavadsky, ethnic Russian journalists who were working for ORT, a Moscow television station. Yeltsin's spokesman publicly stated that, "Russian patience had reached its limit" with Lukashenko and demanded the release of the journalists. Lukashenko dismissed the spokesman as a "nobody." A meeting of Yeltsin and Lukashenko in September 1997 apparently produced an agreement to free the journalists, which Lukashenko then failed to implement. Yeltsin took the unusual step of chiding Lukashenko in public, and Russia cancelled Lukashenko's scheduled trip to the Russian cities of Yaroslavl and Lipetsk. Luka-shenko attempted to shrug off Yeltsin's objections, implying that these were the products of the Russian president's age and ill health.[55] Sheremet was finally released on October 8, 1997, pending trial. After a lengthy trial the journalists were given 18-month suspended sentences.[56]

Momentum on further integration languished again until Yevgeny Primakov, a staunch advocate of integration, was made Russia's prime minister after the August 1998 financial crisis brought down the Kiriyenko government. Primakov's first official foreign visit as prime minister was to Minsk. On December 25, 1998, Yeltsin and Lukashenko met and agreed on a series of documents, ranging from a treaty on equal rights for citizens of both countries in political and economic spheres to a declaration outlining further steps the two countries intend to take in 1999 to advance unification. These steps included drawing up a full-fledged unification treaty by the middle of 1999, the creation of supranational governing bodies, a unified budget, a single legal environment for economic activity, and a single currency.

It is too early to say whether this extremely ambitious attempt at integration will have anything akin to its desired effect, or whether it will, like most efforts at integration that have been undertaken in the CIS, continue to exist more on paper than in fact. Such an outcome is particularly likely now that the strong support of Primakov himself has been removed. There are many sectors of Russia, and even more so, in Belarus, which view the integration of the two states with real enthusiasm. Even the staunchest proponents from both states, however, face a number of serious impediments that must be over-come before integration can be achieved. Without a comprehensive overhaul of the Belarusian economy, any closer integration of the two states would prove extremely costly to Russia; as it is, the

Belarusian economy depends upon Russia's willingness to barter and carry unpaid debt for energy and other key resources.[57] A substantial body of Russian opinion is quite willing to see Belarus become a province of an enlarged Russia, but there is no support for arrangements that would give the much smaller and weaker partner an equal say, a status upon which Belarus insists.

There are also sizeable economic and political circles in Belarus that fear Russia's greater economic power[58] and clearly want to hold on to the advantages they have received from controlling Belarus's political and economic policy. Lukashenko's personal political power depends on his continued ability to deliver political and economic benefits to his supporters, which means that he could not permit a union that would pass the important positions of Belarus's political or economic life to Russian control.

The idea of a Belarusian-Russian union remains immensely popular in both countries, but it is extremely difficult to translate that support into the practical arrangements that would make such a union a reality. The Belarusian elite does not wish to be reabsorbed into Russia, while the Russian elite either does not wish to—or understands that it cannot—subsidize Belarus's attempts to hang onto Soviet-style socialism. Even Russia's communists and nationalists, who admire the closed economic and political system that Lukashenko has created, have no desire to give the charismatic Belarusian president access to Russian politics at the national level. Any agreement short of the total subordination of Belarus to Russia would also seriously destabilize Russia's federalist system. The existing subnational units in Russia would seek to redefine their relations to the whole in light of whatever deal Belarus had struck, and integration would have to give Belarus a voice in those redefinitions. That would introduce such a variety of actors and interests into the federalist process that the original complexities of union might seem simple by comparison.

Rhetorical support for the Belarusian-Russian union may grow or wane, as future political developments in both states dictate, but genuinely substantial movement toward integration seems unlikely. Russia and Belarus are likely to remain strategic and economic partners, but the realities of their different sizes, resources, and willingness to reform mean that the relationship will inevitably remain one in which any advantage Russia might get from Belarus is going to cost more than the benefit obtained, while the price for Belarus will be a loss of sovereignty that the elite of that state cannot countenance. Even in Belarus, the real benefits that independence confers has meant that a sense of sovereignty is growing. In Belarus this sense of sovereignty does not guarantee either prosperity or stability, but it does mean that Russian-Belarusian integration is likely to remain more in the realm of words than in that of fact.

REGIONAL EFFORTS IN PERSPECTIVE

The regional efforts to foster integration explored in this chapter, just like the bilateral security arrangement featured in chapter 3, are in fact an admission that the CIS as a whole is a failure, whatever member states may say about the vitality of that organization. Whatever the rhetoric, the reality is that no country in the CIS has demonstrated a concern for the post-Soviet space as a whole. Russia has seen the CIS and other integrative initiatives as a way primarily to advance its own interests, just as Russia's CIS partners have viewed the organization through the prism of their own problems and the challenges of their own region. Even the countries supporting Russia's desires for integration do so in order to divert Russia's scarce political, economic, and security resources their way and thus, by necessity, away from their partners in other regions of the CIS. The financial constraints on all the member states also impede impulses toward integration; as has been shown, most of the post-Soviet states simply do not have the money to carry out initiatives, whatever their desire to see them implemented.

Regional attempts at integration have suffered from the same problems, as have the attempts to form the CIS as a whole. When Russia is a member of an association, the very dynamics that doomed the CIS—Russia's demands for primacy and non-Russian demands for Russia's resources—are repeated in the smaller body. Frequently these regional and bilateral bodies also show the same pattern of formal agreement followed by informal failure to implement, a tactic that permits smaller states to disagree without defying their larger partners openly.

Even more instructive, however, is the fact that these same patterns also appear in regional organizations to which Russia does not belong. Ukraine, for example, is clearly seeking to extend its foreign policy reach through GUUAM, but Ukrainian officials fear that the country's meager resources will not prove equal to the task of being the senior partner in that relationship. As noted, for all the cooperation that has marked that body, the members of GUUAM also disagree on a number of points of the foreign policy that the body might pursue.

It is no less difficult to build a smaller integrative structure than a larger one, if the participants do not share basic approaches to the tasks and structure of the organization, or if the participants lack resources. A common security structure cannot be built if there is no consensus on threats. Common markets and free trade areas cannot emerge if the tension between cooperation and the primacy of Russia is not resolved.

What the proliferation of bilateral and regional initiatives demonstrates, no less than does the failure of any of these to become viable, is that the similarities that their common birth process gave the post-Soviet states have grown ever more attenuated over time. The huge territory customarily called the "post-Soviet space" is becoming increasingly fragmented and diverse. Republics that were forced by Soviet boundaries to consider themselves parts of a union have become independent states and are learning that there exist other regional and international centers of gravity. This realization has caused the new states to line up in a variety of configurations, without regard for the shared circumstances by which they all received independence.

Countries that were not carved out of the Soviet Union are thus increasingly a part of the mix, as the new states begin to understand that "post-Soviet" is a description of their past, not a single prescription for their futures. The weakness of the CIS states and of their political, economic, and security arrangements has driven them to establish links with stronger partners outside the CIS. To date, none of the CIS states except for Georgia has turned to the outside for its basic security arrangements, although several have greatly expanded their ties to the United States, NATO, Turkey, and China. At the same time, others have gravitated more consciously and decisively toward Russia. The next few years are likely to exhibit a continuation of these trends, causing relations between CIS member states to be increasingly leveraged by the sorts of relationships that each state is forming outside the CIS. Some states in the CIS see this trend as positive and would like to encourage it; others, especially in Russia, see it as a threat that they would like to contain.

As this book has suggested, however, the realities of development in each of the new states are such that—whatever any given state's attitude toward it—the process of redrawing the cultural, economic, political, and military map of the space once dominated by the USSR is likely to continue. The question that this poses to the wider world is whether the present patchwork of larger bilateral and multilateral arrangements into which the CIS states are entering individually can become a stable new pattern.

NOTES

[1] Known as the Central Asian Union until July 1998, it was renamed when Tajikistan joined the organization.

[2] Russian writings on this theme include: G. I. Chufrin, ed., *Integratsionnye protsessy v Azii v kontse XX stoletiia* (Moscow: Institut vostokovedeniia RAN, 1995); A. M. Khazanov and V. P. Pankratev, eds., *Rossiia i Aziia: Sostoianie i perspektivy sotrudnichestva* (Moscow: Institut vostokovedeniia RAN, 1995); A. Malashenko, Alexei Zverev, Bruno Coppetiers, Dmitri Trenin, and Eric Remacle, eds., *Etnicheskie i regionalnye konflikty v Evrazii* (three volumes). Volume 1: *Tsentralnaia Aziia i Kavkaz.* (Moscow: Vesmir, 1997); O. Vasileva, *Sredniaia Aziia: God posle putcha* (Moscow, Russia: Gorbachev-Fond, 1993); *Zapadnaia Aziia, Tsentralnaia Aziia i Zakavkaze. Integratsiia i konflikty* (Moscow: Institut vostokovedeniia RAN, 1995). Western writings include: Daniel Pipes, "The Politics of the 'Rip Van Winkle' States: The Southern Tier States of the Ex-Soviet Union Have Moved the Borders of the Middle East North," *Middle East Insight*, vol. 10, (November/ December 1993), pp. 30–40; *Refuge*, Special issue on Central Eurasia and Eastern Europe, vol. 12 (February 1993), pp. 1–17; Bess Brown, "Central Asia: The First Year of Unexpected Statehood," *RFE/RL Research Report*, vol. 2 (January 1, 1993), pp. 25–36; Paul B. Henze, "Whither Turkestan?" (Santa Monica: Rand Corporation, 1992); David Kaye, "Struggling with Independence: Central Asian Politics in the Post-Soviet World," *Middle East Insight*, vol. 8 (July–October 1992), pp. 27–32; Leon Aron, "The Soviet Union's Soft Underbelly: Muslim Central Asia," *Global Affairs*, vol. 5, special issue (1990), pp. 31–62.

[3] Given Uzbekistan's long shared border and the large diaspora Tajik and Uzbek populations, there is a legitimate fear that it will

engage directly in the Tajik conflict, as Uzbekistan is purported to have done in the November 1998 siege of Khujand by Mahmud Khudoiberdiev. Uzbekistan also declined to become a signatory of one 1998 peace accord between the leading Tajik factions.

4 A fuller account of the Osh riots appears in Eugene Huskey, "Kyrgyzstan: The Politics of Demographic and Economic Frustration," in Bremmer and Taras, eds., *New States, New Politics*, pp. 661–2.

5 *ITAR-TASS*, January 4, 1993, as translated in *FBIS Daily Report*, SOV-93-002, January 5, 1993.

6 Martha Brill Olcott, "Ceremony and Substance: The Illusion of Unity in Central Asia," in Michael Mandlebaum, ed., *Central Asia and the World* (New York: Council on Foreign Relations, 1994), pp. 17–20.

7 Details of these negotiations are in Sergei Gretsky, "Regional Integration in Central Asia," *Analysis of Current Events*, vol. 10, no. 9–10 (September/October 1998), pp. 12–3.

8 *RFE/RL Newsline*, June 25, 1999.

9 As of summer 1998, the bank had $9 million in capital. Sergei Gretsky, "Regional Integration in Central Asia," *Analysis of Current Events*, vol. 10, no. 9–10 (September/October 1998). It has been involved in financing the following enterprises: Regent (Kyrgyzstan), Alisher (Kyrgyzstan), Saiman (Kazakhstan), Metallist factory (Uralsk, Kazakhstan), and the Zharnar (Kyrgyzstan)-Key International (Japan) joint venture. It also served as a transfer point for a loan to Kyrgyzmunayzat from the National Bank of Kazakhstan. Khabar News Agency, January 1, 1998 and April 30, 1998; *Novoe Pokoleniye*, January 29, 1999.

10 *Kyrgyz Radio First Program*, February 4, 1997, in *BBC Summary of World Broadcasts*, February 7, 1997.

11 *Kyrgyz Television First Channel*, July 24, 1997, in *BBC Summary of World Broadcasts*, July 26, 1997.

12 On February 16, 1999, there were six blasts, which have been attributed to religious extremists. On June 28, after almost a month of proceedings, Uzbekistan's Supreme Court sentenced six of the twenty-two accused to death and gave the others sentences ranging from ten to twenty years in prison. Though various groups and even neighboring countries have been purported to conspire against Islam Karimov, the six criminals on death row are of

Uzbek origin. The accused were extradited from Ukraine, Kazakhstan, and Kyrgyzstan. *Tashkent Radio Mashal*, June 28, 1999.

[13] A group of captured rebel fighters claimed they had received training in Uzbekistan from both Uzbek military personnel and Colonel Khudoiberdiev's troops. *RFE/RL Newsline*, November 30, 1998. After the rebellion was quelled, Tajik officials suggested that some of the rebel troops may have escaped to Uzbekistan as well. *RFE/RL Newsline*, November 10, 1998.

[14] Aleksandr Bovin, "Asian Motives," *Izvestiia*, July 21, 1998.

[15] Vladimir Akimov, "Central Asian, US Peacekeepers to Hold Joint Exercise," *ITAR-TASS*, March 11, 1997.

[16] Anatoly Yurkin, "Large-scale International Military Exercise in Central Asia," *ITAR-TASS*, September 16, 1997.

[17] Yury Chernogayev and Boris Volkhonsky, "NATO Paying for CIS Defense," *Kommersant-Daily*, September 23, 1998, p. 4, as translated in *Current Digest of the Post-Soviet Press*, October 21, 1998.

[18] On February 11, 1999, the Kazakh Ministry of Energy, Industry, and Trade announced that, effective March 11, it would introduce tariffs of up to 200 percent on foodstuffs and certain other products from both Kyrgyzstan and Uzbekistan. The ministry cited the need to protect Kazakhstan's producers from the inexpensive, subsidized imports that come out of those countries. Bruce Pannier, "Central Asia: Concern Grows Over Possibility Of Trade War," *RFE/RL Newsline*, February 16, 1999.

[19] The worst of these problems were resolved through a series of negotiations culminating in an agreement signed in Tashkent in November 1996. Kazakhstan agreed to a repayment plan, and Uzbek and Kazakh representatives agreed to negotiate direct contracts for the delivery of Uzbek gas to southern Kazakhstan. *Pravda Vostoka*, November 20, 1996, translated in *FBIS Daily Report*, SOV-97-022-S, February 4, 1997. A recent article in *Delovaia nedelia* suggests that the gas issue has been largely resolved, reporting that deliveries of Uzbek gas are "almost completely" meeting southern Kazakhstan's gas needs. Dmitriy Alyaev, *Delovaia nedelia*, January 29, 1999, in *FBIS Daily Report*, SOV-1999-0215, February 16, 1999.

[20] The Belgian energy group Tractebel took on the responsibility of providing lights and heat to Almaty and the surrounding area when it bought out Almatyenergo in August 1996 for $5 million and pledged to invest $270 million more. The group inherited

outdated generators and encountered numerous problems obtaining fuel to run them, including Uzbekistan's refusal to supply natural gas to its nonpaying Kazakh customers. These and other problems have forced Tractebel to spend more than ten times its initial investment without coming close to realizing the 25 percent profit that its agreement guarantees it. The company threatened to withdraw in the first quarter of 1998 when it was effectively barred from introducing modest rate hikes, but it decided to stay after the Kazakh government issued a public apology.

[21] *Slovo Kyrgyzstana*, May 3–4, 1996, in *FBIS Daily Report*, SOV-96-097, May 17, 1996.

[22] *ITAR-TASS*, December 23, 1997, in *FBIS Daily Report*, SOV-97-357, December 29, 1997.

[23] Peter Sinnott, "Central Asia's Geographic Moment," *Central Asian Monitor*, no. 4 (1997), p. 30.

[24] Roland Eggleston, "Uzbekistan: Conference To Review Environmental Dangers," *RFE/RL Newsline*, September 18, 1998.

[25] As of 1996, Turkmenistan withdrew about 22.8 billion cubic meters of fresh water a year, and Uzbekistan withdrew about 82.2 billion cubic meters. World Bank, *World Development Report 1998/99* (Washington: World Bank, 1999), p. 207.

[26] Almanbet Matubraimov, *Slovo Kyrgyzstana*, July 3, 1997, in *FBIS Daily Report*, SOV-97-199, July 22, 1997.

[27] According to a representative of the Embassy of Turkmenistan interviewed in Washington, D.C., in July 1999, Turkmenistan maintains a presence in Kazakhstan, Tajikistan, Azerbaijan, Uzbekistan; while Kazakhstan, Kyrzyzstan, Tajikistan, and Uzbekistan have embassies in Ashgabat.

[28] Making plain that the revisions did not encourage the stationing of forces or legitimize their presence without the consent of the host nation became an important issue in U.S. Senate approval of the flank revisions. The Senate approved a parallel set of understandings very much in response to the concerns of the GUUAM group.

[29] *TURAN*, November 25, 1997.

[30] "Azerbaijan, Georgia, Moldova, and Ukraine (the GUAM countries) Reiterate Their Intent for Further Development of Cooperation," press release from the Embassy of Ukraine, Washington, D.C., October 19, 1998.

[31] The sweep of Ukrainian-Georgian military cooperation is described in Grigoriy Perepelitsa, "Ukraina v voenoi integratsii sodruzhestva nezavisimykh gosudarstv (SNG)" (Moscow: Carnegie Endowment for International Peace, forthcoming).

[32] *TURAN*, January 21, 1999.

[33] *Nezavisimaia gazeta*, June 30, 1999.

[34] Konstantin Zatulin and Andranik Migranyan, "SNG posle Kisheneva," *NG-Sodruzhestva* [monthly supplement to *Nezavisimaia gazeta*], no. 1, December 1997, pp. 1–2.

[35] They have made little progress since April 1999. *Turan Information Agency*, May 4, 1999. The ministers of defense of GUUAM countries were scheduled to meet in July 1999 to talk about military cooperation and the creation of a GUUAM peacekeeping battalion, but the meeting did not take place.

[36] On Ukraine's efforts in Transdniestr, see Sherman Garnett and Rachel Lebenson, "Ukraine Joins the Fray: Will Peace Come to Trans-Dniestria?" *Problems of Post-Communism*, November–December 1998, pp. 22–32.

[37] This strong sense of limits to GUUAM emerged during author interviews with senior Ukrainian officials and analysts in Kyiv in May 1997 and May and December 1998.

[38] Andrei Zagorski, *SNG: Tsifry, fakty, personaly* (Minsk: PRS, 1998).

[39] Constantine Michalopoulos and David Tarr, "The Economics of Customs Unions in the Commonwealth of Independent States," *Post-Soviet Geography and Economics*, vol. 38, no. 3 (1997), p. 128.

[40] Ibid., pp. 128, 131.

[41] Aleksei Zaiko, "V Tamozhennom soiuze poiavilis' favority," *Russkii telegraf*, January 28, 1998.

[42] Semen Novoprudskii, "Ekonomicheskoe koketstvo/Belarussiia i Kazakhstan reshili stat drug dlia druga dalnim zarubezhem," *Izvestiia*, February 4, 1999.

[43] Michalopoulos and Tarr, "The Economics of Customs Unions in the Commonwealth of Independent States," pp. 128–32.

[44] Russia has long been Belarus's largest trading partner. In 1997 trade with Russia accounted for more than half of Belarus's total trade. International Monetary Fund, *Direction of Trade Statistics Yearbook* (Washington, D.C.: International Monetary Fund, 1998), pp. 912–3.

[45] The "Treaty on the Formation of the Community" was published in *Rossiiskaia gazeta*, October 28, 1996, p. 9. A summary of the

treaty's main points was provided in *Interfax*, April 1, 1996. The statements of Presidents Yeltsin and Lukashenko at the signing ceremony—regarding what the treaty will accomplish and why it is in the interests of the Russian and Belarusian people—was published in translation in *FBIS Daily Report*, April 2, 1996. The 1997 agreement to upgrade this relationship to a union was published in an abridged version in *Nezavisimaia gazeta*, March 29, 1997. "Text of Treaty between Russia and Belarus on Equal Rights for Citizens," *ITAR-TASS*, December 25, 1998 and "Text of Declaration on the Further Integration of Russia and Belarus," *ITAR-TASS*, December 25, 1998.

46 *Nezavisimaia gazeta*, March 26, 1996.

47 Aleksandr Lukashenko, "Speech by the President of Byelorussia at the State Duma Session," *Federal News Service Transcripts*, November 13, 1996.

48 "Vazhneishii proekt utochniaetsia na khodu," *Nezavisimaia gazeta*, April 1, 1997.

49 While the bureaucratic struggles in both countries are reflected in press accounts, this section also relies on interviews conducted in Minsk and Moscow in May and October 1997.

50 Both the approved treaty and an agreed memorandum on how to proceed with the elaboration of a detailed charter through consultation with the public were published in *Rossiiskiaia gazeta*, April 3, 1997.

51 In 1997 the per capita GDP of Belarus was $1,314 while Russia's per capita GDP was $3,056, more than double that of Belarus. *Transition Report 1998* (London: European Bank for Reconstruction and Development, 1998), pp. 209, 225.

52 Author's interviews in Moscow, June 1–4, 1997.

53 Author's interviews in Minsk in May and October 1997.

54 *Belorusskii monitoring*, April 21, 1997.

55 Lukashenko's explanation of Yeltsin's words were that "I am 40 and he is 80." *Belorusskii monitoring*, August 22, 1997; *Belorusskaia delovaia gazeta*, September 25, 1997; *Belorusskii monitoring*, October 7, 1997.

56 *RFE/RL Newsline*, January 29, 1998.

57 As of November 1, 1997, Belarus's debt to Russia for energy resources totaled approximately 823 billion rubles. *PlanEcon*

Energy Outlook: October, 1998 (Washington, D.C.: PlanEcon Inc., 1998), p. 117.

[58] In 1998 the Belarusian economy was approximately 9.1 percent the size of Russia's. Ibid., p. vii.

6
The CIS and the
Outside World

The collapse of the Soviet Union made it possible for each of the successor states to look in its own way for foreign governments, international institutions, private companies, and other actors from the outside world that might provide it with diplomatic recognition, trade and investment, cultural ties, and even political and security assistance. Indeed, each state received more offers of various kinds of assistance and affiliation than it could or should have used, forcing each to factor in global trends and the interests and actions of countries from outside the former USSR in its calculations on how to relate to the CIS. The alternatives that other countries and other affiliations might offer the CIS states were factors contributing to that body's failure. As this chapter will show, it is the interaction between the successor states and the outside world that will increasingly shape the political, economic, and security geographies of the states born out of the USSR.

The multitude of international actors, and the variety of ways in which they have interacted with the CIS states, has meant that the isolation that these areas faced as Soviet republics has been replaced by a staggering level of complexity. Just a partial list of the ways in which various members of the CIS relate to what once was the outside world would include such arrangements as the impressive commercial routes that have developed between various CIS states and China, Turkey, and Poland, and the burst of regional diplomatic activity that has fashioned significant ties between Poland and Ukraine, Iran and Armenia, and China and Kazakhstan. New regional constellations have appeared or are proposed between CIS states and neighboring countries, coexisting and competing with the configurations of the CIS. Western and Chinese energy firms are bidding to develop Kazakh oil fields. International financial institutions, the European Union, and the world's major economic powers have all provided financial and technical assistance to the CIS states, trying to spur economic reform and the integration of the CIS economies into the global economy. From the other side, Russia's Gazprom plans new routes to Europe and to a growing Turkish market. Russia has now become Turkey's largest trading partner, and Turkey has become Georgia's primary market. Army officers from CIS countries are training in Russia—and at NATO facilities.

These few examples give a good sense of the complex new interactions between the CIS and what habit still calls the outside world. Although these interactions are too numerous to be catalogued in a book of this scope, we offer brief examinations of selected representative relationships between CIS member states and various other world actors, such as the European Union, international energy companies, NATO, and China. It is these relationships, and the interplay between them, that are likely to be a strong determinant of the future course of integration within the CIS. This chapter will suggest ways in which that course may move.

POLITICAL CHALLENGES

The end of the USSR opened up a floodgate for contacts between the new states and the outside world. These range from state-to-state diplomatic relations to private links between businesses and cultural organizations. This section concentrates on three important categories of ties with the outside world: the early efforts to win recognition, establish diplomatic ties, and participate actively in global and regional institutions; the attempt to fashion regional institutions that would straddle boundaries between the CIS and the outside world; and the renewal of cultural and civilizational contacts, such as with the Islamic world.

The first impact of the outside world on the new states was the immediate need for formal diplomatic recognition of the new independent and sovereign nations. Such recognition was far from guaranteed. International concern about political instability, worries about the control of nuclear weapons, and an unwillingness to interfere in what was widely interpreted to be a struggle between the old Soviet center and the emerging republics kept most of the world on the sidelines until the new states themselves made the question moot by dissolving the USSR. A brief period of international hesitation followed the declaration of the CIS, but by early 1992 it was plain that the new states were a reality. This set in motion a tide of diplomatic recognitions.[1] Although there were specific concerns about—and conditions attached to—the recognition of certain of the new countries, there was no longer a question that all of them would eventually be recognized by the world community.[2]

The leaders of the new states quickly established a wide range of diplomatic contacts, especially with the major world capitals. New embassies were opened, and ministerial and summit meetings soon followed. These meetings were a further recognition of the legitimacy of each of the new states. Ukraine in particular expanded its outside contacts rapidly, both to confirm its new status and to try to gain leverage in its complicated negotiations with the Russians on numerous issues left unresolved by independence.[3] Other states had their own reasons for the specific destinations that they chose, but all shared the desire to expand foreign contacts, to win foreign economic assistance and investment, and simply to expand their diplomatic options. The following examples give some sense of the enthusiasm with which the new presidents traveled.

Between February 1992 and November 1995 Kazakhstan's President Nazarbayev visited Washington twice (May 1992 and February 1994), Bonn once (September 1992) and Beijing twice (October 1993 and September 1995). In the same period, Ukraine's President Kravchuk visited the United States twice (May 1992 and March 1994), Beijing once (October 1992) and Bonn twice (February 1992 and October 1993), while Uzbekistan's President Karimov visited China once (March 1992) and Germany twice (April 1993 and November 1995). Nor was it only the new leaders who began to travel; these were state visits, which all required many preparatory meetings among senior officials and ministers of both countries. As hectic as these schedules may seem, it should also be noted that the presidents could probably have traveled even more than they did, if it had not been for various international concerns about their countries. Ukraine's initial hesitations about whether to give up its nuclear weapons made Kravchuk less welcome internationally than he and his successor later became once Ukraine firmly advocated nuclear disarmament.[4] Similarly, Uzbekistan's tight political control of opposition groups and restrictions on basic rights and freedoms made its President Islam Karimov an unwelcome international visitor until the world community became more concerned about instability than it was about progress toward democratization.[5]

The rush by the new states to be recognized diplomatically was replicated by their rush to join international organizations. All the states of the former USSR were accepted for membership in the United Nations[6] and became participating members of the OSCE. All of the CIS states have also established formal links with NATO, joining its Euro-Atlantic Partnership Council and the Partnership for Peace.

The new states have been much slower to gain acceptance to international bodies that have more stringent membership criteria. As has been noted, for instance, Kyrgyzstan is the only post-Soviet state to be accepted into the World Trade Organization as a full member; however, all the other CIS states except Tajikistan and Turkmenistan have at least observer status in the WTO. Only Russia, Georgia, Ukraine, and Moldova are members of the Council of Europe. Both Ukraine and Russia had trouble joining the body and have been criticized since. Ukraine could be expelled for its support of the death penalty, and Russia was severely criticized for its war in Chechnya. In general, as this brief synopsis suggests, contacts between the CIS member states and the outside world have followed much the same pattern as they have within the CIS, progressing the farthest in the government-to-government arena where both costs and benefits are slight. It requires little investment by outside powers to recognize independence, receive diplomats and heads of state, and pull up another chair to the table in the United Nations or OSCE. It has been more difficult to obtain and sustain genuine interactions in bodies where the stakes are higher. The WTO, for example, sets standards for its member states that most of the CIS states are simply incapable of meeting, nor have any of them developed the kind of economic clout that might gain them special considerations.

The new states have not only rushed to join existing international bodies; some of them have also attempted to create new mechanisms for cooperation deliberately designed to embrace states inside and outside the former USSR. While on a visit to Hungary in February

1993, Ukrainian President Kravchuk proposed a Central European security zone to fill the security vacuum left after the disintegration of the former Soviet Union, in which member states would pledge not to advance territorial claims on one another.[7] Boris Tarasiuk, Kravchuk's deputy prime minister, subsequently spearheaded this initiative, which he said would help smooth the transition into Europe for states such as Hungary, Poland, Romania, the Czech Republic, Slovakia, and Bulgaria.[8] These countries rejected Ukraine's idea in favor of closer ties with NATO and the OSCE.

President Nazarbayev proposed a Conference on Interaction and Confidence Measures in Asia at the United Nations in October 1992.[9] Unlike the Kravchuk proposal—which was stillborn—Nazarbayev's ideas at least generated preparatory meetings and working groups, even if these have still failed to come up with a basic design for the new forum.[10]

Turkey, Azerbaijan, and the four Central Asian states that are of Turkic heritage have met regularly since 1992 in what is billed as the "Turkic Summit" process.[11] A Black Sea Cooperation Council, embracing the littoral states and key outside parties, has also been formed and meets regularly. These and other regional initiatives seem to suggest at once both the profound redefinition of geography underway in and around the former USSR and the obstacles that stand in the way of its future.

Although it had existed in a different form before the collapse of the USSR, the best example of this type of new organization may be the Economic Cooperation Organization (ECO). Originally called Regional Cooperation for Development, this body was founded in 1965 by Iran, Pakistan, and Turkey and then was renamed ECO in 1985. However, the body had no real function until February 1992 when its membership expanded to include Afghanistan and the Muslim-heritage CIS states of Azerbaijan, Kazakhstan, Kyrgyzstan, Tajikistan, Turkmenistan, and Uzbekistan. At their first expanded meeting the participants signed an agreement to introduce preferential tariffs, set up a development bank, and agreed to cooperate in the modernization of transport, communications, industry, and agriculture. At a subsequent meeting, in July 1993, the ECO leaders agreed to establish a bank to promote trade and investment, a regional airline, a shipping company, and a reinsurance firm. The group's general goal was to create a version of the European Union for the Muslim states of the region.

Although a number of meetings have been held, little of substance has been accomplished in the seven years since.[12] A variety of factors have hindered the ability of ECO to move toward its stated goals. Russia is strongly against the possibility of a viable ECO; senior officials have gone so far as to threaten that the Central Asian nations and Afghanistan would have to choose between ECO and Russia.[13] Though perhaps less blunt in their threats, many of the Western states are nearly as hostile to ECO as is Russia, largely because Iran is one of ECO's most vociferous members. The need of most of the other member states to maintain positive relations with Europe and the United States, as well as to receive Western investment and aid, led to a backlash by certain CIS members of the organization against Iran and stopped much of the momentum toward the regional cooperation that ECO had seemed to promise. After Iran's President Rafsanjani told an ECO meeting of foreign ministers in Tehran in 1994 that members should distance themselves from the West, the next full meeting of ECO heads of state in 1995 failed to reach consensus on key proposals, while previous initiatives languished. A year later, in May 1996, Uzbekistan's President Karimov threatened to withdraw his country from ECO entirely if Iran continued to try to turn the body into an anti-Western organization. His sentiments were echoed by representatives of Kazakhstan, Kyrgyzstan, and Tajikistan, who had by then realized the importance of maintaining good relations with the West.[14] Iran's dominance in the organization has also been a continual source of tension for other ECO members. The need for Western investment in Caspian oil pipelines has become an overriding concern for member countries like Azerbaijan, Kazakhstan, and Turkey, as each has realized that at this time the United States would obstruct any oil transit route involving Iran.

The fifth and most recent ECO summit, held in Almaty in May 1998, also saw little progress. Kazakhstan's President Nazarbayev expressed disappointment at the low level of trade between ECO members,[15] and Uzbekistan's President Karimov once again characterized the organization as ineffective.[16] The meeting also called for a reduction in tariffs and the development of a modern transport and communication infrastructure. The poverty and political instability plaguing most of the ECO member states make those goals unlikely to be realized, at least through the auspices of ECO. However, Western-funded initiatives like the TRACECA project, and the potential for large private and semi-private investment by European and U.S. oil companies, make possible the infrastructure that ECO hopes will be built.

ECO is nevertheless important, because it demonstrates the desire of the Central Asian CIS members and Azerbaijan to realign their trade from the Russian-oriented northern trade routes that have characterized their region since the days of the Russian Empire. At the same time, however, the nature of the organization and the diversity of the political systems represented within ECO make it difficult for that organization to generate consensus sufficient to enact any measurable economic or trade reform. Nearly every document and communiqué that ECO has issued has noted members who abstain or refuse to sign.[17] All the member states wish to increase intra-ECO trade, but none of them has been able to find a formula for doing so. Realistically, most of the member states are too poor, and several of them too distracted by social conflicts, to be able to generate the capital necessary to realize even the most promising of proposals. Even the one attribute that would seem to bind the member nations most closely together—their shared Muslim cultural heritage—is as much a liability as it is a benefit. The leaders of the new Central Asian states and Azerbaijan are generally quite determined to keep the character of their nations secular, and some, like Presidents Nazarbayev and Akaev, are heads of states that also have a large proportion of Russian residents. These leaders have found it difficult enough to incorporate Russian and other European populations into states that are officially secular; shifting toward the Islamic world would merely exacerbate the problem. All of the ECO members, both those from the CIS and the others, are also aware of the hostility and suspicion with which Western governments regard Muslim organizations.

The combination of hesitation and eagerness with which the Central Asian nations have moved to embrace their "Muslim heritage" is representative of a similar impulse in all of the new states: to rejoin a world culture from which their citizens felt cut off by the enveloping ideology and well-guarded borders of the Soviet Union. Both President Yeltsin and then foreign minister Kozyrev frequently characterized Russia's policies in early 1992 as an attempt to "return to the civilized world," while intellectuals and politicians in Ukraine, Moldova, and Georgia have characterized their nations' policies as the attempt to "return to Europe." In addition to the tentative embrace of Muslim identity described above, the Central Asian leaders have also variously characterized their states as part of a Turkic continuum, and as part of Asian civilization.[18]

While such sentiments have undoubtedly widened the horizons of the post-Soviet leaders and their peoples, the substance of cultural reorientation is less dramatic. Each of the new states has proven with time to have a well-established character, which might be significantly disrupted if the nature of the state were forced to change quickly. The various centers of gravitational attraction, such as Europe, Asia, or the Muslim world, have equally been proven to have their own interests, and their own financial, strategic, and political constraints, which mostly have limited their assistance to expressions of goodwill.

Turkey is a case in point. The country's cultural and linguistic affinities with Central Asia, combined with the fact that Turkey is also a member of NATO and an aspiring member of the EU, made many observers, both within Turkey and without, assume that the country would inevitably become the senior partner—indeed, almost the older brother—of Central Asian development.[19] Politicians and intellectuals in Turkey and in Central Asia began to make plans to write the Central Asian languages with Latin script, as Turkey does, rather than with the modified Cyrillic imposed by the Soviets.[20] The religiously inclined began to dream of restoring the Islamic religious institutions and cultural practices of Central Asia to their pre-Soviet status. Once the leaders understood the immense financial investments that would be required to retool all their printing plants and republish all their printed matter, the matter of alphabet reform became less pressing and legislation mandating it is generally being implemented slowly.[21] Similarly, they came to understand that Islam not only provides an alternative for political allegiance, especially for those elements in society who feel most displaced and disenfranchised, but would leave each of the leaders vulnerable to attack as "bad Muslims." The uneasy relationship between Turkey's secular political establishment and the growing Islamic right was also an example that gave cause for concern. Perhaps even more important, Turkey itself proved to have too little capital, either financial or political, to be able to serve as a strong new patron of the Turkic states in Central Asia. As the Central Asian states came to understand that their "long-lost brother state" had more advice than practical assistance to dispense, Turkey became only one of the many states to which they might reach out, along with Iran, the West, Russia, and China.[22]

While perhaps not as clear-cut, Ukraine and Moldova have had similar experiences with their desires to join "European civilization." Eager as they are to be included in the European continuum, these states have been reluctant or unable to introduce the political and economic systems characteristic of modern European states, although Moldova has been making more steady progress in recent years. Europe's general lack of enthusiasm to embrace these new states in their present form is reflected in the limited way that Europe has opened itself to them. Some or all of the new states have been permitted into bodies like the OSCE and the Council of Europe, special arrangements have been set up to allow cooperation with NATO or the EU, and business and diplomatic contacts have expanded enormously. At the same time, the EU has made plain that full membership is at best a distant dream for most of the CIS states, and most of the European countries have kept in place stiff restrictions on travel and trade by citizens of the CIS.

The relations between Russia and Europe, as well as those between Russia and the West, have been characterized by the same ambivalence discussed in the preceding paragraph, but relations have been made even more complex by uncertainties and confusion, both within Russia and without, about whether Russia is a great power, as its size and nuclear capability would argue, or simply another European state, as its Holland-size economy might suggest. For their part, the Russians have found that their early enthusiasm to "become Western" has been tempered by the deep disappointments of Russia's chaotic economic reforms, by the collapse of the Russian economy—which many see to have been part of a deliberate Western design—and by a fear that the West is innately hostile to Slavs and to Orthodoxy, a belief that was strengthened by NATO bombing in Serbia.

While the process of redrawing the cultural map of the former USSR is proving to be far slower and more complex than observers in the early 1990s presumed it would be, the process is nevertheless proceeding. The Russo-centric Soviet education that the present leaders and most of the elite in the various CIS states received disappeared almost a decade ago, as did the comparative economic egalitarianism and tightly closed borders that were equally part of the

Soviet system. The CIS states are increasingly differentiating them-selves from one another, and the populations within each state are rapidly separating into haves and have-nots. Some of the youth in the CIS states are already world travelers, multilingual, and ready to compete in the twenty-first century, while others are sinking back into the poverty, ignorance, and disease of the nineteenth century.

It thus seems inevitable that, as the shared Soviet experience fades further into the past, and even more so as a new generation of leaders who never knew that past comes to power, the ways in which the various new states orient and define themselves will change. Even the relatively short experience of independence that these states have already enjoyed, however, demonstrates that there is nothing inevitable, easy, or self-evident about the ways in which the former USSR will redraw itself.

ECONOMIC CHALLENGES

As chapter 2 has documented, there is an enormous redirection of trade underway throughout the former USSR, as the new states attempt to broaden their trade relationships and to look beyond the inherited Soviet economic patterns. The overall volume of trade between the CIS and the outside world has been kept smaller than most participants would like or had anticipated it would be. The trade has become, however, much more diversified and broad-based. An enormous but largely undocumented expansion of "suitcase trade" has opened up new trade links, bringing Turkish, Polish, Chinese, and other small private traders to the CIS, as enormous numbers of people from the former USSR travel to these neighboring countries. There are more than a million visitors from the CIS in Poland on any given day.[23] Russian markets in China's Heilongjiang Province and Beijing are an essential element in the provisioning of the Russian Far East and Far North, while Chinese traders are a prominent feature of Russian cities like Chita and are found in even Moscow. Chinese goods and merchants are equally visible in markets in Kyrgyzstan and Kazakhstan.

This small-scale trade, of course, is in addition to the larger transac-tions that have been discussed elsewhere in this book. In general, this widening of trade reflects a slow but steady normalization of economic life after decades of Soviet planning, which created inten-sive but unprofitable links within the USSR, and few or none outside it, even with neighboring states. This process of trade normalization will continue, but the still largely unreformed economies of most of the CIS states will slow the pace of change significantly. As this book has already suggested, the expectations of both the outside world and of the CIS member states about what foreign assistance and investment could or should do have generally been exaggerated. We will now detail the interplay of expectation and reality that have characterized three representative initiatives that would have enormous impacts on the economies of at least some of the CIS states, were they to be realized. These are: (1) the possibility of enlargement of the European Union; (2) the development of Caspian energy; and (3) the elaboration of a new east-west trade and transportation corridor.

The European Union

The European Union is the most important regional economic organization in the vicinity of the CIS. It already has fifteen members, with six more countries—Estonia, Poland, the Czech Republic, Hungary, Slovenia, and Cyprus—scheduled to join over the next few years, and another six, including Latvia and Lithuania, at various stages in the application process. None of the CIS states has applied, although the presidents of Ukraine and Georgia have declared that their countries would like to do so. The European response was so immediately discouraging, and all these CIS states are so far from meeting even minimum standards for membership, that it seems extremely unlikely that any of the CIS states will be admitted into the EU within the next fifteen years. At the same time, as a major economic bloc, the EU is going to have a great impact on all the CIS countries, but particularly on Ukraine, Belarus, and Russia.

To date, the impact of the EU on the CIS has come largely in the form of technical assistance, for which the EU committed slightly more than 3 billion ECU (approximately $2.5 billion) to the countries of the CIS between 1991 and 1997. This money has gone into a variety of sectors: nuclear safety, privatization and government reform, education, energy, transport, telecommunications, and agriculture.[24] The EU is also the primary mover behind and one of the major funders of the TRACECA project. However, EU auditors have repeatedly criticized TACIS, the fund-dispersing agency, as being both misdirected and mismanaged.[25]

Europe is the most important Western trading partner for the CIS states. The EU is already a major trade partner for Russia and a partner of increasing importance for most of the CIS countries. Recognizing the position of the CIS countries, the EU has signed numerous trade agreements with several of these countries individually, which serve to minimize protectionist impediments to trade in most kinds of goods.[26] However, the EU is highly protectionist with regard to four kinds of so-called sensitive goods: textiles, agricultural goods, metals, and chemicals. Exporters of such goods face trade barriers in the form of higher tariffs or quotas. The most exposed CIS country is Moldova, whose exports are heavily concentrated in the sensitive goods sectors. Sensitive goods account for roughly two-thirds of Ukraine's exports and about one-third of those of Russia and Belarus. Ukraine and Russia are vulnerable to sudden antidumping actions against their steel exporters. A minor trade war almost erupted in the winter of 1997 when Russia and the European Union threatened retaliatory tariffs against each other in a dispute over Russian-EU textile trade. Although an agreement on the textile issue was reached between the EU and Russia in April 1998, more problems will arise, especially if Poland or any of the Baltic republics are granted admission into the EU, since these countries are now major markets for Russian goods.

The economic prosperity that membership in the EU is likely to bring, as well as the stiff trade barriers that help maintain that inner prosperity, present a real danger that a new "iron curtain" might descend along the borders between the EU and the CIS. Not only would this barrier impede trade between the two regions, it would also be likely to mark a vivid boundary between prosperity and poverty, which could easily have social and political consequences.

The EU has a common labor market, which it protects with a strict visa regime. New members of the EU would be required not only to tighten controls on trade with CIS countries but also to limit the number of CIS citizens admitted into their countries. This would destabilize informal trade and employment patterns that have already become well established. The increase in trade that the eastern and central European countries would enjoy by joining the EU would more than compensate for their losses in the "gray zone" economy, which depends on freelance traders and guest-workers from CIS countries, but the CIS companies and individuals who would find themselves shut out of the newly expanded EU would suffer greatly. Until 1997, for example, citizens of Russia, Ukraine, and Belarus could travel to Poland without a visa. In late 1997, however, Poland introduced visa requirements for Russians and Belarusians, which not only provoked stiff diplomatic protests in Minsk and Moscow, but also prompted local Polish traders and businessmen to block highways in protest of their trading losses.[27] Poland later modified its visa regime somewhat, but visas remained compulsory, leaving its borders open only for Ukrainians. Once Poland actually joins the EU, even that exception will vanish, which may cause further disruption of regional economic, social, and cultural ties. The admission of Poland into the EU would thus result in a major regional realignment, to the detriment of non-EU members.

Even the sorts of assistance projects that interest the EU place significant strains upon the CIS countries. The EU has a limited capacity for policy making and decision making, which tends to make it focus on projects of immediate concern. An example is the vigor with which the EU has pressured CIS states to shut down Chernobyl-style nuclear power stations, including that in Chernobyl itself. While no one in the CIS disputes that these reactors are dangerous, the issues of who would pay to dismantle them, and how the electricity that they generate would be replaced, remain unresolved. Most of the assistance that the EU has provided to the CIS has been directed at issues of nuclear safety. Not all of the money that has been promised has been delivered, however, nor would it come close to paying for the infrastructure changes necessary to shut down the Chernobyl reactors even if all of the funds had been disbursed.

In sum, a strong, successful EU that takes an active interest in promoting investment and trade with its neighbors would have long-term, positive effects on the CIS countries, and particularly on those that are closest, such as Russia, Ukraine, Belarus, and Moldova. In the short run, however, the existing growing pains, which have been further exacerbated by financial crises and currency devaluations in the CIS states, suggest that friction is likely to continue between the EU and the CIS.

Caspian Energy

All positive projections for the development of the Caucasian and Central Asian states depend upon the successful development of

Caspian Basin oil and gas reserves. These reserves are only a fraction of those to be found in the major Persian Gulf producers, but they are still of great interest to Western states that are eager to diversify their potential sources of supply as much as possible.[28]

The oil business requires the constant search for new sources of oil. When the Soviet Union collapsed, the major oil and gas companies inevitably began to compete with each other to secure exploration and exploitation rights in this new market, which the states fortunate enough to have reserves were happy to encourage. Some Caspian leaders played their "oil card" better than others did. President Aliyev, for example, managed not only to draw virtually all the major oil companies into Azerbaijan,[29] but also proved extraordinarily adept at leveraging that interest into diplomatic support from the oil firms' home countries. Even in the less skillfully managed resource-rich states, however, the opening of the Caspian Basin set off a kind of "feeding frenzy," which caused reports of the size of the oil deposits to be exaggerated.

Although preliminary investment has helped slow the collapse of the economies in the new states, actual oil and gas production have not yet made a strong contribution to their economic development. Output in Kazakhstan and Azerbaijan has only returned to its Soviet-era production level, while Turkmenistan's gas sector remains in serious decline.[30]

As has previously been discussed, transportation of oil and gas remains difficult. Until recently, Russia has all but shut Turkmenistan off from world markets for its natural gas and has also made it hard for both Kazakhstan and Azerbaijan to export their resources. New pipelines will be built through the area eventually, but when and how many is still being hotly debated. The Caspian Pipeline Consortium (CPC) from Tengiz, Kazakhstan, to Novorossiisk, Russia, seems almost certain to be built, as is another to the south that will trace an east-west route.[31] But the pipeline from Baku, Azerbaijan, to Ceyhan, Turkey, is unlikely to be built anytime soon, despite strong U.S. government support for a route that would reduce Azerbaijan, Kazakhstan, and Turkmenistan's dependence on Russia. Profitability of this pipeline is also predicated on the completion of a Trans-Caspian Pipeline. There are plans to construct both oil and gas pipelines—the latter is moving forward more rapidly than the former, but industry insiders do not believe that either will be developed any time soon.[32] Until world oil prices rise substantially, Western oil companies investing in the Caspian may not be in a hurry to exercise their exploitation options.

Even if economically attractive pipeline routes are constructed, the Caspian reserves will remain costly to develop. Most problematic are the reserves under the Caspian Sea itself. The similarly sized deposits of North Sea oil, expensive as they were to develop, were still far easier to access than the Caspian deposits would be, because the North Sea is open ocean and submersible rigs were able to be moved in by ship. This is not possible in the Caspian region. The only shipyards on the Caspian are in Russia, and they are already working to capacity. Most Western firms working in the region are thus faced with the prospect of building drilling rigs elsewhere, cutting them down to ship into the region, and then reassembling them, before moving them into drilling position. This entire process takes approximately two years from start to finish.[33]

Before the continued depression in prices and the downward revision of estimated oil reserves made an oil bonanza seem unlikely, there was widespread concern about what the Caspian states might do with their "windfall profits." The fear was that nouveau riche states would succumb to the so-called Dutch disease, meaning that they would use oil rents to support current state expenses, rather than investing the income to develop a diverse, complex, and sustainable national economy.[34] Increasingly, however, the awareness seems to be growing that no bonanza is on the immediate horizon, and that natural resource extraction is going to become at best only one part of economic restructuring.

The economics of Caspian oil and gas development are already changing. In late 1998 Pennzoil, Lukoil, Agip, and the State Oil Company of Azerbaijan disbanded their joint venture, the Caspian International Petroleum Company, which was to have developed the Karabakh deposit, after the exploration phase yielded three dry wells. Earlier in the year Unocal withdrew from a pipeline consortium that planned to ship Turkmenistan's gas east through Afghanistan to Pakistan and India; Afghanistan's lingering civil war played a critical role in that decision, but continued friction between India and Pakistan also made it seem imprudent to ship gas destined for the former through the territory of the latter.

It is not difficult to imagine that the set of international circumstances that provided the geopolitical background for the Caspian oil "feeding frenzy" might change equally quickly. The existing perceptions of Russia as a regional spoiler and the United States as a general savior already seem less accurate. Russia has without question made it difficult for Azerbaijan and the Central Asian states to market their petroleum. The immediacy of this has lessened somewhat, as low prices make Western companies less eager to push quickly, while the United States' inability to move the pipeline and other development issues from discussion to action throws doubt on the seriousness of other U.S. commitments. This is particularly true in the post-Kosovo security environment. The United States and its partners in NATO may be much slower to intervene after their experience in Kosovo; this will certainly reduce enthusiasm to try to play an active role in other parts of the world that are ripe with ethnic antagonisms. Outside interest in the Caspian region, both public and private, has fallen significantly, even though the many battles that have ravaged parts of the area seem now to have ended. Despite the increasing stability of the region, if a new round of fighting were to break out somewhere in the Caspian region, or in the states that stand between the region and world markets, Western interest in the Caspian would certainly diminish further.

The East-West Transportation Corridor

The challenge of transporting Caspian oil led to more general interest in improving other links to the Caucasus and Central Asia, which the USSR had consciously isolated from all points of the compass save the north, where Russia lies. Once they became independent, the states of Central Asia and the Caucasus were acutely aware of their economic isolation and the lack of basic transportation and communication links with potential markets outside the CIS. They also understood the political leverage that Russia gained over them by standing between them and the outside world.

It was to address this isolation that the TRACECA project was formed in 1993, as a cooperative effort between the EU and the CIS republics of Georgia, Armenia, Azerbaijan, Kazakhstan, Tajikistan, Uzbekistan, and Turkmenistan. Later, Mongolia and Ukraine joined in October 1996, followed by Moldova in May 1998. TRACECA's objective is to create a system of trade routes from Europe, across the Black Sea, through the Caucasus and Caspian Sea to Central Asia.

Its goals are to encourage the political and economic independence of these new states and to draw them closer to one another and to the European community.[35] The TRACECA programs are enormously ambitious and would take decades and billions of dollars to complete. In the short-term, TRACECA's importance to the CIS is best measured in its effectiveness as a catalyst for investment and its ability to create a climate for increased involvement between the CIS and outside world.

For now the TRACECA program is focusing on offering technical assistance funded through the EU. To date, TRACECA has spent 30 million ECU (approximately $25 million) on studies but only 20 million ECU (approximately $16.7 million) on investment projects. According to TRACECA officials, the technical assistance it has provided has helped attract larger investments from other financial institutions totaling $200 million from the European Bank for Reconstruction and Development and $40 million from the World Bank. The Asian Development Bank has pledged $50 million toward the modernization of Kyrgyzstan's Osh-Bishkek highway.[36] The technical assistance programs have focused on training local officials in methods of Western-style management and oversight of transportation systems, on promoting a new legal and regulatory framework for the facilitation of cross-border trade, and on rebuilding key elements of transportation infrastructure, such as roads, rail, and ferry links. These technical assistance studies have frequently permitted the preparation of applications to secure full funding for the actual costs of new infrastructure construction from outside financial institutions.

TRACECA's working group meetings have also been the forum for policy initiatives and joint resolutions that have facilitated regional cooperation. Five working group meetings have been held thus far: in Brussels in May 1993, Almaty in May 1995, Vienna in October 1995, Venice in March 1996, Athens in October 1996, and Tbilisi in May 1998. The meetings have become increasingly publicized as the CIS countries, especially Georgia and Azerbaijan, have staked more of their economic future on the growth of transit routes through their countries. A major conference was held in Baku in September 1998, at which all countries and organizations directly and indirectly affiliated with TRACECA were represented, including all EU countries, the United States, and the United Nations.[37] The conference served as a forum for the signing of a major agreement between the TRACECA partners on cooperation and future tasks. The signed document contained clauses dealing with customs tariffs, taxation, highway and cargo safety, supporting services, environmental protection, insurance, and legal safeguards. There were also technical agreements on automobile and railway transport and on customs and shipping procedures. The participating countries also signed an agreement to create an intergovernmental commission to oversee the project's development, the executive secretariat of which is to be based in Baku.[38]

Although it was primarily about intentions and future projects, the Baku meeting did demonstrate that the impulses behind TRACECA can promote the subordination of local conflicts to the larger goal of attracting regional investment. The most vivid demonstration of this was the decision by Azerbaijan's President Aliyev to invite an Armenian delegation to the conference, even though the two states have essentially been at war with one another over the Karabakh region since 1988. The overall effect of the Baku meeting, and of the TRACECA project more generally, has been to demonstrate how outside forces may combine to better integrate some of the CIS republics not only into the world economy, but with one another as well. At the same time, though, the implicit purpose of the TRACECA project is to free several of the CIS states of their dependence upon Russian transportation links,[39] which Russia strongly opposes. If the EU and other supporters of TRACECA pursue the project too aggressively, they risk triggering Russia's suspicions that it is being outflanked and surrounded. Since those same sensibilities are also being goaded by efforts of the OSCE, NATO's Partnership for Peace, and Western military assistance to incorporate the Caucasus and Central Asian republics into broader Western policy, the calculation of how best to stimulate regional cooperation and development in the southern tier of CIS states without setting off a potentially catastrophic escalation of trade protection and other self-defensive measures remains a delicate one.

SECURITY CHALLENGES

Western Europe's basic security structures are highly institutionalized, in broad-based structures of political, economic, and security integration and cooperation. NATO is the leading example, but the European nations also exercise significant security policy coordination through the European Union and the Western European Union, even if the defense capacity of both organizations is underdeveloped.[40] Europe as a whole is integrated into a host of arms control arrangements, largely the product of attempts to regulate East-West security competition. No such security institutions exist in the former USSR. Most states lack the means to fund even basic national security institutions, to say nothing of a collective defense structure. Still more inhibiting is the lack of a basic security consensus among the Soviet successor states.

There has been considerable speculation about the role that the outside world might play in filling this security gap. Some of the new states, such as Ukraine, have actively sought to develop enhanced security ties with countries outside the CIS, of which the U.S.-Ukrainian and Ukrainian-Polish strategic partnerships are examples. Ukraine and Russia have negotiated a special charter with NATO.[41] Turkey and Azerbaijan have cooperated militarily, but on a modest level.[42] Some Belarusian and Russian commentators have noted with alarm instances of U.S. and NATO security interaction within the former USSR. Georgia's declaration in early 1999 in which it stated NATO membership as a future goal of the country's foreign policy has only exacerbated this alarm. A statement by Azerbaijan's foreign minister in early 1999 in which he expressed his country's willingness to host NATO troops on Azerbaijan's territory elicited an outcry among the Russian national security establishment.

What the outside world has tried to do instead is to stimulate greater security interaction and cooperation within the former USSR. Among the policies and programs designed to foster these goals are military-to-military contacts, technical assistance, joint training, and a variety of programs under NATO's Partnership for Peace. The Organization for Security and Cooperation in Europe has become the European security organization concerned with conflicts in the former USSR. This section will examine in greater detail the roles played in bridging the security gap in the former USSR by the Partnership for Peace and the NATO Alliance, by the OSCE, and by the arms control process.

NATO

NATO is the most important security structure in the post-cold war European security environment, and it has flourished particularly following the collapse of the Warsaw Pact and the USSR itself. The extension of NATO membership to Poland, Hungary, and the Czech Republic stimulated broad resentment in Russia and Belarus, both of which warned of unspecified countermeasures. Russian threats took on a greater air of reality during the spring 1999 NATO campaign against Serbia. While Russia's sensibilities were largely appeased by their involvement alongside the NATO peacekeeping force in Kosovo, their resentment is certain to reach potentially dysfunctional levels if future rounds of NATO enlargement come to include former Soviet republics.

NATO enlargement has the capacity to split further the CIS, since Russia and Belarus were the only CIS states that saw their interests threatened or even impinged by NATO enlargement. Many in Ukraine feared the possible consequences of Russian reactions to NATO enlargement, but most senior officials welcomed the actual enlargement itself; during his June 1996 visit to Warsaw, President Kuchma described NATO as "the only real guarantor of security on the continent" and warmly supported Poland's desire to join the alliance.[43] Ukraine also worked to fashion its own special relationship with the alliance. Kazakhstan welcomed enlargement as well; at a meeting in Brussels in May 1998, Kazakh Foreign Minister Tokayev called the decision to enlarge the alliance "evidence of the move towards a united, stable, and democratic Europe."[44]

Although it has established a special NATO-Russian Joint Council, designed to give Russia more access to NATO's deliberations, NATO's day-to-day contact with the rest of the CIS states is through the Partnership for Peace (PFP), a program of cooperation launched at the January 1994 NATO Summit. PFP aims to develop cooperation and close ties between members and nonmembers, both to prepare some of the latter for eventual NATO membership and to encourage security cooperation with those states that will remain outside the alliance. All of the states of the former USSR are members of PFP.

PFP sponsors a wide range of programs aimed at defense and military cooperation in which several CIS states have been active participants. These include joint work between members and nonmembers on air defense and airspace management, crisis management, defense planning, and military education.[45] PFP also sponsors joint exercises to create both the technical bases and the habits of cooperation, which NATO characterizes as "interoperability."

Through the Partnership for Peace and with the support of the United States and other individual NATO members, PFP partners have received communications gear, English language training, computers, and other basic support to enhance their participation in the program. The PFP activities within the CIS have been diverse, ranging from medical evacuation training that Moldovan military and technical units received during Medceur-97 exercises to computer assistance given to the Georgians by the Greek Armed Forces in January 1999. PFP has also inaugurated a regional airspace initiative that it would like to see include members from Central Europe and the CIS, which is aimed at tying the airspace of the partners into the system already established in Western Europe. Additionally, the United States has initiated its own State Partnership Program as a subset of its PFP activities, which is operated by the U.S. National Guard. This program began in 1992 with U.S. National Guard Assistance to the Baltic states and has now grown to include Ukraine, Belarus, Georgia, Kazakhstan, Uzbekistan, Kyrgyzstan, and Turkmenistan.[46]

PFP, with the bilateral support of the United States and other member countries, has sponsored many joint command and field exercises, from platoon to brigade level. In addition to the Central Asian Battalion-97 and Central Asian Battalion-98 exercises that were described in chapter 5, these exercises have included Sea Breeze-97 and Sea Breeze-98, both held in Crimea, and the latter featured live surface-to-surface firing. Ukraine played an active role in the Cooperative-Partner Dragon-99 exercises in the Black Sea in June 1999, and Georgia, Armenia and Uzbekistan each took part in some phase of these operations as well.

Ukraine has been an active PFP member, although it has simultaneously tried to remain sensitive to Russian concerns. Ukraine has hosted several cooperative neighbor exercises, including exercises near Lviv in July 1997 and September 1998 that included Moldovan participation. The Ukrainians and the Poles are forming POLUKRBAT, a Polish-Ukrainian peacekeeping battalion that is being organized under PFP auspices and is going to participate in the NATO operation in Kosovo.[47] Georgia is an extremely active PFP member. Cooperative Partner-2000 exercises are planned for Georgia. The Georgians, who requested admission to NATO in July 1999, participated in 120 PFP activities during 1998.[48]

Not surprisingly, many in the Russian national security establishment have roundly criticized the PFP exercises and the participation of CIS states in PFP activities more generally.[49] Russian observers argue that the PFP and other bilateral military-to-military efforts that have brought NATO into the defense planning and military reforms of many states of the CIS are designed to transform security relations within the CIS. While it is true that PFP has worked to prepare aspirants for NATO membership, it is also true that, at present, no CIS country is even close to being considered for membership.

PFP deliberately tries to achieve interoperability in relatively uncontroversial operations, such as peacekeeping or search and rescue, and makes no attempt to influence basic decisions about doctrines or forces for more serious military operations. PFP offers additional training to a small number of military officers from member nations, but the scope is insignificant compared with the numbers who are trained locally or in Russia; in particular, Belarus and Kazakhstan train a large number of officers in Russia.

It is possible that two CIS states may move toward NATO membership more quickly than the others. Both Georgia and Ukraine have received substantial supplemental bilateral military support from the United States, the United Kingdom, and other NATO states and have correspondingly reduced their military cooperation with Russia. Georgia's assumption of its coastal defense responsibilities (see chapter 3), for example, depends not only on support from Ukraine, but also on assistance from the United States and the United Kingdom.

The most important constraint upon the widening of PFP, and even more so of NATO, is that all of the CIS states still face enormous difficulties in establishing their basic national military structures. None of the CIS states, including Russia, has undertaken systematic military reform, in large part because none of them has the money to do so. Thus, for most of the CIS states, PFP is likely to remain no more than a marginal influence, working toward long-term transformations rather than attempting the immediate reorientation of the CIS security environment that some Russian analysts fear.

The OSCE

The Organization for Security and Cooperation in Europe is the universal European security organization, encompassing all states from Europe and the former USSR, as well as the United States and Canada.[50] The body has a long history of developing norms for the whole of Europe on questions of human rights and economic matters. Among its successes were the confidence-building measures negotiated in Stockholm in 1986, which set new standards of transparency and predictability for conventional armed forces in Europe.[51] Russia considers the body to be the key security mechanism in Europe because of its universality and its practice of making decisions by consensus.[52]

The OSCE itself has adapted to the post-cold war world by finding ways to involve the organization in ongoing conflicts and human rights disputes. But the organization's universality also makes it a weaker and less decisive organization than NATO. Compared with those two bodies, the OSCE is financially weak and lacks basic military and diplomatic assets; resources must be provided by states willing to do so after the OSCE as a whole has agreed on the need for involvement. These strengths and weaknesses have made the OSCE the international actor of choice in many of the problems in the post-Soviet environment. The OSCE has neither the authority nor the resources to impose economic sanctions or to threaten airstrikes; what it offers instead is the possibility to place impartial observers from the outside world into ongoing conflicts. The efficacy of the OSCE's role thus ultimately depends on the acquiescence of the disputing parties.

The OSCE has been active in efforts to resolve the conflict in Karabakh since 1992. Among its initiatives was the Minsk Group, which is the main diplomatic forum attempting to reach a settlement of the conflict. Originally the mediation group included Armenia, Azerbaijan, Belarus, the Czech and Slovak Republics, France, Germany, Italy, Russia, Sweden, Turkey, and the United States, but after the group failed to make progress membership was reduced in 1994 to a troika of representatives drawn from the United States, Russia, and France. Plans put forward at a summit in Budapest that year would have placed 2,000 OSCE-mandated peacekeeping troops on the ground to supervise a cease-fire; this would have been the first time that the OSCE moved beyond mediation and observation to the concrete implementation of agreed cease-fires and settlements. An agreement on the plan was not reached, so no peacekeeping contingent was sent.

In Moldova, the OSCE has tried to broker a deal over the break-away region of Transdniestr. A modest eight-member OSCE mission was created in February 1993, after the Russian-mediated cease-fire of 1992. The pace of efforts to reach a settlement was set by the combatants, with Russian mediation, but the OSCE frequently proved more able to move negotiations forward than did Russia, largely because it was free of Russia's burdens and calculations of interests. The OSCE formulated the settlement plan that the Moldovan government accepted in early 1994. Since then the OSCE has maintained a consistent and useful presence in Moldova, even though the actual negotiation toward a solution is being conducted by the Transdniestrians, Moldovans, and Russians; the Russians ceded part of their role to the Ukrainians in 1997.[53]

The OSCE has had a mission in Chechnya since January 1995. This is particularly significant because Russia permitted the observers to operate in a conflict that both Russia and the international community consider to be an internal matter. At key points these OSCE representatives have functioned as a liaison between Russia, the Chechen commanders, and the Chechen government, and are the only group that has succeeded in doing so. After the 1996 peace agreement, the OSCE monitored the elections of the new government; it remains the only international organization operating in Chechnya. Since 1997 the OSCE has dealt with issues of human rights, crime, and hostage release, and has channeled international donations to the Chechen government.

International Arms Control and Cooperative Security Efforts

There are important international arms control agreements that apply to all or part of the territory of the former USSR. Russia, Ukraine, Kazakhstan, and Belarus are all formal parties to START I, the Intermediate-Range Nuclear Forces treaty (INF), the Stockholm and Vienna OSCE agreements on confidence building, and the CFE treaty. Most of these treaties are intended primarily, if not exclusively, to regulate and restrict the competition between military superpowers and their allies. Some of the provisions of those treaties, such as those requiring data exchange, on-site inspection, and other transparency measures, have not lost their relevance, but others, such as those setting levels for tanks or combat aircraft based on the resources of the Soviet military, have little relevance to the emerging regional military balances.[54]

Regional arms control is far more important in the current circumstances. If it comes to the CIS at all, it is likely to come in agreements that resolve the most serious conflicts, such as that over Karabakh. Presumably such an agreement, if one were ever reached, would include some regional regulation of Armenian and Azerbaijani forces and activities, similar to the restrictions built into the Egyptian-Israeli Sinai Agreement.

In both the near and distant future alike, new arms control and cooperative security arrangements are unlikely to emerge in the former USSR. No matter how much the outside world desires that stability be maintained in the area, there is no international constituency for mounting interventions—even on the small scale of the U.S. intervention in Haiti in 1994—to resolve conflicts or to enforce the terms of a settlement in the former Soviet space. The United Nations, OSCE, and key outside countries are all involved in mediating conflicts or observing existing cease-fires in Tajikistan, Abkhazia, South Ossetia, and Karabakh, but no outside country or organization has expressed interest in expanding these roles, to say nothing of taking on the burdens of peacekeeping operations that Russia and the affected countries now assume.

There is one area where there is growing international security cooperation, at least between those most susceptible to potential conflict. Russia, China, Kazakhstan, Kyrgyzstan, and Tajikistan are working to resolve the demarcation of the old Sino-Soviet border in Central Asia. Russia and China settled issues concerning the small section of their border in the Altai region in 1994 and appear to have come to a long-term solution on disputed sections in the Russian Far East in 1997. The five countries continue to negotiate over demarcation elsewhere in Central Asia. To buttress stability along the old Sino-Soviet border, the heads of these five countries have signed two agreements that regulate military forces and activities in the border regions.

The first agreement, signed in Shanghai in April 1996, focuses on an ambitious set of confidence-building measures governing military forces and their activities in a 100-kilometer border zone. The agreed measures include the exchange of information on troop deployments and planned activities, constraints on the size and number of military exercises in this zone, and notification of troop movements or other activities in this zone necessitated by "an emergency situation."[55] The agreement also requires the parties to invite observers to military exercises. The second agreement, concluded at an April 1997 summit, focuses on military reductions. Originally intended as an agreement to demilitarize the 100-kilometer zone, the agreement now calls for Russia to reduce the size of its forces on the 100-meter border zone by 15 percent. Although the details are still unpublished, press reports suggest the treaty limits a wide range of ground, air defense, frontal aviation equipment, and personnel.[56]

These measures, adapted from existing confidence-building regimes in Europe and elsewhere, represent a unique attempt to fill in gaps in the military transparency and regulation of the post-Soviet space through regionally specific measures. The ceilings set on border activities are so high that the agreement imposes little real constraint on any party, but the principles of cooperation it establishes are important.

LIMITED COOPERATION

As this chapter has shown, the high barriers that once stood between the former USSR and the outside world are gone, and interactions that seemed beyond the wildest fantasy a decade ago have now become routine. The new states of the CIS are taking a variety of roles in the world, carving out new roles for themselves, and in doing so they are also creating new relations with one another. For its part, the world has been drawn much farther into what was once the Soviet space than it ever has been before; private investors, governments, and multilateral organizations all have a variety of interests and involvements in the countries of the CIS.

This chapter also shows, however, that the pattern of relations of the CIS member states with the outside world replicates most of the features of the development of the CIS itself. Large ambitions and high ideals characterize the intentions of most of the contacts between the CIS and the outside world, but the reality of what has been accomplished is shaped much more by financial constraints, internal weakness, corruption, and the inability to make interests coincide, or even to define interests at all. In addition, the leaders of the CIS and of the outside world alike are coming to understand that there are no easy solutions that might overcome the isolation, economic stagnation, and internal shortcomings of the post-Soviet states. Reform and development bring benefits, but they also have costs, as people in the CIS and outside it are constantly reminded.

The interaction of the CIS with the outside world also resembles the processes of the CIS itself, in that the lack of efficacy of the large-scale programs and the intention to create change is accompanied by smaller and slower, but far more sustainable, developments. Time and economic necessity are slowly forging new trade routes and also recreating the old ones that the Soviets closed. Westerners come to the CIS looking for oil and gas, or for other kinds of business, while the youth of the CIS elite study in England, Switzerland, and the United States, learning the languages and habits of the outside world. Even ordinary citizens of many of the CIS states—though not all—are able to travel the world in a way that was unthinkable only a few years ago.

Barring a catastrophic change in the geopolitical condition of the world, the cumulative effect of this wide interaction between the CIS and the rest of the world will be to remake and restore balance to trade and cultural patterns, which in turn will alter the political, economic, and security geography of Eurasia itself. At the same time, however, as history demonstrates repeatedly, the large-scale redrawing of a space once occupied by an extinct political entity is least painful when the parties both within and without work consciously to make the process controlled and evolutionary. The alternative, leaving it to unravel unattended, creates results that are far more likely to be chaotic and revolutionary. Fortunately for the member states of the CIS, the former pattern has been more charac-teristic of recent developments than has the latter.

NOTES

[1] The United States hesitated to recognize formally the indepen-dence of the republics until the Commonwealth Agreement (Almaty Declaration) was signed on December 21, 1991. The Bush administration formally announced its recognition of the new states only after Gorbachev resigned as president of the Soviet Union and the Supreme Soviet enacted a declaration, stating that, "the USSR ceases its existence as a state and subject to international law" and dissolved itself on December 25, 1991. The United States offered to establish diplomatic relations with six republics— Armenia, Belarus, Kazakhstan, Kyrgyzstan, Russia, and Ukraine.

It recognized the independence of Azerbaijan, Georgia, Moldova, Tajikistan, Turkmenistan, and Uzbekistan, but stated that diplomatic relations would not be established until those countries committed to more responsible security policies and democratic principles. The successor states to the Soviet Union all assumed individual seats in the United Nations and became members of the Council on Security and Cooperation in Europe (CSCE) in 1992. James P. Nichol, *Diplomacy in the Former Soviet Republics* (Westport, Conn.: Praeger, 1995), pp. 19, 62–3; John Yang, "U.S. to Recognize Russia, 5 Others," *Washington Post*, December 24, 1991; "Text of President Bush's Televised Speech," *Washington Post*, December 26, 1991.

2 Concerns over the maintenance of a single command and control over Soviet nuclear weapons significantly complicated U.S. and other Western nations' recognition of Ukraine, Kazakhstan, and Belarus, though the delays that resulted were relatively minor.

3 Poland, Hungary, Bulgaria, Latvia, Lithuania, and Canada were among the first to recognize Ukraine's independence after the referendum in Ukraine on December 1, 1991, which approved Ukrainian independence and made Leonid Kravchuk president. Most of the international community, including the United States and Western Europe, welcomed the independence vote but did not extend diplomatic recognition until the Soviet Union was formally dissolved on December 25. The Bush administration was cautious to extend diplomatic relations until three areas of concern were discussed: that Ukraine should adhere to international treaties and standards; that it should take steps to become a nuclear-free zone and adhere to international agreements such as START-I, CFE, and the Nuclear Non-Proliferation Treaty (NPT); and that it should plan to set up a market economy and to service its share of debts of the Soviet Union. Nichol, *Diplomacy in the Former Soviet Republics*, pp. 101–4.

4 Ukrainian President Kravchuk's apparent reluctance to follow through on commitments to disarm strained U.S.-Ukrainian relations between 1992 and 1994. As discussed in chapter 4, Ukraine's wavering on disarmament was an expression of its expectation to be compensated financially by the United States for the cost of disarmament and to be granted security guarantees in the absence of its nuclear arsenal. Although Kravchuk repeatedly told the

West that Ukraine was willing to disarm, no concrete steps were taken to this end until the removal of nuclear weapons from Ukraine was formally linked to specific economic and security conditions in the Trilateral Agreement, which was signed by Ukraine, the United States, and Russia in January 1994. For a discussion of the negotiations leading up to the Trilateral Agreement, see Sherman W. Garnett, *Keystone in the Arch: Ukraine in the Emerging Security Environment of Central and Eastern Europe* (Washington, D.C.: Carnegie Endowment for International Peace, 1997), pp. 113–24; Taras Kuzio, *Ukraine under Kuchma* (New York: St. Martin's Press, 1997), pp. 219–21.

[5] Karimov's debut in Washington did not come until June 1996.

[6] See footnote 1 in chapter 1.

[7] "Hungary, Ukraine View Own Security Policies," *Xinhua*, February 26, 1993.

[8] Chrystia Freeland, "Ukraine Seeks Area Security," *Financial Times*, April 22, 1993, p. 2.

[9] "Kazakhstan Initiates Idea of Collective Security in Asia," *Xinhua*, October 5, 1992.

[10] See Ian MacWilliam, "Kazakhstan's Asian Security Forum Needs More Work," *Deutsche Presse-Agentur*, February 6, 1996; G. Tursunbaev, "Stanovlenie gosudarstvennosti i problema bezopasnosti Respubliki Kazakhstan," *Realnost i mify*, July 5, 1999, as published on the Internet website of Impulse (http://www.impulse.kz/mif/NB_RK1.html). At the June 16, 1999 meeting, experts from 16 states agreed on a draft declaration of principles for a Eurasian security system in the framework of the Conference on Interaction and Confidence-Building in Asia (*RFE/RL*, June 3, 1999).

[11] The eponymous people of Tajikistan are of Persian, not Turkic, origin.

[12] There have been five summit-level meetings of the ECO to date: the first in February 1992 in Tehran, the second in July 1993 in Istanbul, the third in March 1995 in Islamabad, the fourth in May 1997 in Ashgabat, the fifth in May 1998 in Almaty.

[13] *RFE/RL Newsline*, July 14, 1993.

[14] Islam Karimov, remarks broadcast on *Tashkent Uzbekistan Television*, May 15, 1996.

[15] Inter-ECO trade was $1.12 billion in 1997, less than it had been in 1996. "Kazakhstan: Kazakh President Calls for More Trade with ECO Members," *Moscow Interfax*, May 11, 1998.

[16] Islam Karimov, remarks broadcast on *Tashkent Uzbekistan First Channel Network*, May 11, 1998.

[17] During the 1993 Istanbul summit, for example, Pakistan was the only member that signed all the proposed documents and agreements. Uzbekistan refused to sign anything except for a charter on setting up an ECO scientific foundation. No CIS countries signed the ECO air agreement. An agreement on visa simplification was signed by all except for Kyrgyzstan and Uzbekistan. *Economic Review*, "ECO Summit—Exploring New Possibility," no. 4, vol. 26, p. 29. At the May 1998 Almaty summit, the presidents of Turkmenistan and Uzbekistan expressed frustration at some of the ECO's grandiose plans, questioning the ECO's ability to follow through on its agenda and calling for a more limited role of focusing on humanitarian and regional economic problems. *Interfax*, May 11, 1998, in FBIS-SOV-98-131.

[18] For more detailed analysis of the use of ethnicity in the politics of Central Asia, see Martha Brill Olcott, *Central Asia's New States: Independence, Foreign Policy, and Regional Security* (Washington, D.C.: United States Institute for Peace Press, 1996), pp. 21–37.

[19] Historically, Turkey and the five Turkic newly independent countries have been part of a single state or empire.

[20] Initially the Soviet authorities decided to replace the Arabic alphabet with the Latin alphabet, but by 1940 all of the USSR's Turkic languages were being written in Cyrillic.

[21] Azerbaijan began alphabet reform in 1990–1991 and is quite far along. Uzbekistan began in 1995 and also is making steady strides. Kazakhstan began in 1996 and has made little progress; however, there are now plans to have a common Latin alphabet in place by 2005. *Ankara Anatolia*, December 6, 1998, in FBIS-WEU-98-340; *Ankara Anatolia*, July 5, 1999, FBIS-WEU-1999-0705.

[22] For example, even allowing for large discrepancies in reported data, Turkey is just a minor trading partner for all of the Central Asian countries. According to reported statistics, Turkmenistan is the country in the region that engages in the most trade with Turkey; trade with Turkey accounts for only about 10 percent of its imports and 2.5 percent of its exports. International Monetary Fund, *Direction of Trade Statistics Yearbook* (Washington, D.C.: International Monetary Fund, 1998), pp. 276, 285, 427, 445, 461.

[23] *Gazeta Wyborcza*, December 11, 1996, as cited in OMRI Daily Digests, December 11, 1996.

[24] *TACIS Annual Report* 1997, as published on the Internet website of the European Union TACIS (http://europa.eu.int/comm/dgla/ tacis/annualrep97/en/annualrep97_index.htm), 1997.

[25] *Moscow Times*, November 21, 1998.

[26] By the end of 1996 the European Union had signed bilateral Partnership and Cooperation Agreements (PCA) with ten CIS countries. In May 1997 a PCA with Turkmenistan was initialed. By July 1998 PCA agreements with Moldova, Russia, and Ukraine have entered into force. As of July 1998 Tajikistan was the only CIS state that had not signed a PCA. Data from the Internet website of the European Union (http://europa.eu.int/comm/dg1a/nis/ econ/toward_eco_integration.htm).

[27] *RFE/RL Newsline*, February 10, 1998.

[28] Proven oil reserves in the Caspian Basin are currently estimated at 15 to 31 billion barrels, about 2.7 percent of total world proven reserves. Future exploration may show that the region holds more substantial oil reserves, potentially as high as 60 billion to 140 billion barrels. Proven natural gas reserves of 230 trillion to 360 trillion cubic feet represent about 7 percent of total world proven gas reserves. Figures cited in Martha Brill Olcott and Amy Myers Jaffe, "The Geopolitics of Caspian Energy," in Yelena Kalyuzhnova and Dov Lynch Macmillan, eds., *The Euro-Asian World: A Period of Transition* (Macmillian, forthcoming).

[29] The major consortium in Azerbaijan is the Azerbaijan International Operating Company (AIOC). It includes Penzoil, Unocal, and Exxon of the U.S.; British Petroleum/Amoco and Ramco of the U.K.; the State Oil Company of Azerbaijan (SOCAR); Lukoil of Russia; Statoil of Norway; ITOCHU of Japan; Turkish Petroleum Company; and Delta Hess of Saudi Arabia.

[30] Azerbaijan produced 9 million metric tons of oil and 6 billion cubic meters of gas in 1997. The Kazakh government estimates these figures for Kazakhstan at 25.7 million metric tons and 6.1 billion cubic meters, respectively. Turkmenistan, which saw a 50 percent decline in its gas production between 1996 and 1997, saw this figure decline again in 1998 to 11.5 billion cubic meters for the first eleven months of the year. *Economist Intelligence Unit Country Reports*, January 8, 1999, January 29, 1999, and February 22, 1999; PlanEcon, *Energy Outlook for Eastern Europe and the Former Soviet Republics, October 1998* (Washington, D.C.: PlanEcon, 1998), p. 79.

[31] Although figures vary according to different sources, the standard estimated cost of the CPC pipeline is $2 billion; the Baku-Ceyhan route would cost around $2.5 billion, and a pipeline from Baku to Supsa is estimated at $238 million.

[32] Enron, based in Texas, conducted a feasibility study with OPIC funding on a proposed Trans-Caspian pipeline route. Their report estimates that a pipeline carrying natural gas from Turkmenistan to Turkey would cost approximately $2.5 billion. This proposed Trans-Caspian pipeline would go beneath the Caspian Sea and through Azerbaijan and Georgia to Turkey. *Pipeline and Gas Journal*, "International Highlights," March 1, 1999. The construction and management of the pipeline has been assigned to Pipeline Solutions Group International, which is recruiting investors to finance the project.

[33] Amy Myers Jaffe and Robert A. Manning, *Survival*, vol. 40, no. 4 (Winter 1998).

[34] For a thorough analysis of the political and economic effects of oil booms and a more detailed explanation of "Dutch disease," see Terry Lynn Karl, *The Paradox of Plenty: Oil Booms and Petro-States* (Berkeley: University of California Press, 1997).

[35] "What is TRACECA," as published on the Internet website of TRACECA (http://www.traceca.org/whatis.html), February 1, 1999.

[36] This road runs through four of Kyrgyzstan's six regions, making it critical to the Kyrgyz infrastructure. Kazakhstan also sees this road as an important link to its Central Asian neighbors. There is also consideration of a more ambitious trade route across Uzbekistan and Kyrgyzstan to China. It is projected to run from Tashkent via Andijan, Jalalabad, Osh, with side spurs to Irkeshtan and Turugart into China. Uzbek President Karimov and Kyrgyz President Akaev urged that this route be adopted by the TRACECA project at the Baku conference on September 8–9, 1998. *Jamestown Monitor*, September 11, 1998.

[37] The May 1998 TRACECA Group was the last working group meeting to be held to date. The Baku September 1998 meeting, however, was a major TRACECA event, but it was not formally designated as a working meeting.

[38] *Jamestown Monitor*, vol. 4, no. 164, September 9, 1998.

[39] Georgia's President Eduard Shevardnadze used the Baku meeting to castigate "[those who] seek to monopolize transit and dictate

their own terms have spurred us to seek an alternative trade route
. . . we prefer an expansion of foreign capital and technology over
anyone's military expansion into our countries," *Jamestown Monitor*, vol. 4, no. 165, September 11, 1998.

[40] The Western European Union is a defense organization that had its
origins in 1954 when seven countries—Belgium, France, Germany,
Italy, Luxembourg, the Netherlands and the United Kingdom—
signed the Paris Agreements modifying the 1948 Brussels Treaty.
Portugal and Spain became member states in 1990. All the preceding countries are also members of the EU and NATO. Since 1990
the Western European Union has expanded to include twenty-
eight countries by offering access to all EU members and extending
associate, observer, or partnership status to the eastern European
countries and the Baltic states. No CIS state is a member. The
Western European Union itself is weak in terms of defensive
capacity, but it cooperates with NATO and the European Union on
a regular basis. The European Union has no defensive or military
structures, although there have been proposals in recent years to
increase the connections between the two organizations.

[41] The "Charter on a Distinctive Partnership Between NATO and
Ukraine," signed on July 9, 1997, established a NATO-Ukraine
commission that was to meet regularly with top NATO policy
makers to consult on such areas as conflict prevention; nuclear,
biological, and chemical non-proliferation; arms control issues;
and combating drug-trafficking and terrorism. NATO and Russia
signed a similar charter on May 27, 1997, which cleared the way
for NATO to ask Poland, the Czech Republic, and Hungary to
join the alliance in 1999.

[42] Military cooperation between Turkey and Azerbaijan began in
1992 in the form of military training. The defense ministers of the
two countries signed a bilateral agreement on military cooperation
on June 10, 1996, in Ankara that called for an increase in military
training and the sharing of defense technology. In February 1999,
Azerbaijan's foreign minister visited Ankara to discuss the possibility of stationing Turkish armed forces in Azerbaijan, as well as
Turkish assistance in the form of training and air defense, though
earlier rumors of a military pact between the two countries have
thus far been denied by both sides.

[43] *Zycie Warszawy*, June 24, 1996, pp. 1, 6.

[44] "Address of the Minister of Foreign Affairs of the Republic of Kazakhstan, Mr. Kasymzhomart Tokayev," Euroatlantic Partnership Council, Luxembourg, May 29, 1998, as published on the Internet website of NATO (http://www.nato.int/docu/speech/1998/s980529j.htm).

[45] The Defense Resource Management Studies Program, for example, purports to develop defense management systems similar to those of NATO countries with Ukraine, Georgia, and Uzbekistan. The Defense Planning Exchanges Program funds exchanges of military and civilian officials and fosters transparency between Kazakhstan, Uzbekistan, and Ukraine with the United States. The Partner Information Management System Program, which has been developed in Ukraine, Uzbekistan, Moldova, Georgia, Kazakhstan, and Kyrgyzstan, is a network communications system that connects PFP countries to key NATO structures to facilitate exercise planning on-line and to overcome communications barriers in general. *Department of Defense Report to Congress on the Partnership for Peace Developments through July 15, 1998.*

[46] The State Partnership Program pairs each PFP country with a state in the United States. The program's activities are diverse, but include exercises that involve military support activities, humanitarian aid, and peacekeeping. For a more detailed look at the State Partnership Program, see John Groves, "PFP and the State Partnership Program: Fostering Engagement and Progress," *Parameters*, Spring 1999, pp. 43–53.

[47] The Polish-Ukrainian battalion (POLUKRBAT) was formally agreed upon by Poland and Ukraine under the framework of PFP in November 1997 after several years of discussion and debate, although joint exercises between the two countries were held in 1996 under the auspices of PFP exercises Peace Shield-96, Tatry-96, and Brave Eagle-97. In Peace Shield-98, POLUKRBAT was the only combat unit to participate. In early August 1999 plans called for POLUKRBAT to enter Kosovo as peacekeepers. *ITAR-TASS*, August 4, 1999, *FBIS Daily Report*, FBIS-SOV-1999-0804.

[48] They plan to participate in some 160 activities in 1999. *ITAR-TASS*, July 1, 1999, FBIS-SOV-1999-0701.

[49] For a scathing criticism of the Sea Breeze exercises see Aleksandr Shinkin, "Before Nakhimov's Very Eyes," *Rossiiskaia gazeta*, August 23, 1997.

50 Yugoslavia was suspended from participation in 1992 and remains a member in limbo.

51 "Documents of the Stockholm Conference on Confidence and Security Building Measures and Disarmament in Europe," September 19, 1996, *Department of State Bulletin*, November 1986, pp. 20–5.

52 Yeltsin reiterated the Russian government's long-standing view of the OSCE in an interview in *Der Speigel*, where he was quoted as saying that he saw " ... the development and strengthening of the OSCE as the sole really pan-European organization which has the right to act in the security sphere." *ITAR-TASS*, June 19, 1999, FBIS-SOV-1999-0619.

53 For an overview of the twists and turns of negotiations on Transdniestr in 1997–1998, including Ukraine's emergence as an active mediator, see Sherman W. Garnett and Rachel Lebenson, "Ukraine Joins the Fray: Will Peace Come to Trans-Dniestria?" *Problems of Post-Communism*, November-December 1998, pp. 22–32. The OSCE has also organized election monitoring in Moldova, and in other CIS states. In 1998 the Moldovan Mission also assisted in programs teaching Latin script in Transdniestr.

54 See, for example, Provision XI of the Intermediate-Range Nuclear Forces Treaty, the Protocol on Notification and Exchanges of Information of the Treaty on Armed Conventional Forces in Europe, and the inspection and verification sections of the Treaty between the United States of America and the Union of Soviet Socialist Republics on the Reduction and Limitation of Strategic Offensive Arms in the *Arms Control Reporter 1999* (Cambridge, U.K.: Institute of Defense and Disarmament Studies, 1999), pp. 403A9, 407A5, 407A11, 611.A.4–6.

55 "Agreement between the Russian Federation, the Republic of Kazakhstan, the Kyrgyz Republic, the Republic of Tajikistan and the People's Republic of China on Confidence Building in the Military Field in the Border Area," (Moscow: Russian Ministry of Foreign Affairs unofficial translation, April 1996).

56 *Trud*, April 26, 1997, p. 3. Kazakhstan, Tajikistan, and Kyrgyzstan also joined this agreement but declared that they would implement complete troop withdrawals from their borders with China. *Strait Times*, October 10, 1997.

7
What Future Does
the CIS Have?

The drama of building new states has been played out many times this century, and not always with the desired results. The process of creating a new state is exceedingly complex. Old elites are challenged, and new pretenders to power appear, often with nothing to qualify them as elites except their determination to control the societies in which they live. Resources are realigned, creating new winners, and turning old winners into new losers. Loyalties must shift as well, as long-term privileged *colonnes* suddenly become second-class citizens, and the formerly despised become heads of state.

The same shifts occurring in the new states are replicated in the world community. New states create new challenges. One-time patron states lose their ability to sustain old commitments, stranding former allies, and sometimes setting off ripple effects of instability elsewhere. Former patron states can even become international client states themselves, further taxing the abilities of the stronger states to cope with them.

All of these tensions can be found in the new states of the former Soviet Union, making many aspects of state building there the same as they would have been anywhere. However, the transformations that these fifteen states are undergoing are in many ways unique. Because almost all of the Soviet Union had grown out of the Russian Empire, it had some of the attributes of a traditional empire. Therefore, many of the transformations faced by the post-Soviet states are like those of ex-colonial new states in Africa, Southeast Asia, and elsewhere. At the same time, the Soviet Union was also a single state, a world power that had been formed for an array of ideological purposes. Most of its citizens believed in the ideology to some degree, even after the USSR collapsed. One consequence of the ambiguous nature of the Soviet Union is that the states born out of it have had more difficulty than most new states in deciding whether they should be separate entities or should be bound together in some form.

The Commonwealth of Independent States was the first attempt by the former states to answer that question. As this book has shown, most of those states that joined it hoped that the CIS would provide them the security of a group identity, while also permitting them the freedom of individual sovereignty. As this book has also demonstrated, however, most of these states have found the reality of the CIS to be that it hampers and constrains their actions without providing them with the security or assistance they require.

The CIS has generally failed, in a variety of contexts. At the same time, the organization continues to exist. This naturally prompts the question of whether the Commonwealth of Independent States has a significant role that it might yet play, and, if it has, what might that role be. Alternatively, if the CIS has no future, the question then becomes what organization or body might better play the role that the CIS cannot. This concluding chapter seeks to answer these questions, first by cataloguing some of the burdens from the past that the new states must carry into their futures, and then by assessing the problems that the CIS has actually been able to solve. Inevitably, this must be contrasted with the organization's failures, for the purpose of suggesting areas in which the CIS may yet prove to be of value. The chapter concludes with observations about what the West can do about the CIS, and with recommendations about what it should do.

THE LEGACY OF THE PAST

Russia dwarfs all of its post-Soviet neighbors. Many people believe that Russia is only "a strategic paper tiger" in relation to the world's largest, wealthiest, and best-established states. Analyst Raj Menon offers a different view, arguing that in fact Russia has significant advantages in relative power that can be exploited. He believes that power is "dynamic and relational," meaning that in its own backyard Russia far outstrips its immediate neighbors by any conceivable measure of power and is in a position to recover from its problems much faster than any of the other post-Soviet states.[1] Russia is the oldest and best-established independent state in the region. It has a strong elite and a large policy-making community that engage in a wide-ranging public debate. Russia also casts a long shadow over most of its neighbors, for it has the capacity, should it desire to do so, to devote larger reserves of political, financial, or military power to an issue than could any other post-Soviet state.

It is not enough, however, to measure Russia's advantages relative only to the assets of a potential rival; Russia's assets must also be measured against the demands of the country's many problems. The security challenges that Russia is likely to face in the foreseeable future will not come from an organized national army, but rather from the intertwined problems presented by small wars, ethnic conflicts, and unstable regimes. Russia's vast size and wide spectrum of interests also make it difficult for the state to concentrate its assets upon any single problem, therefore diluting its advantages.

Russia has not always treated its new neighbors with respect, but neither has it formally impinged on the sovereignty of any of them, preferring to use bluster and surrogates rather than direct force to get its way. Moreover, Russia's enthusiasm for intervention has waned as its own problems have deepened. This is in part a product of Russia's growing understanding of its own military weakness, but even more so it is the result of the country's economic weakness, which conditions all of Russia's problems, including those of the military. The intractability of the problems that the country faces is increasingly evident in the weariness with which Russia's senior politicians address the wider problems of the CIS.

The failure of the CIS has largely been conditioned by the fear that the states of the CIS have for one another, and which all of them have for Russia. The continued existence of the CIS is driven by the hopes and needs of the member states to receive benefits and support from Russia. Just as their hopes for the CIS were shaped by the belief that Russia is rich, so have their fears been driven by the belief that Russia is strong. As the member states are increasingly disabused of both those notions, it is possible that the CIS may collapse, unable to provide either protection or benefits. If they come to believe that Russia is weak and poor, it is possible that the member states will be stimulated to try to make the CIS better serve the pressing development needs of all. Although interconnections between the CIS states may have attenuated with the passage of time, these states retain significant bonds, created by their shared populations, histories, cultures, and economies, which were unified until relatively recently. The continued similarities of the CIS states make it difficult to gauge the degree to which the antagonisms against Russia—antagonisms that senior officials of the newly independent states express when they meet with Western leaders—are real and to which degree they are simply diplomatic posturing.

The Soviet successor states have not yet resolved the question of what it was they were dissolving; indeed, it is possible that there will never be consensus on this issue. The difficulty of deciding whether the Soviet Union was a colonial power or a unified state in which citizens could receive significant social mobility in exchange for ideological conformity has made the battle over how history is to be written hotly contested everywhere in the CIS. The content of what is taught in each state's schools, and even the language or languages in which the business of each state will be conducted, all depend upon how the past is defined.

Whether it did so as a colonial power or as a single state, the Soviet Union left an important legacy of physical infrastructure and social organization, which was supported by all types of public systems. This book has detailed some of the ways in which that physical infrastructure was both a blessing and a curse. Although the new states began their independence with modern highways, railroads, and telephones, the Soviet-era infrastructure still bound the new states tightly to Russia, making it difficult or impossible for them to interact with the outside world. Even the costs of maintaining the existing infrastructure, to say nothing of trying to replace it with a new infrastructure that would better serve the needs of the new states, are so prohibitive that most of the CIS member states are likely to have to rely upon Soviet-era physical infrastructure for many years to come.

The situation with Soviet-era social organization is even more complex. The educational systems of the post-Soviet states are now evolving in a variety of directions, differing increasingly in how they are structured, what they teach, and even the language of instruction. Most of the new countries have discontinued or have significantly cut back Russian language instruction, often in favor of increased English language instruction. In some states, however, the spread of the new native language is slower than the national advocates hoped, as in Ukraine, where even though Ukrainian is widely accepted as the language of public life, Russian is still a language of private conversation and popular culture. Ukrainian is only now beginning to dominate in higher education. Belarus has gone so far as to make Russian one of its two official languages, and Kyrgyzstan and Kazakhstan have decided to continue to use Russian as a principal language of public discourse. As noted, the features of national education are becoming more distinct from state to state, but a Russian college or advanced degree nevertheless remains a prized credential in the post-Soviet world, particularly for those who lack the resources to get training in the West.[2]

It is precisely the fear that their children will no longer be competitive for obtaining a good Russian education that has led many ethnic Russians from the neighboring states to relocate to Russia (see tables 7.1 and 7.2). Even those living in Ukraine complain that their children lack the Russian language skills, especially in the written language, of their cohorts in Russia, particularly if they live in Kyiv or western Ukraine.

The opportunity for migration has been an important pressure release, of which millions of former Soviet citizens have availed themselves since 1991. Migration will become more difficult as educational systems and the degrees they grant become less interchangeable. It is also going to become harder for non-Russian citizens to find skilled employment in Russia. A CIS-wide labor market has emerged, fed by the different paces at which the various economies are recovering, and also by the surplus labor problems from which some of the CIS countries suffer, and may continue to suffer even after economic conditions improve. Over time, changing patterns of technical and linguistic competence will make this CIS-wide labor market harder to sustain, which may mean that there will be more dissatisfied, underemployed people who feel trapped in the communities and countries in which they are living.

The changes at the elite level of the CIS countries have been less wrenching than might have been expected, primarily because the old Soviet elite was not replaced, but rather reconfigured itself, expanding slightly to absorb new forces as circumstance dictated. The present leaders may resort to the rhetoric of decolonization to whip up their domestic audiences, but their dealings with one

Table 7.1
Population Migration to Russia from the CIS and Baltic States (1992–1997)

Countries of Origin	1992	1993	1994	1995	1996	1997
Belarus	36,212	34,670	43,383	35,377	23,903	17,575
Moldova	32,340	19,344	21,364	18,715	17,847	13,750
Ukraine	199,355	189,409	247,351	188,443	170,928	138,231
CENTRAL ASIA						
Kazakhstan	183,891	195,672	346,363	241,427	172,860	235,903
Kyrgyzstan	62,897	96,814	66,489	27,801	18,886	13,752
Tajikistan	72,556	68,761	45,645	41,799	32,508	23,053
Turkmenistan	19,035	12,990	20,186	19,129	22,840	16,501
Uzbekistan	112,442	91,164	146,670	112,312	49,970	39,620
Subtotal	450,821	465,401	625,323	442,468	297,064	328,829
CAUCASUS						
Armenia	15,750	29,806	46,480	34,112	25,419	19,123
Azerbaijan	69,943	54,684	49,495	43,442	40,310	29,878
Georgia	54,247	69,943	66,847	51,412	38,551	24,517
Subtotal	139,940	154,433	162,822	128,966	104,280	73,518
BALTIC STATES						
Latvia	27,271	25,891	26,370	14,859	8,227	5,658
Lithuania	15,354	19,407	8,456	4,126	3,055	1,785
Estonia	24,440	14,340	11,250	8,591	5,869	3,483
Subtotal	67,065	59,638	46,076	27,576	17,151	10,926
TOTAL	925,733	922,886	1,146,349	841,505	631,173	582,829

Source: Goskomstat of the Russian Federation, quoted in Galina Vitkovskaia, "Vynuzh-dennaia migratsiia v Rossiiu: itogi desiatiletiia," in Zh. Zaionchkovskaia, ed., *Migratsionnaia situatsiia v stranakh SNG* (Moscow: CIS Center on Forced Migration, 1999), p. 171.

another make clear that they consider themselves to be part of the same elite. Indeed, an important part of what may seem to be competition or antagonism between some of them is simply the translation of old rivalries into new arenas. Many of the CIS leaders have known one another for decades, with patterns of interactions that were well established by the corporate culture of the Communist Party of the Soviet Union. Independence and the need for new policy agendas, as well as the new responsibilities that their presidencies have forced upon them, are combining to transform the new states' leaders. Their

Table 7.2
Ethnic Russian Migration to Russia from CIS and Baltic States
(1993–1997)

A. Total Migration to Russia

	1993	1994	1995	1996	1997
Percentage of Russian Migrants	64.5	63.4	60.7	57.8	59.2

B. Total Forced Migration to Russia

	1993	1994	1995	1996	1997
Percentage of Forced Russian Migrants	58.2	72.7	76.9	76.2	76.4

Source: Goskomstat and Federal Border Service of the Russian Federation, quoted in Galina Vitkovskaia, "Vynuzhdennaia migratsiia v Rossiiu: itogi desiatiletiia," in Zh. Zaionchkovskaia, ed, *Migratsionnaia situatsiia v stranakh SNG* (Moscow: CIS Center on Forced Migration, 1999), p. 174.

shared Soviet past still makes it extremely difficult to know what their attitudes toward Russia truly are, and whether their grievances are new, or rather spring from the deep hostilities of ambitious careerists who, as non-Russians, were at a disadvantage until the dissolution of the Soviet system suddenly pushed them to the top. It will probably not be possible to gauge the coincidence and divergence of interests between the various new states and Russia until the present elite passes from the scene.

There is no guarantee that this passing will be gentle. New nationalist elites are seeking power in all the new states; most claim to speak for the majority of their fellow citizens, but some vociferously defend the rights of or demand privileges for the minorities they represent. Each of the post-Soviet states also has an articulate constituency that argues for maintaining or restoring important features of the cultural, historical, and linguistic links that bound the USSR together. Deteriorating economic and social conditions in many of the new states have meant that nostalgia for the presumed benefits of the past is not the exclusive property of the old. In most cases, though, there is no clear way to retrieve the past, nor money to pay for it if there were.

The task of writing the histories of the post-Soviet states is leaving many of these countries with questions as divisive as those raised by the Soviet past. Old rivalries, traditional frictions, and regional ambitions revive as people examine their various myths, religions, cultures, and regional identities. Battles over identity have put Georgia at risk of dividing into four pieces, while the attempt to reclaim their separate versions of their past has led Armenia and Azerbaijan to lock each other into a long-term military stalemate. Armenia's appeals to Russia and Iran, and Azerbaijan's to Turkey, to buttress their conflicting claims also suggest how the return to traditional alliances might create larger regional problems.

TASKS THE CIS HAS RESOLVED

Without question its pacific mediation of the breakup of the USSR was the greatest service that the CIS could have performed. For comparison, witness the violent breakup of the much smaller state of Yugoslavia. This is not to say that the repartitioning of the USSR was entirely bloodless; five of the new states were born with civil conflicts, and Russia has fought a war with Chechnya. In each of these instances, however, the fighting was contained before it escalated to engulf the country as a whole, or the region in which it was located. None of these conflicts has been fully resolved, but neither have they become the catalysts for new wars.

The CIS has also contributed to maintaining peace over many disputed borders. Rather than take advantage of the collapse of the USSR to resolve old border disputes unilaterally, the neighbors of the new states, and the new states themselves, have put most border questions on hold. Many of the boundaries between the new states, and even those between them and more established states, have not been formally accepted, or even demarcated. These border questions will eventually have to be resolved, but for the time being all parties to these disputes seem willing to wait until agreements can be negotiated.

The issues to be resolved are thorny, especially those raised by the transformation of old internal administrative borders into internationally recognized boundaries. For Russia to agree upon firm boundaries with Belarus and Ukraine, for example, is to refute, perhaps forever, the conviction of many Russian intellectuals that the three countries really constitute a single great Slavic nation. Russia and Ukraine have negotiated and begun to demarcate some of their boundaries, and although their governments may be willing to do so, it will be a long time before most Russians are ready to concede that Crimea, or at least Sevastopol, is not Russian territory.

Demarcation of final boundaries between Russia and Kazakhstan would be a similar confession that the several million ethnic Russians who live along Kazakhstan's northern border have been abandoned to a new citizenship. A large part of any continued Russian enthusiasm for a workable formula of deep integration is that the formation of some sort of free trade area would make it possible to put off answering these questions indefinitely.

Similar motivations govern the attempt to create the Central Asian Economics Union. The boundaries in Central Asia are generally even newer and more arbitrary than are those between the European post-Soviet republics, while the scale of history on which Central Asian territorial claims may be based is much longer. All of its neighbors were wary of Uzbekistan even before President Karimov decided to make Timur (Tamerlane) the symbolic founder of Uzbek statehood. Timur's fourteenth-century empire encompassed almost all of Central Asia, something the Kyrgyz in Osh *oblast* surely remember as their neighbors in Uzbekistan steadily expand their household gardens beyond what once were the old administrative boundaries. Turkmenistan's boundaries with both Kazakhstan and Uzbekistan will literally be drawn in sand, and the natural resources that might lie below those shifting sands could be of great value.

Boundaries are likely to prove most incendiary in the Caucasus. Russia already patrols its boundaries with both Georgia and Azerbaijan, a practice it began when neither state was a member of the CIS. The local Lezgin population—found in both Azerbaijan and Russia's republic of Dagestan—periodically protest the imposition of an international boundary between them. Other diaspora populations are also becoming more vocal; the Armenians of Georgia are likely to prove a particular challenge to any boundary-drawing process, particularly since Armenia has chosen to deepen its ties with Russia, rather than to join GUUAM. Armenian membership in GUUAM would make this organization a more effective forum for attaining regional cooperation.

Another astonishing service of the CIS was the division of Soviet property, which the member states generally achieved by agreeing simply to accept whatever Soviet property happened to be on their territory.[3] For legal and technical reasons, it was not possible to divide the Soviet debt, so Russia moved to take responsibility for the whole debt, in return for receiving ownership of payments due the USSR. Ukraine resisted this solution for a time, apparently laboring under the misapprehension that the payments due were larger than the debt. The Soviet debt has proven to be a serious liability for Russia, which has not been able to service even its own debt; presumably most or all of the Soviet debt is eventually going to have to be written off, as the international community agreed to do with the massive debts Poland inherited from the communists.

The British Commonwealth is a reasonable standard by which to judge the success of the Commonwealth of Independent States. Not only did the latter take its name from the first, but it also was contrived to deal with the political and economic transformation of far-flung, disparate territories. The creation of India and Pakistan caused the death of more than one million people, setting up antagonisms that not only continue to this day, but also remain so deep that both sides have raced to develop nuclear weapons as a way to resolve them. Such an example illustrates how much more successful the CIS has been in overcoming the initial challenges of burying a dead empire and dividing up its legacy.

TASKS AT WHICH THE CIS HAS FAILED

As this book has detailed, the list of ways in which the CIS has failed is much longer than is its list of successes. The whole rhetoric of the CIS is modeled on that of the European Union, but the CIS displays none of the features of the EU, or even the potential to develop them. Russia's enormous gravitational distortion either pulls the other CIS states closer to Russia than they wish to be or prompts them to try to keep their distance safely, by agreeing to policies which they never ratify or implement. Rather than becoming the EU, the CIS more closely resembles the CMEA, which in the Soviet years made a show of regulating trade among the Warsaw Pact nations; however, the CIS lacks even the CMEA's pretense of centralized planning. The CIS has had to shelve indefinitely its plans for a common currency, and the Customs Union that some of the members have tried to establish shows no signs of ever becoming what it claims to be. The CIS has not even been able to elaborate a mechanism for resolving trade disputes, so that trade relations among the member states are based almost exclusively on bilateral negotiations, leaving the CIS with no formal role to play in this area.

Russia had great plans for the CIS as a security organization, but it may safely be concluded that those plans are not going to be achieved. Such military initiatives as have been mounted are either openly Russian or make a show at being multilateral, with the greatest part of the exercise borne by Russia. Since 1991 Russia has demonstrated that it is able to intervene in conflicts and to contain them within certain limits, but it increasingly proves unable to extinguish conflicts entirely or to impose settlements. Russia can force its CIS partners to adopt a decision, but it cannot make them implement it, because Russian power is spread too thinly across the entire post-Soviet space.

The goals that Russia elaborated in 1993 for military bases and border guard deployment assumed that its resources and needs were the same as those of the Soviet Union. It is increasingly clear that memories of greatness have made Russia seriously overstretch itself; the state will be unable to keep the commitments it has made in Central Asia or the Caucasus if any of the problems that now lie dormant should awaken. The imbalance between Russia's ambitions and its ability to execute not only affects Russia's calculations of interest and response, it also makes its neighbor states more determined than perhaps they need to be to supplement or replace the security commitments that Russia has offered them.

REMAINING CHALLENGES

The failure of the CIS to become an effective body has left many of the issues that the group attempted to address unresolved. To the extent that it allows the leaders and senior officials of the member states to meet on a regular basis in a controlled environment, the CIS has been an effective political forum. Judged by the policies it has actually been able to put into place, however, the CIS has been a political failure.

The same is true of the attempt to make the CIS a regional trade organization. Any number of policies and principles have been declared, but the reality is that trade barriers and protectionist practices have proliferated among CIS states. What is worse, the CIS has proven to have no means to counteract these impediments to free trade, even when they are blatant violations of CIS agreements.

The pattern of failure is replicated even in the smaller bodies that CIS member states have attempted to form in part in response to the ineffectiveness of the larger body. To a certain extent this syndrome extends even into the international bodies that the CIS member states have joined; the actual effectiveness of the various bodies is generally inversely proportional to the ease with which the new states have been able to join them.

When the CIS was first conceived, fear that the other states had for Russia paralyzed the body's development. Increasingly, however, weakness rather than fear causes this paralysis. Even Russia is now accusing the CIS, the other regional bodies, and even most of the bilateral agreements of existing primarily on paper.

The political and economic needs of the CIS member states are enormous, but it is the pattern of spreading weakness that is truly alarming. Western analysts and theorists argue increasingly that it is weak and failing states that shape the contemporary security environment. "Wars today," wrote Phillipe Delmas, "are caused not by the strength of states but by their weakness. The primary problem of security today is not the desire for power or expansion, but rather the breakdown of states."[4] Lawrence Freedman also sees regional conflicts, especially those caused by weak states, as an important engine of future wars, which are most likely to arise "from within weak states—countries caught on the margins of the global economy, released from colonial rule but suffering from compound social fractures that cannot be healed when resources are scarce and political institutions feeble."[5]

Weak states offer a number of potential triggers for future violence. By definition, they fail to provide such basic building blocks of social stability as economic sufficiency, adequate health care, widespread education, and dependable public order. The world being what it is, most of the discontent that such failure engenders can also seem to have ethnic or religious dimensions, which further exacerbate social tensions. This makes weak states a breeding ground for factional violence.

Many of the CIS states already manifest these symptoms. Georgia, Azerbaijan, and Tajikistan have gone through periods when political factions had active paramilitary wings and political killings were common. Some of the states, such as Belarus, Uzbekistan, Turkmenistan, and Azerbaijan, have tried to avert or keep the lid on chaos by embracing authoritarian or paternalistic presidents, but such an approach is likely to make these states more vulnerable to chaos when the present leaders pass from the scene, as inevitably they will.

Individual weak states of any dimension are potentially destabilizing, especially if they become failed states. In this case, however, size matters; the failure of a state like Ukraine or Kazakhstan would magnify the risks of failure enormously. The most alarming possibility of all, of course, would be the failure of Russia; this would create a continent-sized maelstrom of chaos and instability bordering an expanding European Union, a rising China, a potentially troubled Japan, and an unstable Persian Gulf region.

The post-Soviet space is shared by a concentration of weak states, several of which seem reasonable candidates to become failing states. Their collapse would set off serious economic and humanitarian pressures, regional conflicts, or large-scale violence. Even if Russia manages to strengthen sufficiently to become a fully democratic and stable country, it will nevertheless continue to inhabit a very difficult neighborhood. The failure of one or more of the new states would almost certainly prompt interventions from outside powers and could even rekindle major power rivalries that are not now in evidence.

Russia's security environment will inevitably be shaped for years to come by the fact that it stands between two different geopolitical environments, one of which is characterized by the highly developed European mechanisms of cooperation, and the other of which reflects the instabilities and the use of force that mark old-fashioned notions of international competition that often dominate in other parts of the world. The outside world may interpret Russia's security concerns as a disguised desire to expand its hegemony, but to Russia itself, the weakness of its neighbors is a problem of great concern, likely to undercut the security and financial stability of Russia for decades to come.

It is not enough that the states of the former Soviet Union must face all the risks to their security that have confronted other newly independent nations before them; they also confront a dizzying array of less traditional threats, all of which have developed into major problems in contemporary international relations. The weakness of modern states particularly feeds terrorism, narcotics trafficking, and organized crime, all of which have mushroomed in the new states. For the most part, the criminals of the new states are significantly better armed, better organized, and better financed than are the government forces that attempt to combat them. The corruption that drug money breeds further corrodes public confidence, while the weakness of central authorities makes it difficult to assist international efforts to cooperate in stopping terrorism, crime, or drug running.

Soviet industrialization and the arms race have left a legacy of environmental catastrophe across broad swathes of the former USSR. In addition to posing a major threat to public health and imposing budget-busting costs for their cleanup, some of the post-Soviet environmental problems could also become genuine security challenges to states both inside and outside the region. Examples of such problems are the regional competition for water in Central Asia, the degradation of chemical, biological, or nuclear weapons storage sites, and the unchecked spread of infectious diseases.

The patterns of military power in Eurasia are also changing, which could exacerbate the risk of conflicts. The collapse of the Soviet Union has greatly increased the flow of arms, military technology, and know-how from the old center of power to ambitious states on the rim of Eurasia. American, European, and Israeli firms are also deeply involved in this lucrative weapons trade. The involvement of Russia, Ukraine, and other post-Soviet states in this trade is of particular concern because of the weakness of their state regulatory institutions. Moreover, their weak economies encourage deals of questionable wisdom, as long as they provide cash. Russia has sold a broad range of weapons and material to both China and Iran, including a variety of advanced ground, air and sea systems, air defense and missile systems, and—it is rumored—key components of cruise and ballistic missile guidance systems. The effect of this arms competition is to permit countries like China, India, Pakistan, Iran, and Iraq to project their power farther out into the open oceans and much deeper into the European landmass. Their growing strength makes it increasingly possible that in the decades to come Russia and the United States alike will be confronted by more ambitious and more capable Eurasian powers.

The continued weakness of the post-Soviet states, and the increasing military capabilities of the regions surrounding them, may also serve to stimulate a resurgence of great power rivalry. The post-Soviet space is increasingly open to the outside world, making it easier for instability and violence to spill from Afghanistan into Tajikistan, or for possible troubles in China's Xinjiang province to spread to Central Asia. If, however, a new "Great Game" were to break out, the players would unlikely be Russia's old competitors in Europe, or the United States and its NATO allies. Russia's weakened political and economic situation has already stimulated the appearance of new, more interested competitors in parts of the former USSR, such as Turkey in the southern Caucasus and China in portions of Central Asia and even in areas of Russia itself. Iran and Pakistan are two other neighbors who may be tempted by Russia's weakness to seek additional advantages for themselves in what once was Soviet territory.

LOOKING AHEAD

It seemed easier to predict the future when the Soviet Union first broke up than it is now. The immediate tasks of dismantling the huge state appeared relatively straightforward, even if they were extremely complex. As the process of differentiation and development continues, however, it becomes increasingly clear that the establishment of new connections between the states, and the establishment of the states themselves, is a complicated process that has only begun. All the post-Soviet states are still controlled by men who reached political maturity in the days of the USSR, which means that it will take at least one generation, and quite possibly two, before the natures of the new states, and of the relations between them, become fully defined.

The CIS was most effective at its birth; it has steadily declined in effectiveness ever since. This suggests that it will probably prove to be a transitory phenomenon, which will either disappear or be radically restructured well before the last ties that held the Soviet states together are dissolved. The next generation of leaders is unlikely to find the CIS a usable vehicle for their state needs, and the following generation would find it even less so. For one thing, succeeding generations will not have the shared socialization experiences of the present leaders; indeed, they may not even have a language in common, and if they do, it is unlikely to be Russian.

For all their probable divergence, however, these states will still be neighbors. Most are landlocked, and so will still have to ship goods through others to reach markets; each is also likely to remain a major market for the others. This will require close trade cooperation of some sort. It is possible that this will come through existing international bodies like the WTO, but the current slow pace of economic restructuring suggests that it will be a long time before most of the CIS countries are granted membership in the world's primary trade and financial bodies.

This suggests that there will be continual pressure to try to create customs unions or free trade blocs within the region, or with states just beyond it. It is difficult to see how these potential formations will avoid being crippled by the growing economic discontinuities across what used to be a single economic space. Similar efforts have failed to overcome these obstacles.

It is also possible that nothing will emerge to fill the void left by the collapsing CIS. At a certain point the CIS states of today may grow so certain of their individual identities that they will be able to define the geography of their regions and their interests without any regard for the ghostly boundaries of the vanished Soviet state, and so manage their mutual business as needed through a series of bilateral and multilateral arrangements.

The disappearance of the CIS is not necessarily good news for U.S. policy makers, or for the states themselves. A void will not make it easier for the member states to sustain their independence, to reform their economies, or to develop the political institutions necessary for the peaceful transfer of power. At no point in its history has the CIS succeeded in helping member states manage their economic and political reforms. To be sure, the simple existence of the CIS seems to have helped the new states sustain their independence, allowing their leaders to grow accustomed to the notion that they were no longer one whole union. The CIS has fostered the understanding that the temptation of one new state to dabble in the sovereignty of a neighbor might tempt others to follow the same course, thus making it seem wiser to respect the sovereignty of all. It was not the CIS itself, however, that insured this sovereignty. Its existence did not cause or exacerbate the conflicts that developed between or within these states. With the minor exception of some mitigation in Tajikistan and Moldova, the CIS also did not solve any of these conflicts.

In a perfect world the international community would fill the gap left by the failure of the CIS. In reality, however, the new millennium is dawning with such a clamor for the attention of the international community that it seems unlikely that foreign states or institutions would step forward as guarantors of peace in any of the CIS states, even if Russia had no objection to such intervention. If Russia did object, as it likely would, any enthusiasm for foreign intervention in the region might vanish entirely.

Certainly, the United States will be reluctant to intervene, despite the fact that current U.S. policy is strongly oriented toward support-ing projects that aim to strengthen the independence of the new states and to reduce their dependence upon Russia. For several years it has been the conviction of the Clinton administration that the post-Soviet states must be bolstered against potential Russian med-dling, so that, to the degree that the CIS has been an instrument of such meddling, the organization's slow fade toward oblivion will be seen as a positive development. The death of the CIS will only serve U.S. goals, however, if the member states prove to be suffi-ciently mature to cope with the challenges of their individual state building in ways that do not threaten or hinder their neighbors.

The United States must be prepared for the post-Soviet world to evolve in any of a number of directions, including one in which many of the new states weaken or even fail. It has been a frustrating process to try to encourage the development of democracy and market reforms among the member states of the CIS even when they were stronger, so that the option of giving up on such efforts entirely as the states grow weaker will be very tempting. As the history of Yugoslavia's dissolution has taught, however, the costs of intervening after states fail is far higher.

For this reason it is especially important not to give up on the prospects for reform in Russia, no matter how bleak these may sometimes seem. A stable and reformed Russia would certainly serve as an anchor for the post-Soviet space as a whole, but the world should not grow impatient when this cannot quickly be achieved. Russia would be aided in its attempts to solve the tasks confronting it if the international community were not so quick to suspect that superpower nostalgia lies behind so many of its actions and attempted policies.

Nor should the United States expect that Russia could cope alone with the problems posed by weak and unstable states on its periphery. A manageable neighborhood is the most important external requirement for Russian stability and reform. This requires that U.S. policy be regionally focused, rather than built exclusively upon a series of bilateral agreements.

The United States must recognize that integration and disintegration of various kinds will occur simultaneously throughout the region. U.S. policy has to define more clearly which kind of integration to encourage and which kind to resist as not being in the interests of or inimical to long-term stability. Beyond ensuring that an arrangement has the consent of all parties, U.S. policy has to recognize the impact of these integrative arrangements on the immediate neighborhood and Eurasia as a whole. Economic integration has to favor free markets and WTO-compatible trade regulations. Other interested Western powers also have important roles to play in this regard; there is an urgent need, for example, to shape long-range policies of the European Union in ways that will not erect new barriers between its members and nonmembers in the former USSR. The EU needs to anticipate the effect that enlargement will have on crucial regional ties, such as those between Poland and Belarus, Ukraine, and Russia, respectively.

Security relations are an area of great sensitivity as well. The West, and the United States in particular, should also do all it can to encourage the recent, still fragile experiments that are transforming conflict management in the former USSR from being a unilateral Russian operation to including neighboring states and international institutions. Ukraine's role as a co-mediator in Transdniestr and the U.S.-French-Russian initiative on Karabakh are modest but promising beginnings, which should be encouraged, not just with words, but also with the financial and technical assistance necessary to sustain the agreements that these initiatives produce.

U.S. policy also must think more carefully about what Eurasia will come to look like as the notion of "post-Soviet" continues to fade. This will require a broad-based engagement with the new states and regions emerging there. Russia will remain a key state in all the emerging regions of the former USSR, but outside actors will increasingly play a larger role in the various new regional definitions that emerge. Some of the new states, such as Ukraine, Georgia,

Kazakhstan, and Uzbekistan, are going to become important regional actors in their own right and will require special attention.

As it moves to devise its policies, the United States must remember that in the decade to come the former USSR will require large-scale doses of developmental assistance, in the forms of both traditional aid and outside investment. The new states themselves have a crucial role to play here, for neither form of assistance will materialize if corruption and weak state institutions complicate a genuine partnership between donors and recipients, or investors and local businesses.

Even if the new states do a poor job of helping themselves, the huge dimensions of the crises in health, education, and environment that are growing in the post-Soviet states—and the consequences if any of these were to spill out beyond the CIS—mean that the United States cannot afford to stand back from continued efforts at reform and development. The United States must work to design aid that can help forestall these crises before they become devastating, even if the recipient nations themselves sometimes seem to be working at cross purposes to these attempts. Successful intervention through aid will not only reap large benefits in terms of long-term U.S. influence in the region, but would also be far cheaper than a massive and urgent intervention in a failing state.

Probably the most pressing immediate task in this regard is the expansion of bilateral and multilateral efforts to combat drug trafficking and terrorism in the new states. The weak states of the region are already tempting safe havens for both activities and will only become more so if the states weaken further. Neither druglords nor terrorists respect international boundaries, which could quickly transform a penny-wise foreign aid stature today into a pound-foolish disaster in a not-so-distant tomorrow.

At the same time, though, the problems of the post-Soviet states are so great that they surpass the ability of even the richest of single states to combat. For that reason the United States ought to increase serious efforts to elaborate complementary policies with its European allies and Japan. Notwithstanding the existence of current donor programs, the West has simply not yet done enough to coordinate its efforts to help the post-Soviet states; consequently it is wasting both time and money.

That said, it must also be concluded that outside actors, including the United States, have only a limited number of ways in which they can affect the course of events in the post-Soviet space. All the CIS members need new incentives to strengthen their statehood, to engage in reforms that result in economic restructuring, and to develop political institutions that permit an orderly transfer of power. Suggestions for those incentives can come from outside, but the will to put them into effect must come from within the states themselves. Foreign actors have done a great deal to ease and to shape the transformation of the Soviet republics into independent states, and there is still more that they can do. Ultimately, the most important issues concerning the future of the region as a whole, and the fate of each state individually, must be resolved by the CIS member states themselves.

NOTES

[1] Raj Menon, "After Empire: Russia and the Southern 'Near Abroad,'" in Michael Mandelbaum, ed., *The New Russian Foreign Policy* (New York: Council on Foreign Relations, 1998), p. 104. As our book demonstrates, we differ from Raj Menon somewhat on Russian power, but his essay is a unique and powerful overview of Russia's ties to a complicated region.

[2] In 1997–1998, 1,000 students from Azerbaijan studied in the Russian higher education system, as did 1,100 from Armenia, 3,100 from Belarus, 1,400 from Georgia, 10,700 from Kazakhstan, 1,200 from Kyrgyzstan, 1,600 from Moldova, 400 from Tajikistan, 400 from Turkmenistan, 3,300 from Uzbekistan, and 6,500 from Ukraine. *Rossiiskii statisticheskii ezhegodnik, 1998* (Moscow: Goskomstat, 1998), p. 291.

[3] One conspicuous exception to this was the division of the Black Sea Fleet, which was decided through bilateral negotiations between Russia and Ukraine.

[4] Phillipe Delmas, *The Rosy Future of War* (New York: Free Press, 1997), p. 7.

[5] Lawrence Freedman, "The Revolution in Strategic Affairs," *Adelphi Paper 318*, (London: Oxford University Press, 1998), p. 34.

Appendix
Chronology of Key Events

1991

October 18   **Moscow:** Armenia, Belarus, Kazakhstan, Kyrgyzstan, Russia, Tajikistan, Turkmenistan, and Uzbekistan create an Economic Community.

December 8   **Minsk:** Heads of State of Belarus, Russia, and Ukraine sign an agreement on the creation of the CIS.

December 13   **Ashgabat:** Heads of State of Kazakhstan, Kyrgyzstan, Tajikistan, Turkmenistan, and Uzbekistan express their surprise at the creation of the CIS, but then express their desire to join it.

December 21   **Almaty:** Heads of State of eleven former republics sign the declaration which incorporates the five Central Asian states, as well as Armenia, Azerbaijan, and Moldova into the CIS.

December 30   **Minsk, First CIS Summit** (Heads of State/Heads of Government): establishes CIS governing bodies (Council of Heads of State and Council of Heads of Government); fails to agree on the monetary arrangements in the aftermath of the collapse of the Soviet Union.

1992

January 16   **Moscow:** Heads of State discuss military affairs, agree to coordinate CIS foreign policy and to establish an organizational group to prepare future meetings of CIS leaders.

February 8   **Moscow:** Heads of Government name Russia the legal successor and guarantor of the foreign credit agreements of the Commonwealth member states.

February 14   **Minsk:** Heads of State sign an agreement that seeks to regulate trade and economic cooperation and calls for the ruble to remain the sole monetary unit of the CIS.

March 13	**Moscow:** Heads of Government agree to accept joint responsibility for repaying the Soviet debt. Russia is to repay about 61 percent, Ukraine 16 percent, and the balance to be divided among the remaining six members.
March 20	**Kyiv:** Heads of State sign Declaration of the Non-Use of Force or Threat of Force in Relations Among CIS Members, Agreement of Groups of Military Observers and Collective Peacekeeping Forces, Agreement on the Joint Command of the Border Troops, and Agreement on the Status of CIS Border Troops.
May 15	**Tashkent:** Heads of State/Heads of Government; Russia, Kazakhstan, Kyrgyzstan, Uzbekistan, Tajikistan, and Armenia sign a Collective Security Treaty, as well as agreements on manning and financing frontier troops, on forming peacekeeping forces, and on fulfilling the USSR's obligations on chemical weapons control.
July 6	**Moscow:** Heads of State sign agreements creating a CIS Economic Court and a CIS Council of Commanders of Border Forces, along with agreements on dividing USSR property and on coordinating new currencies when member states depart from the ruble zone.
October 8–9	**Bishkek:** Heads of State/Heads of Government agree to send humanitarian aid to Tajikistan.
November 13	**Moscow:** Heads of Government unable to reach an agreement on CIS charter.

1993

January 3–4	**Tashkent, Central Asian Regional Summit:** Establishes Central Asian Commonwealth.
January 14	**Bishkek:** Heads of Central Asian States sign Central Asian Treaty recognizing the inviolability of existing borders and establishing diplomatic relations and embassies within the region.
January 22	**Minsk, Second CIS Summit:** Creates CIS Inter-State Bank and debates CIS charter.
March 12	**Moscow:** Heads of Government agree to create Inter-State Council for the Protection of Industrial Property.
April 16	**Minsk, Heads of State Emergency Summit:** Hold general discussion on strengthening the CIS; sign no documents.

April 28   **Minsk:** Heads of Government adopt the Statute of the Coordinating and Consultative Committee.

July 10   **Moscow:** Prime Ministers of Russia, Belarus, and Ukraine create Slavic Monetary Union to ensure free movement of goods, services, and capital among their countries.

September 24   **Moscow:** Prime Ministers of Armenia, Azerbaijan, Belarus, Kazakhstan, Kyrgyzstan, Moldova, Russia, Tajikistan, and Uzbekistan initial Conception of an Economic Union, which provides for the free flow of commodities, services, capital, and work force; and coordinates fiscal, budget, tax, price, and foreign economic policy.

December 24   **Ashgabat, Third CIS Summit:** Agrees to begin implementing Economic Union despite some signatories' failure to ratify it.

1994

April 15   **Moscow:** Heads of State create a free trade zone among the member states. Ukraine joins the Economic Union as an associate member.

April 30   **Cholpon-Ata:** Presidents of Kazakhstan, Kyrgyzstan, and Uzbekistan create common economic space.

August 4   **Almaty, Central Asian Union:** Kazakhstan, Kyrgyzstan, and Uzbekistan sign an agreement on the creation of the Central Asian Union—a defense and economic formation.

September 9   **Moscow:** Heads of Government agree to create the Inter-State Economic Committee. Azerbaijan and Turkmenistan abstain from signing the document.

October 21   **Moscow:** Heads of State create Inter-State Economic Committee as the executive body of the CIS Economic Union; sign an agreement on the payments union; adopt a convention on guarantees for minorities.

December 9   **Moscow:** Heads of Government sign 20 documents and create a collegium of the Inter-State Economic Committee.

1995

January 28   **Moscow:** Prime Ministers of Russia, Belarus, and Kazakhstan create a Customs Union.

February 10	**Almaty:** Heads of State sign memorandum pledging that the countries will not use political, economic, or military pressure on other CIS members to achieve foreign or domestic goals. Armenia, Belarus, Georgia, Kazakhstan, Kyrgyzstan, Turkmenistan, Uzbekistan, Ukraine sign Agreement on Creation of a Unified Air Defense System.
May 26	**Minsk:** Heads of Government agree to establish a regional currency committee. Kazakhstan, Kyrgyzstan, Russia, and Belarus approve a unified border security system; extend the peacekeeping mandate in Abkhazia and Tajikistan. Russia and Belarus sign a customs union agreement. Seven states sign Convention on Human Rights and Basic Freedoms.

1996

January 19	**Moscow:** Heads of Government sign an agreement to reduce the value-added tax by 5 percent and to establish common legal principles in national customs policies. Also adopt guidelines for conflict prevention and settlement on the territory of CIS member states.
March 29–31	**Moscow:** At Heads of State meeting, Kyrgyzstan joins the Customs Union of Russia, Belarus, and Kazakhstan. Presidents of the four countries create an inter-governmental council of presidents, prime ministers, and foreign ministers; an integration committee; and an inter-parliamentary committee within the Customs Union framework.
April 2	**Moscow:** Presidents of Russia and Belarus sign an integration treaty and form a community of sovereign states.
April 12	**Moscow:** Heads of Government discuss economic integration.
May 17	**Moscow:** Heads of State endorse Yeltsin's candidacy for president of Russia.
October 18	**Moscow:** Heads of Government sign an agreement granting the Inter-State Bank the right to conduct banking operations and transactions on the member-country territories and ensuring its access to the internal currency market in accordance with the requirements of their national legislation.

1997

January 17   **Moscow:** Heads of Government approve a draft concept of the economic integration.

March 28   **Moscow:** Heads of State discuss military, political, and peacekeeping issues; approve a concept of economic integration.

April 2   **Moscow:** Presidents of Russia and Belarus sign Union Treaty.

October 9–10   **Bishkek:** Heads of Government sign 24 documents, including one on the concept of CIS integrated economic development.

October 10   **Strasbourg:** Presidents of Georgia, Ukraine, Azerbaijan, and Moldova issue a joint communiqué creating GUAM to address issues of regional security and cooperation, and to establish a transport corridor for Caspian oil.

October 23   **Chisinau:** Heads of State create a common agricultural market.

1998

January 6   **Ashgabat:** At meeting of Central Asian Heads of State, Turkmenistan, citing its neutral status, declines an invitation to join the Central Asian Union, but Tajikistan's bid to join finds support among the members and Turkmenistan does not rule out an observer role later.

January 22   **Moscow, Customs Union Summit:** Produces signed documents on joint customs tariffs, coordination of tax systems, creation of a transport union; fails to reach an agreement on common economic space.

March 6   **Moscow:** Heads of Government sign 11 documents, including accords on a common agricultural market. Sign an accord on cooperation between law enforcement agencies.

April 28   **Moscow, Customs Union Summit:** Presidents of Belarus, Kazakhstan, Kyrgyzstan, and Russia agree in principle to admit Tajikistan as a new member.

April 29   **Moscow:** Heads of State deal with administrative issues (appoint Berezovsky CIS executive secretary and decide that Yeltsin will remain chairman of the CIS Heads of State Council until 2000; appoint Uzbek Prime Minister

Utkir Sultanov chairman of the CIS Council of Heads of Government). Fail to adopt a draft Declaration on Further Equal Partnership and Cooperation as well as a document on Single Economic Space and Free Trade Zone.

July 17 **Issyk-Kul, Central Asian Union Summit:** Tajikistan joins the Union and it is renamed the Central Asian Economic Community.

November 25 **Moscow:** Heads of Government debate Berezovsky's blueprint for CIS reform.

1999

February 26 **Moscow, Customs Union Summit:** Tajikistan formally joins as a full member.

April 2 **Moscow:** Heads of State discuss CIS reforms and progress establishing the free trade area; fire Berezovsky from the post of CIS executive secretary and appoint Yuri Yarov.

April 25 **Washington, D.C., GUAM-GUUAM Summit:** Uzbekistan formally becomes the fifth member of the Georgia-Ukraine-Azerbaijan-Moldova alignment. The presidents affirm their support for one another's territorial integrity, and back regional cooperation— including creation of regional transport corridors—as well as cooperation within the framework of international organizations such as NATO's Euro-Atlantic Partnership Council.

June 4 **Minsk:** Heads of Government create two new administrative bodies: the Commonwealth Executive Committee, which replaced the Executive Secretariat, and the Economic Council, which consolidated the Inter-State Economic Committee and most of the CIS economic bodies.

June 24 **Bishkek:** Central Asian Economic Community discusses further economic integration that would include a free trade zone and a common market for goods, services, and capital. Georgia, Turkey, and Ukraine are granted observer status.

Selected Bibliography

Adams, Jan. *Will the Post-Soviet Commonwealth Survive?* Columbus, Ohio: Mershon Center, Ohio State University, 1993.

Aron, Leon. "The Soviet Union's Soft Underbelly: Muslim Central Asia," *Global Affairs*, vol. 5, special issue (1990), pp. 31–62.

Åslund, Anders. *How Russia Became a Market Economy.* Washington, D.C.: Brookings Institution Press, 1995.

Aukutsionek, Sergei. "Barter v rossiiskoi promyshlennosti," *Voprosy ekonomiki*, vol. 70 (February 1998), pp. 51–60.

Baev, Pavel. "Peacekeeping and Conflict Management in Eurasia," in Roy Allison and Christoph Bluth, eds., *Security Dilemmas in Russia and Eurasia.* London: Royal Institute for International Affairs, 1998.

Becker, Abraham S. "Russia and Economic Integration in the CIS," *Survival*, vol. 38 (Winter 1996–1997), pp. 117–36.

Beloff, Max, ed. *Beyond the Soviet Union: The Fragmentation of Power.* Aldershot, U.K.: Ashgate, 1997.

Billingsley, Dodge. "Georgian-Abkhazian Security Issues," *Jane's Intelligence Review* (February 1996), pp. 65–68.

Bonesteel, Ronald M. "Viability of a CIS Security System," *Military Review*, vol. 72 (December 1993), pp. 36–47.

Bremmer, Ian and Ray Taras, eds. *New States, New Politics: Building the Post-Soviet Nations.* Cambridge, U.K.: Cambridge University Press, 1997.

Brzezinski, Zbigniew and Paige Sullivan, eds. *Russia and the Commonwealth of Independent States.* London: M.E. Sharpe, 1997.

Chufrin, G. I., ed. *Integratsionnye protsessy v Azii v kontse XX stoletiia.* Moscow: Institut vostokovedeniia RAN, 1995.

Corden, Warner Max. *Integration and Trade Policy in the Former Soviet Union.* Washington, D.C.: Trade Policy Division, World Bank, 1992.

Crow, Suzanne. "Russia Promotes the CIS as an International Organization," *RFE/RL Research Report,* vol. 4 (March 18, 1994), pp. 33–38.

Dawisha, Karen and Bruce Parrott, eds. *Conflict, Cleavage, and Change in Central Asia and the Caucasus.* Cambridge, U.K.: Cambridge University Press, 1997.

Delmas, Philippe. *The Rosy Future of War.* New York: Free Press, 1997.

Ehrhart, Hans-Georg, Anna Kreikemeyer, and Andrei V. Zagorski, eds. *Crisis Management in the CIS: Whither Russia?* Baden-Baden, Germany: Nomos, 1995.

Freedman, Lawrence. "The Revolution in Strategic Affairs," Adelphi Paper 318 (London: Oxford University Press), 1998.

Frankel, Jeffrey. *Regional Trading Blocs in the World Economic System.* Washington, D.C.: Institute for International Economics, 1997.

Gaddy, Clifford and Barry W. Ickes. "Russia's Virtual Economy," *Foreign Affairs,* vol. 77, no. 5 (September/October 1998), pp. 53–67.

Garnett, Sherman. *Keystone in the Arch: Ukraine in the Emerging Security Environment of Central and Eastern Europe.* Washington, D.C.: Carnegie Endowment for International Peace, 1997.

———. "The Integrationist Temptation," *The Washington Quarterly,* vol. 18, no. 2 (Spring 1995), pp. 35–44

———. "Russia's Illusory Ambitions," *Foreign Affairs,* vol. 76, no. 2 (March/April 1997), pp. 61–76.

Havrylyshyn, Oleh and Hassan Al-Atrash. "Opening Up and Geographic Diversification of Trade in Transition Economies," IMF Working Paper no. 98/22 (Washington, D.C.: International Monetary Fund), 1998.

Henze, Paul. "Whither Turkestan?" Santa Monica, Calif.: RAND Corporation, 1992.

Jackson, Robert. *Quasi-states: Sovereignty, International Relations, and the Third World*. Cambridge, U.K.: Cambridge University Press, 1990.

Johnson, Lena. "The Tajik War: A Challenge to Russian Policy," Discussion Paper 74 (London: Royal Institute for International Affairs), 1998.

Karatnycky, Andrei, Alexander Motyl, and Charles Graybow, eds. *Nations in Transition 1998: Civil Society, Democracy and Markets in East Central Europe and the Newly Independent States*. New York: Freedom House, 1999.

Karl, Terry Lynn. *The Paradox of Plenty: Oil Booms and Petro-States*. Berkeley: University of California Press, 1997.

Kaye, David. "Struggling with Independence: Central Asian Politics in the Post-Soviet World," *Middle East Insight*, vol. 8 (July–October 1992), pp. 27–32.

Khazanov, A. M. and V. P. Pankrat'ev, eds. *Rossiia i Aziia: Sostoianie i perspektivy sotrudnichestva*. Moscow: Institut vostokovedeniia RAN, 1995.

Kuzio, Taras. *Ukraine Under Kuchma*. New York: St. Martin's Press, 1997.

Lapidus, Gail W. and Victor Zaslavsky, with Philip Goldman, eds. *From Union to Commonwealth: Nationalism and Separatism in the Soviet Republics*. Cambridge, U.K.: Cambridge University Press, 1992.

Mandlebaum, Michael, ed. *Central Asia and the World*. New York: Council on Foreign Relations, 1994.

———, ed. *The New Russian Foreign Policy*. New York: Council on Foreign Relations, 1998.

Medvedev, Sergei. "Security Risks in Russia and the CIS: A Case Study," *International Spectator*, vol. 29 (January–March 1994), pp. 53–87.

Michalopoulos, Constantine and David Tarr. *The Economics of Customs Unions in the Commonwealth of Independent States*. Washington, D.C.: International Bank for Reconstruction and Development, 1997.

Mozaffari, Mehdi, ed. *Security Politics in the Commonwealth of Independent States: The Southern Belt*. London: Macmillan, 1997.

Nazarbayev, Nursultan. *Piat'let nezavisimosti: iz dokladov, vystuplenii i statei Prezidenta Respubliki Kazakhstan*. Almaty, Kazakhstan, 1996.

Nichol, James. *Diplomacy in the Former Soviet Republics*. Westport, Conn.: Praeger, 1995.

Noren, James H. and Robin Watson. "Interrepublican Economic Relations after the Disintegration of the USSR," *Soviet Economy*, vol. 8 (April–June 1992), pp. 89–129.

Olcott, Martha Brill. *Central Asia's New States: Independence, Foreign Policy, and Regional Security*. Washington, D.C.: United States Institute of Peace Press, 1996.

_____ . *The Kazakhs*, 2nd ed. Stanford: Hoover Institution Press, 1995.

Pipes, Daniel. "The Politics of the 'Rip Van Winkle' States: The Southern Tier States of the Ex-Soviet Union Have Moved the Borders of the Middle East North," *Middle East Insight*, vol. 10 (November/December 1993), pp. 30–40.

Priakhin, V. "On the Economic Integration of the CIS," *International Affairs*, vol. 43, no. 1 (1997), pp. 106–13.

Pushkov, Alexei. "The Commonwealth of Independent States: Still Alive though Not Kicking," *NATO Review*, vol. 40 (June 1992), pp. 13–18.

Rogov, Sergei, et al. *Commonwealth Defense Arrangements and International Security*. Alexandria, Va.: Center for Naval Analysis, 1992.

Rybakov, O. "CIS: Five Years of Existence," *International Affairs*, vol. 42, nos. 5/6 (1996), pp. 95–104.

Rywkin, Michael. *Moscow's Lost Empire*. Armonk, N.Y.: Sharpe, 1994.

Sakwa, Richard and Mark Webber. "The Commonwealth of Independent States, 1991–1998: Stagnation and Survival," *Europe-Asia Studies*, vol. 51, no. 3 (May 1999), pp. 379–415.

Shirin Akiner. *The Formation of Kazakh Identity from Tribe to Nation-State*. London: The Royal Institute of International Affairs, 1995.

Smith, Graham, Vivien Law, Andrew Wilson, Annette Bohr, and Edward Allworth, eds. *Nation-Building in the Post-Soviet Borderlands*. Cambridge, U.K.: Cambridge University Press, 1998.

Smith, Mark. *Pax Russica: Russia's Monroe Doctrine*. London: Royal United Services Institute for Defence Studies, 1993.

Snyder, Glenn. *Alliance Politics*. Ithaca, N.Y.: Cornell University Press, 1997.

Valdivieso, Luis. "Macroeconomic Developments in the Baltics, Russia, and Other Countries of the Former Soviet Union, 1992-97," IMF Occasional Paper no. 175 (Washington, D.C.: International Monetary Fund), 1998.

Vitkovskaia, Galina and Alexei Malashenko, eds. *Vozrozhdenie kazachestva: nadezhdy i opaseniia*. Moscow: Carnegie Moscow Center, 1998.

Sheehy, Ann. "The CIS Charter," *RFE/RL Research Report*, vol. 2 (March 19, 1993), pp. 23–27.

Walt, Stephen. *The Origin of Alliances*. Ithaca, N.Y.: Cornell University Press, 1987.

"Will CIS's First Anniversary Be Its Last?" condensed from *Nezavisimaya Gazeta* and *Migapolis-Express*, December 22, 1992–January 6, 1993, as translated in *Current Digest of the Post-Soviet Press*, vol. 45 (February 3, 1993), pp. 8–10.

Woff, Richard. *The Armed Forces of the Former Soviet Union: Evolution, Structures, and Personalities*. London: Brasseys, 1996.

Zagorski, Andrei. *SNG: Tsifry, fakty, personalii*. Minsk, Belarus: PRS, 1998.

_____ . "Regional Structures of Security Policy within the CIS," in Roy Allison and Christoph Bluth, eds., *Security Dilemmas in Russia and Eurasia*. London: Royal Institute for International Affairs, 1998.

Zemskii, V. "Collective Security in the CIS," *International Affairs*, vol. 45, no. 1 (1999), pp. 97–104.

Index

CONFERENCE PARTICIPANTS

As part of the work on this book, the authors convened a conference on the state of CIS integration. It was held at the Carnegie Moscow Center on March 5–6, 1998, with the following participants:

Leila Alieva, Institute of History of the Academy of Sciences, Azerbaijan

Can Altan, Embassy of Turkey, Moscow

Anders Åslund, Carnegie Endowment for International Peace

Nadija Badykova, State Commission for Statistics and Forecast, Turkmenistan

Keith Bush, Center for Strategic and International Studies

Ara Darbinian, Institute of Management and Economic Reforms, Armenia

Yuri Fedorov, Moscow State Institute of International Relations

Sherman Garnett, Carnegie Endowment for International Peace

Thomas Graham, RAND Corporation

Almond Gutmanis, Presidential Office, Latvia

Arnold Horelick, Carnegie Endowment for International Peace

Zhao Huasheng, Shanghai Institute for International Studies

Sabit Jusupov, Institute of Social and Economic Information, Kazakhstan

Kyoji Komachi, Embassy of Japan, Moscow

David Kramer, Carnegie Endowment for International Peace

Djumaly Kubatov, Security Council, Kyrgyzstan

Gail Lapidus, Stanford University

Aleksei Malashenko, Carnegie Moscow Center

Jessica T. Mathews, Carnegie Endowment for International Peace

Nurbulat Masanov, Soros Foundation, Kazakhstan

Constantine Michalopoulos, World Trade Organization

Arkady Moshes, Institute of Europe, Russian Academy of Sciences

Kathleen Newland, Carnegie Endowment for International Peace

Ghia Nodia, Caucasian Institute, Georgia

Martha Brill Olcott, Carnegie Endowment for International Peace

Muzaffar Olimov, Scientific Informational Center "Sharq," Tajikistan

Anatoli Rozanov, Belarusian State University

Alan Rousso, Carnegie Moscow Center

Rafik Saifulin, Institute for
Strategic and Regional Studies,
Uzbekistan
Natasha Segev, Embassy of
Israel, Moscow
Andrei Smokine, International
Independent University,
Moldova
Andrei Sobilev, National
Institute for Strategic Studies,
Ukraine
Angela Stent, Georgetown
University
Marin Strmecki, Smith
Richardson Foundation
Henryk Szlejfer, Polish Ministry
of Foreign Affairs
Roman Szporluk, Harvard
University

David Tarr, World Bank
Dmitri Trenin, Carnegie Moscow
Center
Natalia Udalova, Carnegie
Endowment for International
Peace
Marat Umerov, Carnegie
Moscow Center
Vladimir Yevstigneev, Institute
of World Economy and
International Relations,
Moscow
Andrei Zagorsky, Moscow State
Institute of International
Relations
Irina Zvyagelskaya, Russian
Center for Strategic and
International Studies

About the Authors

Martha Brill Olcott is a senior associate at the Carnegie Endowment for International Peace and a professor of political science at Colgate University. She has written numerous studies on Central Asia and the Caucasus and on ethnic relations in the post-Soviet states, including *Kazakhstan: A Faint-Hearted Democracy* (Carnegie Endowment, forthcoming). She has also served as a special consultant to then-Acting Secretary of State Lawrence Eagleburger and is a director of the Central Asian American Enterprise Fund.

Anders Åslund is a senior associate at the Carnegie Endowment for International Peace. He is the author of numerous books and articles on the post-Soviet economic transition, including *How Russia Became a Market Economy* (Brookings Institution, 1995). He has served as an economic advisor to the Russian government, to the Ukrainian government and to President Askar Akaev of Kyrgyzstan.

Sherman W. Garnett is dean of James Madison College, an undergraduate institution at Michigan State University that provides liberal education in public affairs. A specialist on the foreign and security policies of Russia and Ukraine, he was formerly a senior associate at the Carnegie Endowment for International Peace. He is the author of *Keystone in the Arch: Ukraine in the Emerging Security Environment of Central and Eastern Europe* (Carnegie Endowment, 1997) and editor of forthcoming books on Russian-Chinese relations and on Belarus.

About the Carnegie Endowment

The Carnegie Endowment for International Peace is a private, non-profit organization dedicated to advancing cooperation between nations and promoting active international engagement by the United States. Founded in 1910, its work is nonpartisan and dedicated to achieving practical results. Through research, publishing, convening and, on occasion, creating new institutions and international networks, Endowment associates shape fresh policy approaches. Their interests span geographic regions and the relations among governments, business, international organizations, and civil society, focusing on the economic, political, and technological forces driving global change. Through its Carnegie Moscow Center, the Endowment helps develop a tradition of public policy analysis in the states of the former Soviet Union and improve relations between Russia and the United States. The Endowment publishes *Foreign Policy*, one of the world's leading journals of international politics and economics, which reaches readers in more than 120 countries and several languages.

Carnegie Endowment
for International Peace
1779 Massachusetts Ave., N.W.
Washington, D.C. 20036
Tel: 202-483-7600
Fax: 202-483-1840
E-mail: carnegie@ceip.org
Web: www.ceip.org

Carnegie Moscow Center
Ul. Tverskaya 16/2
7th Floor
Moscow 103009
Tel: 7-095-935-8904
Fax: 7-095-935-8906
E-mail: info@carnegie.ru
Web: www.carnegie.ru

| 271